Square Dancing in Wisconsin

>–‹›–•–O–•–‹›–‹

A Historical Anthology
1948-1998

by Agnes Thurner

Published by Patchworks Publishing
P.O. Box 23160
Brown Deer, WI 53223

Printed in the United States of America by:
Palmer Publications, Inc.
318 North Main Street
Amherst, WI 54406

Dedication

This book is dedicated to the Square Dance Association of Wisconsin, in honor of its 50th anniversary, and to the State of Wisconsin in celebration of its sesquicentennial year.

Contents

Dedication. iii
Preface ix
Acknowledgments. xiii

Chapter 1: *Square Your Sets* 1
    Square Dancing in Wisconsin. 2
    The Square Dance—*by Anne Campbell* *3*
    How It All Began—by *Dale Wagner* 3
    Wisconsin Square Dance Pioneers. 9

Chapter 2: *All Join Hands, Make a Big Ring* 11
    The Square Dance Association of Wisconsin
    Our Pledge—*by Sally Conger*. 12
    Getting Organized 12
    1948 Officers 13
    First SDAW President 14
    First Vice President 15
    Our Creed—*by Sally Conger* 15
    The First Four Years—*by Irene Qually* 16
    Reorganization. 19
    Organizational Committee. 21
    1949 Calendar of Events 22
    Member Groups of Square Dance Association of Wisconsin—1949 . . 23

Chapter 3: *Wheel Around*. 25
    Early Square Dance Clubs
    History of the Green Bay Squares—*by Ann Krueger* 26
    EMBA—*by Dolores Tock* 28
    Square Dance Miracles—*by Dolores Tock*. 29
    Petunia City Squares—*by John and Gloria Rindfleisch* 31

Chapter 4: *Star Promenade*. 33
    Pioneers of the Wisconsin Square Dance Movement
    The Sky's the Limit—*by Agnes Thurner*. 34
    Where Would We Be Without Callers?—*by Agnes Thurner* 35
        Doc Newland 35
        Herb Johnson. 36
        Howie Bernard 37
        Bert Rietz 38
        Chet Wangerin. 39
        Elmer Hamann 39
        This is Your Square Dance Life, Paul Ratajczyk 40
        Clarence Freis 43
        Ode to Clarence—*by Romaine Wellhoefer* 43
        In Remembrance of Clarence—*by Romaine Wellhoefer*. 44
        Ben Blankenheim 45
        Johnny "Red Vest" Toth—*by Louise Toth* 45
        George Ziemann 47
        Bill Williams 47
        Martha Clark. 48
        John Eagan 48
        Bob Dawson. 49

Contents

Chapter 5: *Peel Off* 51
  Area Associations
    SDAW-South East Area, Inc. 52
    Milwaukee Area Callers' Council 52
    SDAW-South West Area (SDAW-SWA) 54
    Wolf River Area Callers' Association 55

Chapter 6: *Grand Square* 58
  Wisconsin State Square and Round Dance Conventions
    First Wisconsin Convention 59
    Overview—*by Agnes Thurner* 61
    Left Allemande in Dairyland—*by Vera Schreiner* 62
    Highlights of the 1979 Convention 63
    Wisconsin's Square Dance Flag 66
    Convention Memories—*by Agnes Thurner* 67
    Exhibitions and Demonstrations 69

Chapter 7: *Go Red Hot* 81
  Square Dancing at its Peak 1950-1980
    What is a Caller?—*by Harold Silvers* 82
    Bill and Betty Kersey 82
    Harry and Barbara Jashinsky 84
    Irv and Pearl Pasch 84
    Following Dad's Footsteps 85
    Our Square Dance Life—*by Howie Reoch* 86
    Jack and Lolly Gaver 87
    Bob and Pauline Holup 88
    Howard and May Donna Gilmore 89
    Dave and Nancy Hussey 90
    Pat and Bob Kelm—*by Pat Kelm* 91
    Why We Square Dance—*by Margaret Leatherman* 92
    The Hodag Twirlers 92
    The M-T Saddles 95
    "R" Squares 96
    Happy Twirlers of La Crosse—*by Sue and Skip Comeau* 97
    Circle 'n Star 98
    The Westport Squares—*by R. Lecheler* 99
    The Swingin' Singles Squares 101
    The Square Benders Square Dance Club 103
    T-P Taws & Paws—*by Doris Palmen* 105
    Diamond Squares—*by Art and Helen Anhalt* 106
    Country Swingers 108
    Dudes and Dolls Square Dance Club—*by Mary Edge* 109
    The Tale of Loyal Circle 8's—*by Nathan and June Noeldner* 110
    Hartland Hoedowners—*by Ann Dow* 111
    Kettle Moraine Squares—*by Lloyd and Joyce Gatzke* 112
    Paddock Lake Squares—*by Gladys Elda Bishop* 113
    Shadow Viners Round Dance Club—*by Mary Edge* 113
    History of the NorJen Dancers—*by Sue and Skip Comeau* 114
    Grand Squares—*by Royal and Joan Gibson* 115
    Art and Dorothy Wegner 116

Brownie and Regena Brown 117
Win and Jo Ann Erlandson 117
Jim and Jeanette Conner 118

Chapter 8: *Explode the Wave* 119
National Organizations
A Caller's Life For Me—*by Agnes Thurner* 120
CALLERLAB 121
What Does CALLERLAB Do? 122
ROUNDALAB 123
LEGACY 123
ECCO 125
History of the National Square Dance Campers' Association 125
The Overseas Dancer Association 128
The Lloyd Shaw Foundation 132

Chapter 9: *Take a Little Peck* 133
Memories, Reminiscence, and Poetry
Looking Back 134
Her Grandpa Was a Caller! 134
A Square Move—*by Norma DeBoer* 135
Reminiscence of a Square Dance Brat—*by Ann Ratajczyk Buck* . . 136
Fun in the Fifties—*by Leona Klemp* 138
How I Became Involved in Square Dancing
   —*by Elizabeth (Betsy) Isenberg* 140
The Floral Organdy Dress Speaks—*by Judy Berg Hogan* 142
Square Dancing Keeps Me Young!—*by Phil Koch* 146
An Unusual Square Dance Program—*by Ann Krueger* 148
Our Hobby—*by Norma Mader* 149
Mom and Me!—*by Sue Ruf* 149
They Square Dance To Belgian Calls—*by Ann Krueger* 150
Russell's Hustle–A Tribute to Russell Burss—*by Judy Hogan* . . . 152
The Dance of My Life—*by Agnes Thurner* 153
Come Dance With Me!—*by Olive "Skippy" Giese* 161
Square Dance Stories—*by Judy Barisonzi* 161
It's Fun To Be Square—*by Jean and Bob Brisk* 164
Salvation—*by Caroline Cook* 167
Haiku's—*by Olive "Skippy" Giese* 170
A Couple of Squares—*by Margaret L. Been* 171
What is Square Dancing?—*by Dolores Tock* 172
Northwoods Square Dance Stories—*by Judy Hogan* 173
Welcome To Our World—*by Doug Kindschuh and Judy Barisonzi* . 175
A Grateful Square—*by Olive "Skippy" Giese* 176

Chapter 10: *Wheel and Deal* 177
Square Dance Enterprises
Getting The News Out 178
Square Dance Fashions—*by May Donna Gilmore* 182
Where Do They Buy Those Fancy Outfits?—*by Agnes Thurner* . . . 184
In Days Gone By—*by Dolores Rabe* 189

Contents

Chapter 11: *Cross-Trail Thru* 191
    Promoting the Fun
      Havey-Sauer Tours—*by Don Sauer* 192
      What Kind of People Are Square Dancers?—*by Judy Barisonzi* . . 193
      Thirty-Eight Years Ago—*by Don Niva* 195
      Badges, Rings, and Thieves—*by Agnes Thurner*. 196
      The Promotion Committee 200
      Flail Tail—*by Don Niva* 202

Chapter 12: *Crossfire* 203
    Squaring Off
      Introduction to Square Dancing—*by Don Niva* 204
      The Community Dance Program—*by Dennis Leatherman* 205

Chapter 13: *Passed Thru* 209
    In Memoriam

Chapter 14: *Promenade Home* 215
    What Were We Doing in 1998?
      The Square Dance Association of Wisconsin 216
      1998 SDAW Officers. 216
      Area Associations 217
      Callers' Associations. 219
      1998 Club News 222
      Vern and Billie Weisensel. 223
      Tim and Charlotte Manning 224
      Dale "The Auctioneer" Ryan. 225
      Thanks for the Memories—*by Jim Noonan* 225
      The Lightning Trio. 227
      Crosstrails Square Dance Club—*by Vern and Billie Weisensel* . . . 228
      Cream City Squares—*by Don Dilges* 229
      Joyce and The Yellow Rocker's—*by Joyce Gibour*. 230
      Wisconsin Square and
        Round Dance Convention 233
      The 50th Anniversary of the SDAW—
        The Sesquicentennial of Wisconsin—*by Agnes Thurner* 234
      Memory Quilt Contributors 236
      Trail's End 238

Glossary. 239
Index 243

Preface

A non-square dancer reading this book for the first time may think it has been written in a foreign language. Terminology such as "flip the diamond", "pass the ocean" and "trade the wave" are familiar phrases to experienced square dancers but would certainly be confusing to a square dance novice. The average person hears the words "recycle" and "circulate" mentioned just about every day. They have a perfectly ordinary meaning. But on the square dance floor those words tell the dancers to execute a particular dance movement. "Hash" is not something you eat, and a "tip" is not something you leave to a waitress for good service.

Most people were exposed to some form of square dancing while in high school and may recognize the Allemande Left and Grand Right and Left. Modern square dancing goes far beyond what we learned in school. Forty years ago a school recreation director would teach a few calls and lead a few simple dances. Callers would do the same thing, perhaps using only twelve calls during an entire evening of dancing. And you didn't need to know how to square dance beforehand. The caller would teach or workshop the calls at the beginning of the dance and use the same calls throughout.

Every caller had his own repertoire, some gleaned from other callers, and some originating with him. For example, a "do-si-do" in Wisconsin was not necessarily done the same way in Illinois. As square dancing spread across the country, callers realized that some standardization was needed. An organization known as CALLERLAB was formed to work with callers to identify and standardize square dance calls. Now the same commands result in the same reaction no matter who is calling or where. Today's square dancers can travel anywhere in the world, find a square dance hall and have no problem understanding the caller because all the calls are done uniformly and in English.

There are many different skill levels in square dancing. Currently, the Basic level has about fifty calls and requires about ten to twelve weeks of two-hour lessons. That's the starting point. From there, dancers move into the Mainstream level. Most clubs in Wisconsin dance at the Mainstream level. To learn more, dancers can continue into Plus, Advanced, or Challenge level.

A companion dance form is Round Dancing. Round Dancing is done with couples moving in a circle around the dance floor using familiar ballroom rhythms. The dances are cued or prompted so each couple is doing the same dance steps at the same time. Square dances usually include round dancing between "tips". "Square Dancing" integrates and encompasses many other dance forms. Just as this country has been referred to as the "melting pot" of the world, the square dance might be called the "dance of the world." People from almost every European country arrived in America during our first 200 years. They brought with them their customs, skills, and dances. As they traveled across the country, migrating from one city to another, the different dance movements blended together. Mountain dances, Quadrilles, Contras, and Mescolanzas are some of the dance forms that comprise the American Square Dance.

In the 1980s President Ronald Reagan signed a document proclaiming square dancing as "America's Folk Dance." Although it has not been ratified in Wisconsin, thirty-three states have made square dancing their state "Folk Dance." People the world over have come to know square dancing as "America's Dance."

Why do people square dance? Many surveys have asked that question. The top four answers are always the same:

The number one answer is FUN. Whether married or single, teenager or senior citizen, everyone seems to have fun at a square dance. It's an activity the whole family can do together. In this age where both parents are working, and kids are torn between homework, and music or sports competitions, square dancing is an enjoyable, non-competitive way to spend time as a family.

Number two is FRIENDSHIP. Bonds have been forged all over the world between people that went to a dance as strangers, and left with lifelong friends. You are always among friends when you're on a square dance floor, whether in your hometown or thousands of miles away.

Number three is FITNESS. Square dancing is a great aerobic exercise. Many doctors recommend it to their patients with arthritis and as a cardiovascular workout. It provides mental stimulation and challenge and helps to improve memory.

Four—it's AFFORDABLE. 1998 costs are between $2.50 and $3.00 per person per dance, and most clubs offer family rates. A family of four could dance all night for under ten dollars with snacks thrown in.

In the 1930s and '40s most clubs were "caller run." A caller would rent a hall, advertise, and workshop square dances, and acquire a dancer following. Eventually this following coalesced into a club with no officers, and the caller doing all the work. As new callers came on the scene and square dancing became more popular, dancers wanted more say in how clubs were run. They began organizing their own clubs, electing officers, and hiring "club callers." Soon dancer run clubs began to outnumber caller run clubs. The swift growth of square dance activity in Wisconsin brought about another change. Dancers and callers wanted more interaction with other clubs and groups in the state. So, in 1948, the Square Dance Association of Wisconsin was organized, and square dancing continued to prosper well into the 1980s.

Square dance businesses also thrived. The advent of modern sound devices and recorded music did away with the need for live musicians, and created a demand among callers who wanted to upgrade to new equipment. Men needed boots, western shirts and pants, bolo or string ties. Ladies had to have special shoes, costumes, pettipants, crinolines, even coats to fit over the newly bouf-fant skirts. Even those who did their own sewing found it easier to purchase the multilayered petticoats and ruffled pettipants than to spend time making them. When it became commonplace for men's outfits to match the ladies, the garment industry kept pace by stock-ing men's and women's clothing and accessories in matching colors.

At one time there were several square dance specialty shops doing business in Wisconsin. Today there is only one shop left deal-ing specifically in square dance attire. Dancers either make their own, wait for a square dance convention to buy in the retail sales area, or order by catalog. Gone are the days when ladies could buy a complete square dance outfit at J. C. Penney's or Sears Roebuck.

Nothing ever stays the same and so it is with square dancing. The activity has been in a downward spiral since the mid-1980s. Square dance lessons are attracting fewer new dancers. The cur-rent square dance population is aging. Although some people con-tinue dancing well into their eighties, eventually dancers leave the activity when they can no longer physically participate. Many smaller clubs have been forced to disband due to declining mem-berships and lack of club leadership.

Where once there were forty to fifty clubs in the southeastern area of Wisconsin, there are now only twenty. In the seventies and eighties, there were numerous teen clubs; all but a few have dis-banded. State conventions that used to attract over 4,000 dancers now register less than half that number at the annual event.

Square dance callers and leaders nationwide have been strug-gling for more than a decade to stop the decline in square dance activity. Some believe that reducing the number of calls required to get into the Mainstream dance program would help. Learning the Mainstream program currently requires a considerable time com-mitment. Many demands on free time are made through work, church, and school, and there are numerous other social options that may offer more immediate gratification.

Many different proposals are being discussed by various square dance leadership groups to address the concerns of dancers and callers. Major changes are expected to be made in the activity by the year 2000.

Despite our current problems square dancing has many posi-tive elements. In addition to the fun, friendship, and feeling of physical well-being that dancers experience, square dancing also offers challenge, and teamwork—eight individuals all doing their part to bring the dance to a successful conclusion, each one an essential part of the square. And at the end of a tip, when the dancers join hands to bow to the others in their square they are saying "We did it together—thanks for being there."

Agnes Thurner
Mequon, Wisconsin
June 1998

Acknowledgments

Many people helped to compile this history of square dancing in Wisconsin: Committee members who wrote and edited articles, dancers, callers, and round dance leaders from all over the state; some that have retired to warmer climes. Their articles, pictures, and reminiscences have contributed greatly toward making our history come alive. Information came from folks who are retired from the square dance activity and those who only remember hearing about it from parents, grandparents, aunts or uncles. My thanks to all of you for your contribution to this anthology, especially to the members of my committee for their help and support. Most importantly, I want to say thank you to my husband, Max, who cheerfully assisted and encouraged me in this project and boosted my spirits when necessary.

My fervent hope is that fifty years from now historians will look to this book as a comprehensive reference to Square Dancing in Wisconsin. However, it is more than a history book. It is a book about people. People from right here in Wisconsin who willingly shared their dreams, hopes, and memories about an activity they truly enjoy and believe in.

Agnes Thurner, Chairman

Anthology Committee

Judy Barisonzi
Karen and Ellery Gulbrand
Judy and Tom Hogan
Wayne and Lucy Mattson
Marilyn and Ray Steinich

CHAPTER 1

Square Your Sets

Honor your partner, swing and whirl
Then promenade with the corner girl.
Throw in the clutch, put her in low.
Swing your partner and away we go!

Square Dancing in Wisconsin

Square dancing in Wisconsin? Of course! Even before statehood, "sets-in-order" was a familiar sound. Early settlers from eastern states and New England brought to the midwest the house party and the barn dance. These friendly neighborhood gatherings would have a local "caller" with a fiddle or organ supplying the music. Wisconsin had many rural organizations and lodges which kept the movement alive. Granges, co-operatives with recreation programs, church groups, as well as 4-H Clubs developed a program of play party games and other traditional forms of square dancing to keep membership interested and active throughout the state from the 1840s until the present time.

> *—May Donna Gilmore*
> *1979 Square Dance Convention Booklet*

The following record from the Milwaukee County Genealogical Society documents square dance calling and teaching in Wisconsin as early as 1838.

Mrs. Rosalind Peck was the first white woman in Madison, and the first to cross the Baraboo Bluffs to locate in the valley. She died in 1898 at age 90. She and her husband, Eben, settled down in a log cabin that had previously been used as a hotel, in the year 1837. Nelson Dewey was present on September 14, 1837, at the christening of her daughter, Wisconsiana Victoria, the first white child to be born in Madison. Sculptor, Vinnie Ream (Hoxie) was born in the cabin in 1847.

In a reminiscence of her early life. Mrs. Peck said, "we had a regular dancing school twice a week the first winter in the old cabin. There was quite a number of young ladies and middle-aged people. Mr. Stoner brought four daughters, Esquire Bird had a young lady sister; and there were two Brayton girls. A. A. Bird used to call at our dances and trip the light fantastic, too. Visitors from Milwaukee, Fort Winnebago, Galena and Mineral Point, frequently attended our dances."

The Square Dance
by Anne Campbell

Talk about the modern dance, fox trot, an' the rest,
Did you ever have a chance dancin' when 'twas best?
Lanterns hangin' on a string high above your head,
Grand march was a bang-up thing if 'twas you who led!

Violin a screechin' high "Turkey in the Straw;"
All the gals a-steppin' by, best you ever saw!
Ol' man Perkins shoutin' out "Choose your partners now!
Allemande, an' turn about, make a little bow!"

"All hands join an' don't be slow. Circle to the right.
Dance with all the gals you know! (Watch out fur that light!)
Ladies in the center! Quick! Shake your feet awhile!
Gents, go in an take your pick! Swing 'em round in style!"

In the days of long ago, never had to speak
'Bout the young folks dancin' so spoony cheek to cheek!
Had no dancin' censor gent eyeing couples there,
For I guess square dancin' meant dancin' on the square!

Reprinted from *Fiddle and Squares* magazine,
November 1952

How It All Began
by Dale Wagner

American Folk Dancing has a strong English ancestry. The dignity and elegance of the stately contras and quadrilles were brought to America and became popular in the early history of New England. Because we lacked the customary elegant ballrooms of our early history there was a long period of time when it was difficult to maintain the dignity and beauty of the once stately dances. As our pioneers moved west with its rough and tumble lifestyle, the fiddle rather than the musical ensemble became the basic instrument for dancing. It's been said that dancing moved from the ballroom to the brawl room.

Many, many years later Mr. and Mrs. Henry Ford revived the beauty and dignity of folk dancing by building a fine dance hall with teakwood floors and crystal chandeliers in Greenfield Village in Dearborn, Michigan. Mr. Ford hired a dance instructor, Benjamin Lovett, to reestablish the charm and gentility of folk dance, and Mr. Lovett's published book became a much sought-after text.

Once again the Contra and Quadrille with elegant costumed dancers graced the beautiful ballrooms. I believe the hall in Greenfield Village is to this day carrying on the traditional dance programs, featuring the old classical styles of dance as well as dress.

Dr. Lloyd "Pappy" Shaw

One who welcomed Mr. Lovett's book was Dr. Lloyd Shaw, superintendent of Cheyenne Mountain School in Colorado Springs, Colorado. Aware that the book covered only half of America's folk dancing he spent the next three years researching square dancing nationwide. His resulting book *Cowboy Dances*, standardized square dance calls for all parts of the country.

Its instant success spawned, in 1947, the first of ten years of Shaw Square Dance Fellowships at Cheyenne Mountain School. The demand necessitated week long classes in June, July, and August for beginners, intermediate, and experienced leaders. Over the years many nationally recognized callers established their own caller/dancer seminars featuring the traditional Shaw qualities, values, and style. The resulting popularity and success of square dancing led it to be proclaimed by President Ronald Reagan as America's official folk dance.

Cowboy Dances *and* The Round Dance Book

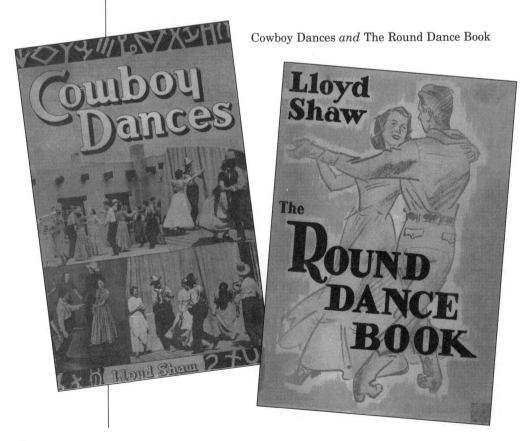

We have Dr. Shaw to thank for not only the rebirth of square dancing, but for its perpetuation, through his research and caller-leader fellowships. Much of his success is rightly attributed to his devoted, dedicated, wife Dorothy, who did much research and writing about many phases of the art of dance. Long after Dr. Shaw's death in 1958 she continued to contribute articles on their mutual love, square dancing.

It should come as no surprise that their granddaughter Enid Cocke, a one-time Cheyenne Mountain dancer, is president of the Lloyd Shaw Foundation. From her hometown of Manhattan, Kansas, she also edits the quarterly publication *The American Dance Circle*. This publication is the Bible for the disciples of today who are carrying on the rich, well-grounded Lloyd Shaw traditions —sponsoring and supporting workshops, seminars, and fellowships covering every phase of American Folk Dancing.

Prior to the founding of the Square Dance Association of Wisconsin (SDAW), Milwaukee and Wisconsin were introduced to square dancing in several Milwaukee area schools. Night school beginners' classes were held at the schools' social centers, and later a weekly open square dance was held, with live music featuring Marge Merhoff's Band. Many an aspiring caller got a start at these classes, including this writer.

Marge Merhoff and her Orchestra — Marge is at the piano, Dale Wagner calling.

Coleman "Doc" Newland, a caller who had recently moved here from Colorado initiated the square dance programs. Mel Schoeckert, a resident of Wauwatosa, introduced a similar program in the Wauwatosa school system. Forgive me for not naming and praising the countless number of similar pioneers who contributed greatly to the early growth of square dancing in Milwaukee and Wisconsin.

A huge boost was given square dancing when, at the 1945 or '46 Wisconsin State Teachers Convention at the Milwaukee Auditorium, Dr. Lloyd "Pappy" Shaw and his touring Cheyenne Mountain Dancers put on an impressive, exciting performance. This high school group demonstrated with beautiful style and enthusiasm the quadrilles and contras, folk and square dances taught them by Dr. Shaw. Wherever they performed he had requests from interested leaders who wanted to learn more about square dancing and its history. Milwaukee was no exception. Those of us privileged to meet him backstage, after the show, were delighted to learn that he was beginning a series of classes generated by the sincere interest of enthusiastic square dance leaders.

The activity received another unexpected boost when service men and women returned after World War II looking for opportunities to learn more about the square dancing they had been exposed to at the various USO's, and found to be so much fun.

At a local level we here in eastern Waukesha County were fortunate when "Doc" Newland announced at a PTA meeting that he was interested in starting square dancing in the area. Doc had already established classes and a successful dance at Wisconsin Avenue School. Basement recreation rooms soon were filled with square dance parties. Many a prospective caller purchased an amplifier, a few records, and began his own basement sessions.

The demand for square dancing prompted Doc to search for a suitable hall. Thus the birth of Calhoun Hall, on Calhoun Road in New Berlin, Wisconsin, as a square dance mecca.

Milwaukee with its many, many, tavern dance halls found owners anxious to have square dancers use their facilities. Many clubs took advantage of this opportunity and to this day many such halls are being used by square dancers. Nationwide, associating square dancing with taverns was frowned upon, but over the years this has presented no problem. After "Doc" Newland left Calhoun Hall in 1947, we took over the popular open Friday night dances and for the next 34 years Calhoun Hall was associated with square dancing every night of the week, but Saturday.

The success of the Friday night dances led to beginners classes, round dance classes, refresher classes, and more advanced dances.

One of the most successful ventures was family dancing on Sunday afternoons, using simple squares, circle dances, songs and family type games learned at a popular guest ranch in the Colorado Rockies, Peaceful Valley Lodge. This opened up a whole new scenario for Wisconsin leaders and dancers.

The owner of the lodge near Estes Park, Colorado, toured the country in search of prospective guests, interviewing callers and leaders, offering his beautiful lodge with its adequate square dance hall for family square dance vacations. At that time it took only twelve to twenty couples to fill the camp. Among the amenities offered square dance families were pack trips, trail rides, ghost town trips, breakfast on the mountain, family rodeo events, evening barbecues, family sing-a-longs, games and dances, plus incomparable food, proving the whole week to be a true mountain-top experience.

Many Wisconsin callers and their families became the backbone of the summer leadership staff, and hundreds of Wisconsin square dance families over the years found this to be a memorable way to share their love for square dancing combined with all the ranch activities. Some of Wisconsin's outstanding leaders served on the staff at Peaceful Valley: Bert Rietz, Dale Wagner, Art Radoll, Bill Barr, Ray Quade, Ken Johnson, Art Weisensel, Herb Johnson, Elmer Elias, Lew Snyder, Earl Thompson, Buzz Kaczmarek. Each one usually teamed up with top nationally acclaimed leaders such as Ray Smith, Manning Smith, Ed Gilmore, Bob Osgood, and Pancho Baird. The square dance season was eventually extended to twelve to fifteen weeks. Local TV stations found square dancing to be an attractive addition to their live shows. In the late '40s Channel 4 WTMJ, included it in their successful noon show, and Channel 12 WISN, used square dancing as a fill-in on a Saturday sports show. The next year a full half-hour show was taped on Saturday to be shown on Monday night. This scheduling featured clubs and callers from all over the Channel 12 WISN viewing area.

In those early days square dance records were scarce. In this area we were fortunate to have Art Knobloch of Midwest Records on 34th and North Avenue, Milwaukee. He became our chief source of supply. All available records were of the 78 RPM variety, some 12-inch size. I don't remember when the small 45s appeared but they were most welcome.

Again we were fortunate to have an enthusiastic caller named Howie Bernard publish the state's first square dance magazine called *Fiddle and Squares*. Mr. Bernard also sponsored the first week long square dance seminar led by a nationally recognized caller. Another popular caller, Bob Dawson, filled the void when *Fiddle and Squares* ceased publication. *Here 'Tis* became an equally successful source of square dance information.

SDAW Jamborees were held in various cities with a square dance following the meeting. Many gimmicks were used to encourage visiting by the statewide clubs. One was banner stealing which involved visiting a club with several couples to steal or retrieve a banner. During the polio epidemics huge crowds of square dancers supported the benefit dances held at the Milwaukee auditorium with local TV and radio personalities acting as master of ceremonies.

Square Dance Jamboree in Sheboygan — Florence and Dale Wagner, Front left position 3 & 4.

In the same vein, Allen Bradley, one of Milwaukee's most noted manufacturing plants, sponsored a huge benefit dance for the Boys' Club in their beautiful gymnasium atop the plant on 2nd and Greenfield. Live music with Harry Moertle's Band was also featured when State Fair Park held free open air dances on the midway. These were very successful with as many as 50 to 100 squares of dancers in attendance. Milwaukee parks also sponsored outdoor dances at Garfield Park Pavilion with Marge Merhoff's Band and at Washington Park with Chet Cholka's Band.

The world of square dancing, Milwaukee and Wisconsin in particular, will always be grateful to Bob Osgood and his nationally acclaimed magazine *Sets in Order*. It became the most popular source of square dance coverage for leaders as well as dancers. After the release of the movie "Three Guys from Milwaukee," featuring Pat O'Brien and two other Wisconsin stars, *Sets in Order* came to Milwaukee to record an album of square dance records called "Three Callers from Milwaukee." Recording artists, Doc Newland, Dale Wagner, and Mel Schoeckert were thus introduced to the intricacies of record production.

One of my proudest moments came when *Sets in Order* presented me with the Silver Spur Award given in recognition of long-time leadership in square dancing.

One of the outstanding recognitions given our city and state was the awarding of the prestigious National Square Dance Convention in 1979, the result of our great support of the many state conventions. What a privilege to host this impressive event. Over 23,000 dancers and leaders were in attendance setting a still unmatched attendance record for a three day convention held at Milwaukee's MECCA Convention Center.

Summing Up

Milwaukee and Wisconsin have an enviable record in support of square dancing. As a dedicated disciple of Dr. Lloyd 'Pappy' Shaw let me close this editorial effort by quoting some of his ideas that we were taught when square dancing was in

The Silver Spur Award.

its infancy. He left it to us to appreciate them and practice them wherever and whenever we were given the opportunity.

"Let us never forget that the main ingredients in square dancing are the dancer on the one hand and the dance on the other. It is the privilege of the caller to stand in the middle and bring the two together. If he is merely a 'caller' he is relatively useless. He must be a caller, teacher, and leader.

"After mastering the three prime requisites of calling—rhythm, clarity, and command—he must follow to the best of his ability for a fun-filled evening of square dancing: keep it simple, keep it folk."

I'm taking the liberty of naming those callers whom I think were the early pioneers and helped to organize the Square Dance Association of Wisconsin. The danger, of course, lies in the fact that in all probability someone is going to be overlooked. That would be regrettable. As one who considers himself to be a charter member of that list I'm submitting these names in the hope that it's complete at least for the state-wide leaders. Whoever is qualified to be on that list deserves recognition for having laid the foundation for what is now a fifty year old organization that contributed greatly to the success of square dancing in Wisconsin. It is my hope that many of the unsung, little recognized leaders that did so much during the early promotion of square dancing will get recognition.

Wisconsin Square Dance Pioneers

R. W. Beauchamps	Irv Kickbusch
Howie Bernard	Lyle Leatherman
Ben Blankenheim	Coleman "Doc" Newland
Martha Clark	Jim van Pietersom
Bob Dawson	Irene Qually
Elmer Elias	Paul Ratajczyk
Carl Faelten	Bert Rietz
Joe Fugina	Carlton Schneider
John Gardner	Mel Schoeckert
Vic Graef	Dale Wagner
Herb Johnson	Chet Wangerin
Elsie Kerkhoff	Art Weisensel

*Dale and
Ruth Wagner*

Dale and Florence Wagner started dancing in 1944 and later came into calling by way of basement parties, parent-teacher associations, church groups, youth gatherings and social center classes. Dale called in cities throughout the state and in Chicago and he and his taw, Florence, attended Dr. Lloyd Shaw's August class at the Cheyenne Mountain School, Colorado Springs, Colorado. In February 1947, they began regular open dancing at Kuney's Hall in Calhoun, a small community ten miles west of Milwaukee. (Calhoun was eventually annexed to New Berlin, and the name of the hall was changed to Calhoun Hall. It was located just south of Greenfield Avenue on Calhoun Road). The Wagners' held a fall-winter program there that included beginners, intermediate, and advanced dancers.

Florence Wagner played an important role in Dale's square dance career. She was at every dance and lesson, lending support and helping demonstrate the dance steps. She became known for her beautiful dresses and was helpful in showing the new dancers the value of appropriate and pretty costumes. She shared sewing hints and patterns with the ladies, and her suggestions and instructions for making petticoats and skirts was published in Sets in Order, a national square dance magazine.

One of the couples in the Wagner's 1948 beginners class was Art and Ruth Ulichny. They became avid supporters of square dancing and worked hand in hand with Florence and Dale on many occasions. Art Ulichny was instrumental in arranging for the recording session when Dale, Mel Schoeckert and Doc Newland made the record "Three Guys from Milwaukee."

Florence Wagner and Art Ulichny passed away in 1975 within months of each other. Dale was devastated but continued his square dance activities. One Friday night a friend brought Ruth Ulichny to a dance at Calhoun Hall, and she and Dale became reacquainted. They were married in 1979 and reside in Wauwatosa. Dale retired from calling in 1981 but still keeps abreast of what is happening in the square dance world.

The Lloyd Shaw Foundation, Inc.
"To Recall, Restore and Teach the Folk Rhythms of the American People"

March 29, 1998

Aggi Thurner
1711 West Fiesta
Mequon, WI 53092

Dear Aggi:

Congratulations to the Square Dance Association of Wisconsin on its 50th anniversary. And thank you for asking me to write a few words about my grandfather, Lloyd Shaw. I am sure that he would be pleased to know that your association has continued for fifty years, giving many people in Wisconsin the chance to experience the joy of dance and the fellowship that goes with it.

In 1948, when your association began, Lloyd Shaw was near the height of his influence in making square dancing a popular recreational activity across the nation. He was conducting summer classes for dance leaders in Colorado Springs, and those leaders returned home inspired to bring square dancing to their areas. At those summer classes they learned square and round dances and how to teach them in the clearest, most succinct way. More important, they learned to treasure this American dance tradition and to believe in its power to bring people together and to bring out the best in everyone.

Lloyd Shaw had not planned to become a dance leader. He was first and foremost an educator, having become superintendent of Cheyenne Mountain School in Colorado Springs a few years after he graduated from Colorado College. He created a curriculum at that school that won national attention for its innovative techniques. Among the activities that he explored to engage the students was international folk dancing. He then stumbled upon square and round dancing as it was then done in Colorado, and this exposure started him on a lifelong quest to research the old dances and get people to dancing again.

The key to spreading these dance forms was his exhibition team of high school students, the Cheyenne Mountain Dancers. They traveled from coast to coast, inspiring people with the joy and beauty of their dancing. The summer classes followed and also the publication of two books, Cowboy Dances in 1939 and The Round Dance Book in 1948. These books have become classics and are still a valued resource to anyone interested in traditional American dancing.

Square dancing has evolved in many ways since Lloyd Shaw passed from the scene in 1958. While he encouraged innovation, he could not have foreseen the explosion of new figures or the increasing complexity in both rounds and squares. I think, however, that he would take great pleasure in knowing how many people have been touched by this great activity. My congratulations to the Square Dance Association of Wisconsin for carrying on the tradition.

Best wishes and happy dancing,

Enid Cocke

Enid Cocke

PRESIDENT	ARCHIVES	SALES	ADC/RMDR
Enid Cocke	LSF Dance Center	LSF Sales Division	
2924 Hickory Ct.	5506 Coal Ave., SE	P.O. Box 11	Ms. Diane E. Ortner
Manhattan, KS 66502	Albuquerque, NM 87108	Macks Creek, MO 65786	929 NW South Shore Dr
(913) 539-6306	(505) 255-2661	(314) 363-5868	Kansas City MO 64151-1443

CHAPTER 2

All Join Hands, Make A Big Ring
The Square Dance Association of Wisconsin

All join hands and circle to the South
Let a little sunshine in your mouth.
Apples in the cellar, peaches on the floor,
Grab your honey and you swing some more.

OUR PLEDGE
by Sally Conger — Chaplain (1948)

We, the Square Dance Association of Wisconsin, do pledge ourselves:

To "March Forward " in the revival and preservation of American Square and Folk Dances;

To "Circle Round" in a spirit of sincerity, democracy, harmony, joyous living, and good fun;

To "Intermingle" with other clubs and their dancers in a spirit of understanding and mutual helpfulness;

To "Honor" and perpetuate the dance by maintaining an active interest in, and an eagerness to learn "Performance" of new "Patterns" and "Movements;"

To "Balance" carefully all propositions for presenting a dance to the general public and to "Cut Away " participation in competition or awards;

To be always on the "Square," in our "Set" or community.

>─┤◆>─O─<◆┤─<

Getting Organized
As compiled from association minutes and the 1949 Association Handbook

The Official Emblem of the Square Dance Association of Wisconsin (SDAW)

The year 1948, having been a Centennial year of the State of Wisconsin, it was very appropriate that something as important as the formation of the Square Dance Association of Wisconsin should take place in that year.

On May 1, 1948, about thirty square dance callers and leaders were invited by Elsie Kerkhoff to meet in Kenosha, which was the day of their First Anniversary Jamboree, to talk over the forming of an organization that would be helpful in spreading the gospel of square dancing. Vic Graef brought up the suggestion that instead of a group of callers, an association of square dance groups would be most influential in spreading the movement.

The next meeting of the group was held in Sheboygan on May 16, in connection with their Second Anniversary Jamboree. At that time a steering committee was selected to further study the advisability of forming a state organization.

Another meeting was held in Milwaukee on July 18 before the jamboree sponsored by the State Centennial Committee of Milwaukee County. At this meeting the callers who had attended Dr. Shaw's June class gave a report on the meeting they'd had with him on the subject of state organizations. His advice was to go slowly and not to over organize, with the primary object of the association to be SERVICE. At this meeting those in attendance were given mimeographed lists of names and addresses of all known callers, leaders, and groups, with data on meeting places and dates.

The fourth meeting, which was the organizational meeting, was held in Oshkosh on August 29, and at that time information was brought back by those callers who had attended Dr. Shaw's August class. Dr. Ralph Piper, of the University of Minnesota, was also present and gave a summary of the organization and function of the Minnesota Federation. Much was accomplished at this meeting. The name was chosen, the bylaws drawn up, and the officers elected.

The Square Dance Association of Wisconsin became a reality. Membership in the Association was open to all groups interested in the promotion of Square Dancing, Folk Dancing, and related arts. Two delegates from each member club served on a council to conduct the business of the association. Monthly Jamborees were held, on the 4th Sunday of each month, with member clubs bidding for their turn at sponsoring such Jamborees in their area. Proceeds from the Jamborees remained with the sponsoring club to be used for promotion purposes.

>-!-◆>-·O-·◆>-!-◁

1948 Officers

President—"Vic" Graef, Sheboygan, Wisconsin

Vice President—"Mel" Schoeckert, Wauwatosa, Wisconsin

Recording Secretary—Dolores Fuerst, Sheboygan, Wisconsin

Corresponding Secretary—Irene Qually, Oshkosh, Wisconsin

Treasurer—Dale Wagner, Milwaukee, Wisconsin

Historian—Agnes Phillipson, Oshkosh, Wisconsin

Director of Publicity and Extension—Irv Kickbusch,

     Milwaukee, Wisconsin

*(Dwight Rice of Racine was elected Historian and served until January 1949, when he resigned because of being transferred to Iowa.)

First SDAW President

Vic Graef, an avid square dance caller, was the first president of the newly formed association. In the summer of 1945, Vic accompanied his brother Henry, to Colorado Springs, where they attended the August class conducted by Dr. Lloyd Shaw. Vic went to observe, but returned to Wisconsin an enthusiastic square dance advocate. He immediately contacted the Recreation Department in Sheboygan and began a study of folk and square dancing with the physical education instructor, Miss Alice Nimocks. They formed a small group, and soon many other groups were formed throughout that area.

Vic returned to Colorado each year to learn under his good friend, "Pappy" Shaw, and to mingle with other top leaders and callers throughout the country. He was a strong advocate of "visiting around" among groups and leaders, and encouraged many other Wisconsin callers to attend the Shaw classes, thereby promoting good dancing throughout the state.

Vic and his groups created public interest in square dancing by exhibiting for organizations, convention groups, church groups, and by sponsoring jamborees. He was responsible for bringing Dr. Shaw and his Cheyenne Mountain Dancers to Wisconsin in 1946, for exhibitions in Sheboygan, La Crosse, and the State Teacher's Convention at the Milwaukee Auditorium.

Because of Vic's personality and born leadership, it was only natural that the Square Dance Association of Wisconsin should elect him as their president.

Vic Graef and family (wife Ida, children, Nancy age 14; Billie, age 12.)

First Vice President

Mel Schoeckert began his calling career in 1941. With his wife, Loretta, he conducted dances and classes in both squares and rounds, and instructed for the Milwaukee Recreation Department. For several years the Schoeckerts instructed for the Wauwatosa Recreation Department, for private groups, and clubs in the Milwaukee area. Mel was the first vice-president of the Square Dance Association of Wisconsin, and was elected president in 1950. He was also the first president of the Wisconsin Square Dance Leaders' Council. Among his many dancing and teaching activities, he served on the steering committee of the March of Dimes Polio Benefit Jamboree, held at the Milwaukee Auditorium in 1950.

Mel was born into a square dancing family in Watertown, Wisconsin. Memories of his childhood days just naturally led him into calling. Mel was an alumni of "Pappy" Shaw's classes and Herb Greggerson's Milwaukee Ranch Dance Institutes.

Sources: The 1949 SDAW Handbook (Irene Qually) and Fiddle and Squares *magazine*

Mel Schoeckert

>─┼─◆>─○─<◆>─┼─<

Our Creed
by Sally Conger, Chaplain

Dear God, grant us the power to be
Always in perfect harmony;
Our hearts, our hands, our feet, our minds
With singing calls or spoken lines.
Let us ever do our duty
And make the dance a thing of beauty.
Teach us that fun and laughter gay
Can banish all life's cares away.
Help us to keep our dance amusing
So folks will come of their own choosing.
We must not dance for gain or greed.
Let this, Square Dancers, be our Creed.

>─┼─◆>─○─<◆>─┼─<

The First Four Years

The following paragraphs were prepared by Irene Qually depicting the outstanding events in the life of the Square Dance Association of Wisconsin from May, 1948 to 1952.

1948

May: A meeting of about thirty square dance leaders and callers at Kenosha. Discussion centered around the need for an organization to help promote square dancing in Wisconsin. A second meeting at Sheboygan. A steering committee was selected to study the merits of an organization that would best serve the interest of square dancing.

July: Third meeting at Milwaukee where the first jamboree of state-wide proportion was held under the sponsorship of the Milwaukee County Recreation Department in conjunction with Centennial celebration on lake front. Reports from several callers and leaders who attended Dr. Lloyd Shaw's June class indicated his thoughts on organization were: (1) to go slowly, (2) not to over organize, (3) to keep it simple, (4) to let SERVICE be the objective. Mimeographed lists of all known callers and groups were given to all present.

August: Oshkosh. This was the organization meeting. After discussion and reports, a vote was taken indicating that those leaders present felt that square dancers and leaders were definitely interested in an organization. It was voted that this be an association of groups rather than of leaders and callers. The bylaws were drawn and the following officers were elected: Vic Graef, president; Mel Schoeckert, vice president; Irene Qually, corresponding secretary; Dolores Fuerst, recording secretary; Dale Wagner, treasurer; Agnes Phillipson, historian; Irv Kickbusch, director of publicity and extension.

December: Twenty-five groups had joined by the end of the year. With the keynote of SERVICE the following plans were outlined: (1) to publish a yearly handbook which would primarily be a directory of groups throughout the state; (2) to be a clearing house for jamborees; (3) to sponsor monthly meetings and jamborees in various cities as a means of spreading and creating a greater interest in square dancing; (4) to encourage groups and couples to visit around among other groups to foster friendship, fellowship, and fun. Sally Conger of Cascade was appointed chaplain.

Inquiries were sent to Chambers of Commerce and recreation departments in all cities in Wisconsin. The replies revealed that there were several groups which were not known, and a good picture of the extent of square dancing in the state was obtained. The official emblem of the Square Dance Association of Wisconsin was adopted.

1949

March: First handbook off the press. Features included a letter from Governor Oscar Rennebohm, Bylaws, Creed and Pledge by Sally Conger, History, biographical sketches of Vic Graef and of "Pappy" Shaw, list of member groups and Directory of all groups.

Letter from Governor. Rennebohm.

Stationery with Square Dance Association letterhead was printed.

May: Election of officers. Replacements: Martin Roltgen, treasurer; Art Petri, director of publicity and extension. Martha Clark appointed Chaplain upon Sally Conger's resignation.

Amendment to bylaws changing election month from May to September and month of taking office to October.

Membership now consisted of thirty-three groups.

Mel Schoeckert headed a committee to study the advisability of a callers and leaders council as an auxiliary to the association.

Bibliography of books, magazines, and records was compiled and mimeographed for distribution to all individuals and groups who requested information.

WTMJ Television broadcasts of "Square Dance Jamboree" on Monday night gave many groups an opportunity to appear and spread square dancing through this medium.

July: Amendment to bylaws, allowing the formation of Wisconsin Square Dance Leaders' Council as an auxiliary group.

November: Hobby show at Milwaukee. SDAW booth with attractive lighted sign, showing map of Wisconsin with location of member groups.

December: Placards for all delegates used for the first time (printed by Jim Cecil).

1950

January: Adoption of bylaws and election of officers of Square Dance Leaders' Council: Mel Schoeckert, president; John Gardner, vice president; Hermine Sauthoff, secretary; Martha Clark, treasurer.

February: 1950 Handbook distributed. Added feature—Calendar of Events.

March: Report of plan for first International Square Dance Festival, sponsored by WLS—Prairie Farmer Station in Chicago in conjunction with Chicago Park Board. Vic Graef called to meet with leaders from nine central states and selected to represent Wisconsin.

September: Election of officers: Mel Schoeckert, president; John Gardner, vice-president; Lois Rogge, recording secretary; Roland Braun, corresponding secretary; George Ziemann, treasurer; Jim Cecil, director of publicity and extension; Eleanor Gotoski, historian.

Leader Council of officers: John Gardner, president; Elmer Elias, vice president; Les Grandine, secretary; and Martha Clark, treasurer.

October: SDAW officers did "committee calling" for hash number at Wisconsin exhibition at First International Square Dance Festival at Chicago Stadium in Chicago.

There were now forty-five groups.

John Gardner, chairman of the Emblem Pin Committee, announced that pins were now ready for distribution.

1951

January: 1951 Handbook distributed. More improvements in
            arrangement and content. New bibliography compiled
            for distribution.

February—October:

            Meetings, jamborees, new member groups. Second
            International at International Amphitheater in
            Chicago, Wisconsin's Grand March exhibition
            arranged by Roland Braun, and directed by Vic Graef,
            carved another notch for SDAW.

December: There are now fifty-five member groups and one
            application pending. There are seventy-one members
            in the Wisconsin Square Dance Leaders' Council.

>─┼─◆>──O─<◆┼─<

Reorganization

In a similar manner the next years rolled by. Square dancing
increased and new groups or clubs were formed, many joining the
association. With the addition of new clubs and callers in the
square dance association many soon felt the necessity to form area
associations to help callers and clubs work more closely together.

As the activity grew and expanded, 1961 found the SDAW
faced with a decision on re-organization and a transition in the
original formation took place. And so it was resolved that the
SDAW would function more successfully as an organization of
areas rather than individual clubs. The following is a report from
the SDAW Reorganization Committee— March 1961.

Wisconsin is recognized throughout the country as a
leader in all phases of round and square dancing. The right
combination of circumstances makes this possible. Genuine
interest on the part of dancers, sound leadership, and a
spirit of cooperation to mention a few. In addition we are
fortunate in having the finest and most progressive group
of round and square dance callers available anywhere.
Wisconsin was one of the first states to form an association
of square dance clubs. This association contributed greatly
to the stature we now hold. We have been fortunate and
should feel proud of these accomplishments.

In the next few paragraphs we would like to explain
briefly what is happening around our state, and especially
how all the clubs in Wisconsin will benefit as a result of the

reorganization of the Square Dance Association of Wisconsin.

The SDAW was formed in 1948. From the start there was an exchange of ideas between clubs. Member clubs cooperated with each other; they worked together with the caller groups toward standardizing on the same type of calls, etc. Clubs began to spring up everywhere. The square dance movement had direction and leadership under the guiding hand of the SDAW.

During the early years of formation there were just a few clubs scattered around the state. Now in the Milwaukee area alone you will find over sixty active clubs. Many more are concentrated in other areas, such as Madison, Wolf River, and Wausau. As a result the SDAW felt that changing the territory structure, to allow smaller groups of clubs to work together would be more harmonious than continuing on a statewide basis. At the same time, other changes will be made to tie in with this reorganization.

Although the reorganization plans are not quite complete, the following general changes are being set into motion. The state will split into several areas: Milwaukee, Madison, Wolf River, and Wausau for example; Each area will form its own group of clubs. Individual club members will choose a representative for their area. The area group of clubs will function under the bylaws of the SDAW. Each area will elect its own officers and will be guided by their own set of local operating rules.

Several times a year each area will send delegates to a state level meeting. Instead of holding twelve jamborees a year, there will be four large area jamborees sponsored by the SDAW (this includes the state convention).

The area groups will be free to promote any type of square dance activity within their area. Individual clubs are members of the SDAW by belonging to an area group. Those clubs located on the fringe of two areas may join the area of their choice.

At this point it should be understood that SDAW is going to be a Dancer Club and Caller Club organization. This is a service organization only—service to and for the clubs within each area and on a broader scale at the state level. Topics for discussion, ideas, and suggestions will be voiced by the clubs through representatives at both area and state meetings.

But, you may ask, "How will all this benefit our club?" Like most other organizations consisting of many groups that share a common interest, it has proven advantageous to the group as a whole to have a central body that can knit the pieces together for the good of all.

These are the aims (or benefits) of belonging to the SDAW: To maintain a spirit of cooperation and harmony between clubs, dancers, and callers. To combine the collective efforts of all clubs in the presentation of square dancing to the public. To make information available that will serve the best interest of square dancing. To support the efforts of new clubs and those clubs who may be in distress. To have a voice in decisions effecting general policy. To take an active part in conducting large jamborees and conventions. To share in the proceeds resulting from these efforts and decide to what purpose they are to be channeled. To discuss in a friendly way items of mutual interest with caller groups.

Please give this your serious consideration and talk it over with your club members. When you have received their approval, join with us to reach these goals.

>—•⟩—O—⟨•—◁

Organizational Committee
Milwaukee Area — SDAW

Based on the Organizational Committee recommendations, area caller and dancer associations were formed in the South East, South West, Wolf River, and Central areas of Wisconsin. Membership in the dancers association was growing as clubs met together to discuss common goals. And so it was resolved that the SDAW would function more successfully as an organization of areas rather than individual clubs.

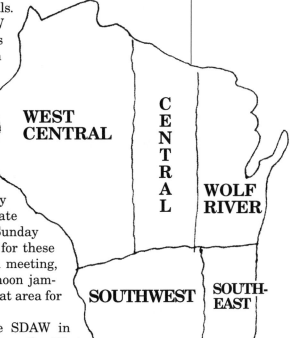

The governing body of this reorganized SDAW is made up of two couple delegates, one from the dancers association, and one from the callers association in each area. Meetings are held quarterly, alternating from area to area. The 4th Sunday in February and May, the Sunday of the State Convention in August, and the 1st Sunday in November have been designated for these meetings. At all but the Convention meeting, the sponsoring area hosts an afternoon jamboree, with proceeds remaining in that area for the promotion of square dancing.

After the reorganization of the SDAW in 1961, a 5th area joined the ranks, as the West

Central area was organized with a Dancers and Callers organization.

One of "Pappy" Shaw's suggestions to the group working toward organization back in 1948 was to let SERVICE be the objective. SERVICE has been emphasized from the beginning. The meetings and jamborees have been planned so that they spread outward throughout the state. Workshop sessions at the leaders' council meetings have helped spread good dancing and given an opportunity to callers and leaders to take new dances and techniques back to their groups. Help has been given immeasurably by individual callers and groups to many beginning groups. Friendship and fellowship have predominated at the meetings and at the jamborees. We have moved slowly, avoided over organization and the keynote has been "not what you can get out of the association, but what you give to it."

Above information was compiled from early handbooks and Summer 1966 Here 'Tis *by May Donna Gilmore, secretary 1965-66*

>─◄►─○─◄►─►<

1949 Calendar of Events

Sunday, February 27
  SDAW Council Meeting and Hoedown in Oshkosh

Thursday, March 17
  Kettle Moraine St. Patrick's Day Dance at Tony Wester's
    Resort, Lake Ellen

Sunday, March 27
  SDAW Council Meeting and Hoedown at Madison

Sunday, April 24
  SDAW Council Meeting and Waukesha Square Dance Club
    Hoedown at Waukesha

Saturday, April 30
  EMBA (Elec. Co.) Second Anniversary Jamboree at Public
    Service Building air-conditioned auditorium, Milwaukee

Saturday, May 7
  Kenosha Square Dance Club Second Anniversary Jamboree
    Southport Park Club, Kenosha

Sunday, May 15
  SDAW Council Meeting and Sheboygan Square Dance Club
    Third Anniversary Jamboree at the Sheboygan Armory

Sunday, June 5
  Winnebago Dip and Dive Club, First Anniversary Jamboree at
    Brothertown

Sunday, June 19
SDAW Council Meeting and Kettle Moraine Square Dance
Club Open Air Jamboree and Picnic at Lake Ellen

Saturday, July 2
Green Bay Fourth Anniversary Jamboree at Bay Beach

Sunday, July 17
Milwaukee County Recreation Department Open Air Square
Dance Festival on the Lake Front, Milwaukee

Sunday, July 24
SDAW Council Meeting and Calico & Kerchief Dance Club
Jamboree at Two Rivers

Sunday, August 28
SDAW Council Meeting and Green Bay Hoedown at Green Bay

Sunday, September 25
SDAW Council Meeting and Hoedown at Brothertown

Sunday, October 25
SDAW and Milwaukee Area Jamboree at Nightingale Ballroom

Sunday, November 6
Turner Square Dancers, Third Anniversary Jamboree at
Sheboygan

➤⎯◆⟩⎯○⎯⟨◆⎯⎯◅

Member Groups of Square Dance Association of Wisconsin—1949

BELOIT:
Beloit Square Dance Club

BROTHERTOWN:
Winnebago Dip & Dive Square Dance Club

CASCADE
Kettle Moraine Square Dancing Club

COLGATE
Lazy L & N Riding Club

FOND DU LAC
Fond du Lac Square Dance Club

GREEN BAY
Green Bay Square Dancers
The Gardner's Square Dancers

KIEL
Bar-None Square Dance Club

MADISON
- Co-op Recreation Group
- Community Center Group

MARINETTE
- Marinette KC Square Dance Club

MILWAUKEE
- Brown Deer Park Square Dancers
- Cream City Buckaroos
- EMBA Square Dancing Club
- Harvey's Square Dance Club
- J.F. Square Dance Club

OMRO
- Omro Square Dancers

OSHKOSH
- Oshkosh Square Dancers

PLYMOUTH
- Plymouth Square Dance Club

SHEBOYGAN
- Circle 8 Club
- Docey Doe
- Elm City Dancers
- Sheboygan Square Dancing Club
- Swingsters
- Turner Square Dancing Club

SHEBOYGAN FALLS
- Sheboygan Falls Square Dancers

TWO RIVERS
- Calico & Kerchief Square Dancers

WAUKESHA
- Waukesha County Square Dancers

WAUPUN
- Waupun Old Time Square Dancers

WAUWATOSA
- Wauwatosa Fundamentals
- Hawthorne Square Dancers

WHITEFISH BAY
- Whitefish Bay Square Dancers

WEST ALLIS
- West Allis Recreation Department Dancers

CHAPTER 3

Wheel Around
Early Square Dance Clubs

*A little bit of heel, a little bit of toe
Grab your honey and away we go
Look over yonder and what do you see
Mo' folks comin' in a Model T.*

Before the Square Dance Association of Wisconsin was established there were many clubs dancing in Wisconsin with names like Winnebago Dip and Dive (Brotherton), Cream City Buckaroos (Milwaukee), Docey Doe Club (Sheboygan), Calico & Kerchief (Two Rivers), Bar-None Club (Kiel), along with more straightforward names like the Marinette KC Club, Fond du Lac Club, and Kenosha Club. Many were simply named for the club caller such as Gardner's Square Dance Club (John and Mil Gardner) in Green Bay, and Harvey's Square Dance Club (Harvey Stipe) in Milwaukee. There were clubs that began in schools and recreation centers: West Allis Recreation Department Dancers, Badger School (Cold Spring Road, Milwaukee), South Milwaukee Recreation Department, and Wisconsin Avenue Social Center.

One of the oldest clubs in the state is the Green Bay Squares. They were the first club in northeastern Wisconsin and one of the first in the state to promote and furnish public square dancing. Club members have been dancing on Thursday nights for over half a century.

>─┤◆├─○─◄◆├─◄

History of the Green Bay Squares
by Ann Krueger

Mr. and Mrs. Gardner honored at 25th anniversary dance.

The club was organized in 1945 by John Gardner, a city mail carrier, and his wife, Mildred. John and "Mil" were introduced to square dancing in the summer of 1935, and by 1940 were conducting programs wherever invited to do so. John was successful in

persuading the Green Bay Recreation Department to sponsor a square dance party every other week. The dancers from that group formed the nucleus of the Green Bay Squares. At the end of the school year the new club held its first dance at Pamperin Park. Later, club members and visiting couples danced at Bay Beach Pavilion.

Square dancing at Bay Beach became very popular, and gradually the crowd grew too large for the dance hall. A smaller, adjoining hall was then used as a backup to accommodate the four- to five-hundred people who came each week. With the extra space, another caller was needed. Neil Thayer, one of the original members, became the assistant caller.

Another member, Charles (Grandpa) Allen, had learned to call square dance numbers at the age of twelve by listening to the older callers. He called a few tips each Thursday night at the club dance, and was still calling in his late eighties.

Gradually, new clubs were formed in the area, and in 1948 members of the Green Bay Squares helped to organize the Square Dance Association of Wisconsin.

Throughout those fifty-three years, club members danced at a number of halls, which included Riverside Ballroom and Bastens Hall, and presently, Wertels Hall, in east Green Bay.

Ann and Milt Krueger

After Gardner, a number of other callers took their place at the mike. Ivan Draize, the late Lloyd Bungert, and Clayton Pigeon each called for a number of years, along with many visiting callers. Now, Larry Cockrum and Lloyd Vertz call for the club twice a month on alternate Thursdays.

In those early years, live music was furnished for dancing, but by the middle fifties it was replaced by recorded numbers.

When the club members started to square dance, a couple could take one half hour of instruction and dance with the group. Gradually, the calls had more intricate steps, with the entire square in action, which called for increased instruction time for new dancers.

Some of the earlier dancers are still dancing with the club. They recall those good old days and Gardner's words:

"Square dancing is an American heritage. It is one of the few forms of entertainment where a couple can spend an enjoyable evening and meet new friends, either in their hometown or some distant city."

Ann Krueger of Greenleaf, Wisconsin, and her husband Milt joined the Green Bay Squares in the mid-1950s and danced with the group for many years. When Milt passed away Ann continued to dance as a single, usually taking the part of the man. Ann is an accomplished writer, and has been published in local newspapers, and American Square Dance *magazine. She has won several awards for her writing. Ann is a thirty-five year member of the Wisconsin Regional Writer's Association.*

>–◇–○–◇–◁

One of the strongest clubs in the Milwaukee area was the EMBA which began as a social club for employees of the Electric Company. The club was formed in 1946 and is still going strong. Here are some "tidbits" gleaned from reports, minutes, and news articles of the club.

EMBA Anniversary Poster

EMBA
Submitted by Dolores Tock

EMBA ♣

Square Dance Club
1946-1996

Please join us as we celebrate
50 years
of friendship, fun, and square dancing!

September 29, 1996

Knights of Columbus Hall
3200 So. 103 rd St.
Milwaukee

Len and Ruth Siegmann : M.C.

12:30 Dinner
and Dance - $14.00 per person

Dinner only - $12.00 per person
Reservations by August 31.

2:30-5:00 Square Dance only -
$4.00 per person at door

Send reservations to:
Ray and Donna Luber
4806 W. Midland Drive
Greenfield, Wi. 53219
Tel. - 414-327-3646

1946—The Electric Company established a Square Dance Club in Milwaukee for the benefit of their employees. Hence the name— Employee Mutual Benefit Association or EMBA. Irv Kickbusch was the first president and instructor. Elmer Elias was the first secretary. The first dance was held in the Public Service Auditorium of the Electric Company. The first year had 14 couples. Women wore long dresses and men wore western shirts.

1948— A report states that the Club had a large deficit. Membership dues of 25 cents augmented the treasury. A newspaper picture shows EMBA dancers featured on WTMJ-TV, a regular 10 pm. Tuesday program.

1949—The Club bought its own calling equipment in November. Elmer Elias was appointed club caller. Elmer, together with his wife Rosemarie, taught and choreographed square and round dancing.

They were well-known for the Roselle Dancers, also known as the Black Light Dancers because they used black lights for special effects.

1950—Admission to an EMBA dance was 75 cents. There were good and lean times. In 1950 there were 32 new dancers—in 1953 there was only one new dancer!

1963—Club dances were regularly held at Todd American Legion Post on the second Friday of the month. This is still true.

1986—Elmer retired as EMBA Club caller. However, his leadership in square and round dancing is still very evident.

1988—Len and Ruth Siegmann are now club caller and cuer. Elissa and Bob Pischke are club instructors.

1996—A special dance was held in honor of the 50th year of the EMBA. Dancers from all over Wisconsin attended the dance. Elmer Elias was presented with a special award—a handmade wood carving of himself.

⊱─┤ ◆⟩─•─�‹◆─┤ ─⊰

Square Dance Miracles
Written by Dolores Tock in honor of EMBA's 50th Anniversary

> Square Dancing—a strange name for fun, fitness,
> friendship. Yet today a gathering of dancers,
> friends, family, here to celebrate 50 years of
> square dancing !
> Is this not a miracle?

> Square Dancers—not so square, but certainly
> dancers, smiling as they happily respond in
> rhythm and movement to a caller's direction!
> Is this not a miracle?

> Square Dancers—always ready to welcome each
> other to a circle or to a square. Yes, they recall
> that "a stranger is just a friend to be."
> Is this not a miracle?

Yellow Rock? Yellow Rock! Tell your friends and neighbors about that one! But to a square dancer this call is always greeted with cheers, smiles, and warm hugs!
Is this not a miracle?

Callers, Cuers, Teachers—men and women who give time, energy, talent, yes and patience, so that the rest of us can promenade in fun and fitness.
Is this not a miracle?

Dancers all—what would callers and cuers do without you? Would they not be down-sized? Your enthusiasm attracts new members who help to keep the tradition of squares and circles moving forward into the future.
Is this not a miracle?

EMBA Square Dance Club—all present and former members—truly a circle of friends. You have shown the meaning of caring and cooperation as you shuffled and twirled through the years. And you have done this for 50 years!
Is this not a miracle?

The Siegmanns—Len, one of our favorite callers! Ruth, just as favorite a cuer! You keep us on our toes. Yes, you make our feet dance, our voices sing, and our faces glow with happy smiles. We just can't help it!
Is this not a miracle?

Elmer Elias—a fellow dancer, a caller, a cuer, a friend! You celebrate with us today your own 50 years of leadership in square and round dancing. We applaud your life and contribution to one of our favorite activities.
Is Elmer not a miracle?

Petunia City Squares
submitted by John and Gloria Rindfleisch

The Petunia City Squares originated in 1946. The club was started as a recreation for teachers in the Beloit schools in 1946. Dances were held alternately at Lincoln and Roosevelt Junior High Schools. Callers were few and instructions were given half an hour before a dance. Dances were of the "visiting" type where the first couple would lead out to the second couple, execute a move, then move on to the third and fourth couples to repeat the move(s).

Live music was used entirely at that time. Instruments were guitar, accordion, piano and violin. About 1952 the membership was so large that dances had to be held in both schools simultaneously. This caused problems with dancers moving between schools looking for friends since the schools were on opposite sides of town. The problem was solved when Roosevelt Junior High was enlarged and the dances could once again be held in one facility. Later on the club moved to Converse School and then to Aldrich Junior High where it still dances today. Old club records would always indicate the date of the dance, the name of the caller, the number in attendance, and the weather conditions. Lou Harrington and Robert McCarthy were two callers used by the group.

In the beginning, refreshments were simple (donuts and coffee). The coffee was boiled in a large copper boiler with a faucet soldered onto it and the coffee was put into a cloth bag and then into the boiler to cook. Since it took a long time to make the coffee, the first duty of the "serving" committee was to fill the boiler with water and start the coffee boiling over two gas burners.

The club was originally known as the "Beloit Square Dance" club. That name was changed by the presiding officers in the '60s, around the time the City of Beloit was named an "All American" city. Over the years, attendance and membership has been good at times and in decline at other times, much as it has been with other clubs in the surrounding area. We would

Petunia City Squares Poster.

1946 1996

Petunia City Squares

50th Anniversary Dance

| Bob Wild | Nancy Hills |
| Bob Lindemann | Leta Thomas |

Sunday October 27th, 1996 - - 1:00 - 4:00 pm
Aldrich Junior High School (Commons)
1859 NorthGate, two blks. north of Cranston Rd.
Beloit, Wisconsin

Refreshments 50/50

Admission
.50¢
per
person

608-365-1907

hope that in another 50 years, the club will still exist and provide the same wonderful entertainment it does today.

The history of Petunia City Squares was provided by club members, John and Gloria Rindfleisch of Clinton. John and Gloria have only been square dancing about ten years, but during that time have taken an active role in state square dance leadership. They have served on various committees with their area association, were general chairmen of the 1991 State Convention in Madison, and currently are historians for the SDAW.

CHAPTER 4

Star Promenade
Pioneers of the
Wisconsin Square Dance Movement

Hand over hand, and heel over heel,
The more you dance, the better you feel.
Applejack and home brewed corn,
Listen to the caller and dance 'til morn.

The Sky's the Limit
by Agnes Thurner

An alien from the planet Mars
    passed by a country inn.
He stopped awhile to listen
    to the music from within.
The song was nice and peppy
    but the words weren't very clear,
So he sneaked inside to eavesdrop
    where he could see and hear.
He stayed there all throughout the night,
    then silently withdrew,
And returning to his spaceship
    this is what he told his crew.

"There was a big room full of people,
    men and women, two by two.
And a man up in the front
    was telling them what they should do.
But he spoke a funny language,
    things I couldn't understand
Like allemande left your corner,
    do-si-do, and weave the land.
I've never seen such strange maneuvers,
    twists and turns across the floor.
And when he hollered "yellow rock"
    you should have heard the people roar.
Then someone saw me hiding there
    and dragged me to the ring.
A woman grabbed me in an armlock,
    showed me how to do the "swing."

Back at home our Martian friend
    became a hero far and near.
He loves to talk of his adventures
    and he has a new career.
He is giving square dance lessons,
    teaching how to "shoot the stars"
And planning for a World Convention
    to be held someday on Mars.

Where Would We Be Without Callers
by Agnes Thurner

Where would we be without square dance callers? In the days before sound equipment, a square dance often meant that several among those present shared in the calling, for it was quite likely that each dancer knew a call or two. At larger dances, where a single caller could not be heard by everyone it was common practice to have a caller in each square to direct the dancers. Can you imagine twenty squares of dancers, each with its own caller, each doing a different dance?

By the beginning of the twentieth century, the early dance styles such as the Contra, (from the English Country Dance), and the Quadrille, (which came from France), had blended together and taken on different attributes. The traditional, or visiting couple style dance came into vogue. Inexperienced dancers would be placed in the number four spot in the square, where they could watch the head couple as they "visited" each couple in the square to execute a specific pattern with that couple. Number two would follow suit, then number three. When the time came for number four to go "visiting" they had memorized the pattern.

Long before recorded music became available, and long before clubs were instituted, there were fiddlers and other musicians who traveled from town to town playing and calling for dances. Wisconsin had its share of these traveling minstrels. When one of them arrived in the area, word was sent around, families and neighbors would gather in someone's home, where the largest room, usually the kitchen, was commandeered for a square dance. The caller would stand on a chair and call out his commands. These "kitchen junkets" were purely American, and are an excellent example of the friendliness and neighborliness that has become synonymous with American Square Dancing.

The formation of the SDAW was the first step in bringing the callers and dancers of Wisconsin together into a cohesive group. A roster of callers and clubs was compiled and distributed throughout the state. With the aid of square dance magazines, and caller and dancer recollections we have been able to profile many callers who played an active role in the first years of the new association.

⊱─◆─◦─◆─⊰

DOC NEWLAND had his first contact with square dancing in southeastern Colorado in 1930. In Denver, Colorado, from 1938 to 1940 he did considerable dancing with various groups sponsored mainly by the Denver city recreation department. 1940 found "Doc" attending a class for callers, which was sponsored by the Denver Recreation Department. "Doc" began calling late in 1940 and

*Doc Newland
and Eunice*

through 1943 he called and instructed for school and church groups. Along about this time, "Doc" moved his family to Milwaukee and from 1944 to 1949 he called and taught in Milwaukee at the Wisconsin Avenue Social Center. From 1948 on "Doc" was kept busy with private classes, open dances and club groups. He attended the "Pappy" Shaw Institutes of 1949 and 1950 at Colorado Springs, Colorado. For several years "Doc" conducted an open dance every Saturday night at Mother of Good Counsel School auditorium, where more than forty sets on occasion cavorted to his calling.

>→⋅◆→⋅○⋅◆→⋅◄

HERB JOHNSON hailed from Oshkosh, Wisconsin. He was a well-known caller and leader whose first experience at calling dated back to the early 1930s. From 1931 to 1936 Herb was a leader of an old-time dance band. During this time dances were made up of circle two-steps, waltzes, the schottische, hop-waltzes and a few square dances. His repertoire of square dances totaled about a dozen.

Herb and his lovely wife were married in 1934 and he soon realized that being a member of a dance band was no place for a family man. Tilda and Herb discontinued their dance activities until 1948, during which time they were raising two daughters.

Herb enrolled in a special class in square dance calling at the University of Wisconsin under the leadership of Mr. Max Casper. Herb was doing post-graduate work at the same time. He and Tilda also entered a square dance class sponsored by the Madison Recreation Department at that time.

Soon after, Herb formed his first club. It was known as the Capitol Squares and they danced in a little town between Madison and Oregon. By 1952 he had taught nine beginners classes, and was calling regularly for six clubs in Madison, Evansville and Freeport, Illinois. In March of 1952 he moved to Oshkosh and started his first beginners class there that fall.

One of Herb's most important activities was a monthly program at Winnebago State Hospital, where he conducted dances with and for the patients. Square dancers from throughout the area, assisted in this program by two Oshkosh clubs, Timber Toppers and the Square Swingers, helped immensely with this program.

HOWIE BERNARD began dancing in 1943 at the Wisconsin Avenue Social Center under Barbara Shipps, who at that time was the caller-instructor for the school board recreation department. After several years of dancing Howie began calling for small basement groups, PTA's, and private parties. Thereafter came a series of square dance promotions. The first and most spectacular was the first Wisconsin Square Dance Festival, sponsored by the Wisconsin State Centennial committee of Milwaukee County and staged at Juneau Park, Sunday, July 18, 1948. Several hundred thousand spectators viewed this outdoor spectacle and it immediately gave square dancing in the Milwaukee area a terrific impetus. Then came several huge outdoor square dances at the opening of a number of Milwaukee's newest paved streets including North 3rd Street, West Greenfield Avenue, West North Avenue, North Green Bay Avenue, and the opening of the "Magnificent Mile" in downtown Milwaukee, for which Herb Greggerson of El Paso, Texas, was the featured caller. A million people were said to have been on Milwaukee's "Magnificent Mile" that evening with square dancing smack in the middle of the "mile."

Howie Bernard

In August of 1952 and 1953 Howie Bernard promoted and organized free Public Exhibitions, (three hour shows) presented on stage at the Temple of Music, Washington Park. These events were sponsored by the Milwaukee County Recreation Department. Howie attended "Pappy" Shaw's 1949 class, Herb Greggerson's Ranch Dance Institutes in 1950, '51, '52, '53, '54, '55 and with the help of his lovable and efficient taw Hildegard, sponsored many Herb Greggerson Ranch Dance

Herb Greggerson Ranch Dance School — 1951

HERB GREGGERSON MILWAUKEE RANCH DANCE SCHOOL

Dancers at Capitol Pladium — 1954.

Institutes in Milwaukee at the Capitol Pladium.

In addition, this energetic promoter and organizer for square dancing in this area issued the first edition of *Fiddle and Squares*, Wisconsin's square dance magazine. Howie also held dances twice a week at the Capitol Pladium and called for clubs in various parts of the state and in Chicago.

>─┤◄►─•─O─•─◄►─┤─<

Bert Rietz

BERT RIETZ started square dancing in 1946 under Chet Wangerin. In 1947 he began calling with the Shorewood Recreation Department. He was caller for the Gateway Square Dance Club of Kenosha, Wisconsin, for several years and conducted open dancing at Club Garibaldi on Milwaukee's south side, taking over the dancing started by Bill Barr after Bill's departure for Sacramento, California. Bert taught and conducted clinics at Appleton, Wisconsin, in 1951 and 1952, and caller clinics at Memphis, Tennessee, in August 1964, under the auspices of the Memphis Park commission. He made three cross-country trips covering all of the western states and attended Greggerson's Milwaukee Institute, 1960, and Ray Smith's school, 1961. He held public dances at Clark's Woods from 1948-1961. He was a member of the faculty of the first Wisconsin Square Dancer Leaders' Council (WSDLC) Work Spree at Green Lake in September 1964. In 1953 he made a record album of four records under the RCA label.

CHET WANGERIN began dancing back sometime before 1945 and started calling in October 1946, when he organized the Whitefish Bay Square Dancers. Square dancing was just beginning to be popular and Chet was surprised at how many people were interested in this pioneer recreational activity. More than four sets danced regularly every week during that first season. That winter Chet also organized the St. Paul Square Dancers.

In 1949 he organized the Shorewood Square Dancers, which became famous for their annual "Open House." Dancers and callers came from all over Milwaukee as invited guests of the group, to dine and dance at no charge. Chet was athletic director for the Shorewood school board, he also served as "Mike Boss" at the square dance celebrating the first anniversary of the Southgate Shopping Center, held Wednesday, September 10, 1952. Dancing was on the macadam adjacent to the center.

*Chet
Wangerin*

In the spring of 1946 **ELMER HAMANN** and his taw, Ruth, were invited to join a group of square dancers at Greendale, a suburb of Milwaukee. That night was the beginning of eight years of dancing and calling pleasure. For several years prior to taking up square dancing, Elmer was already using a public address system for entertaining at weddings and private parties. Quite naturally, therefore, calling squares followed. Elmer joined "Doc" Newland's 1946 fall class for callers at the Wisconsin Avenue Social Center, Milwaukee, and from there was on his way to happy dancing and calling. He taught beginners at Auer Avenue and Park Lawn social centers for over five years. In addition he was the regular caller for the Belles and Beaux Square Dance Club in the fall of 1949.

Elmer attended two Herb Greggerson Milwaukee Institutes and was general chairman for the March of Dimes polio benefit jamboree for five years running.

The following pages are taken from a speech written for Paul Ratajczyk by his wife Marie in 1956. It was for a party to celebrate his tenth anniversary in square dancing. (Information provided by Ann Buck, daughter).

This is Your Square Dance Life, Paul Ratajczyk

It was late 1946—World War II had ended and you were working at the Allis-Chalmers "Supercharger Plant" with a fellow who came from Colorado. This fellow, whose name is "Doc" Newland, was a square dance caller. He was always after you to join a square dance group he was forming but your wife, Marie, just wasn't interested. Dorothy Baldwin, one of the members of Doc's group, talked to Marie, and she finally agreed to come to one dance. You attended your first square dance one Friday night at Calhoun Hall. Doc Newland was calling not to records, as we do now, but to a piano player and a fiddler.

Then it was January 1947, the year of the great storm. Fourteen inches of snow fell. You were frustrated that Friday when all traffic was stalled and you couldn't get to your next square dance. You couldn't stop telling all your friends how much fun square dancing could be.

Paul Ratajczyk

The rest of 1947 was spent square dancing with Doc, and taking calling lessons from him at the 27th Street Social Center. There was very little square dancing being done in Milwaukee County at this time, and none on the south side of Milwaukee.

In January 1948 you had a chance to conduct your first class at South Milwaukee High School. Many of the folks in your first class were people you had known for years, and it was fun teaching them this new source of entertainment. At that time square dancing was done a little differently—let's say it was a little more strenuous than it is today.

In June 1948, you and Doc attended "Pappy" Shaw's Cheyenne Mountain School in Colorado. Here they were teaching a new, smoother type of square dancing, and you had to change your entire style of dancing. When you came back you

The Log Cabin Dancers.

changed the method of teaching in your classes to the smooth Western style of dancing. Many square dancers objected to the change, but eventually they accepted it, and today everyone is doing it that way.

In the fall of 1948 you held classes in many different locations: in South Milwaukee, Cudahy, the Town of Lake, and at Odd Fellows Hall in Bay View. You and Doc jointly ran an open dance at Odd Fellows Hall on Saturday nights. By this time you had quit working and spent three glorious years doing nothing but square dance calling and teaching. Immaculate Conception School, Allen-Bradley Company, and the Craig-Schlosser Post, were some of the other places you taught.

In May 1949, you started open square dancing on Friday nights at the Log Cabin (restaurant and hall) on North Avenue and Calhoun Road. The following June you attended Pappy Shaw's classes again, as you did for the next five years.

In September you decided to have a beginners class at the Log Cabin, in conjunction with the Friday night dance. It was from this class that the '49ers Square Dance Club was formed. The '49ers is one of the oldest clubs in Milwaukee, and one you still call for. Many members of that first class are here tonight. It was a busy life, and all your evenings were taken but you loved every minute of it. It gave you a chance to do something you enjoyed and still be with your family all during the day.

You kept your classes at the Log Cabin for six years, and later taught advanced as well as beginner classes there. You had a chance to get acquainted with many people in the area. After introducing a party theme to your square dancing, Irene Hastings and Mary suggested adding food to make it a real party. Since then your Christmas, New Year's, Halloween, and Valentine parties have become legend. They were made up of people who had become friends while attending your classes.

At this time, you also had a group of 200 high school students at Shorewood who had formed a square dance club. This was something unusual at that time.

You attended all but the last of the International Square Dance Festivals in Chicago, and renewed friendships made at Pappy Shaw's classes. You also attended three of Herb Greggerson's classes in Milwaukee. Herb was a traveling caller from Texas who used to teach classes all over.

In 1954 you flew to Dallas to attend the National Square Dance Convention, where you met more acquaintances from the West.

You will always have wonderful memories of square dancing. Remember dancing at the Broadmore Hotel overlooking Cheyenne Mountain during a full moon. Remember the picnic with the class at Austin Bluffs overlooking Palmer Park. It was here that Pappy Shaw, surrounded by his class, told the legends of the West. And you will surely recall the trip to Pappy's cabin in the mountains, and the chuck wagon dinners held at the foot of the mountains in the Garden of the Gods.

Last year you conducted classes at Dixon School in Brookfield, and this year you are holding classes on Tuesday evenings at St. Mary's in Hales Corners. On Wednesday evenings you are holding classes at St. Veronica's in Milwaukee, and on Friday evenings in Elm Grove.

One of the classes you especially enjoy calling at is the Craig-Schlosser Legion Post. You have been calling there every Sunday night for the past seven years. This group also visits the Veterans Home in Waupaca, and the mentally affected veterans at Downy, Illinois.

And so Paul, you can look back with pride on the past ten productive years, and the hundreds of enjoyable hours spent calling and teaching square dancing. You can be proud of your role in preserving this important part of our American Heritage.

You can reflect on the many friendships you formed while teaching your classes, and in your calling activities. You can take satisfaction in knowing that you have been instrumental in providing many happy occasions where dancers could band together, meet new people, and develop lifelong friendships.

Paul Ratajczyk continued to call for square dances and lessons until late 1958 when he suffered a double brain aneurysm. Doctors were unable to operate. When home from the hospital, Paul had to stay in bed for six months to allow the aneurysms to heal by them-

selves. He lived for ten more years, long enough to see his first grandchild. Unfortunately he was never able to call or dance again. He passed away in late 1968, leaving behind him a legacy of fun and friendship set to music.

>━┼━◆>━O━<◆━┼━<

Pat Kelm, a caller, cuer, and prompter from Deerbrook, Wisconsin, shared these memories of one of her favorite callers, Clarence Freis.

CLARENCE FREIS and his wife, Adeline, lived and farmed in rural Sheboygan County. Clarence was born on May 15, 1906. He called his first square dance at the Palladium in Sheboygan in 1946. He studied calling under the tutelage of Betty McGinnis in Sheboygan.

In 1959 the Clar-Adel Dancers was formed. That club danced every Friday night until November 1, 1986. During those years his business card read "Dairyland's Singing Cowboy." He did have a very good voice. The evening of the club's last dance one of the club members, Romaine Wellhoefer, read aloud the following poem she had written:

Ode to Clarence

I think it was back in '73,
That our friends the Pausigs said to me
"Come on along to the Clar-Adels dance
And let's find out, if perchance
You'd like to learn a thing or two
And meet our caller, Clarence, too."

Well, we came, we saw, we met, we stayed.
We heard "do-si-do" and "partner trade."
I said to Louie—"I wonder if my poor old head
Can assimilate all this before I'm dead."

For months we plodded thru the "teach"
And I never thought that we would reach
The point where we could dance at all
And learn to execute on call!

I began to hate the word "beginner,"
It made me feel like some old sinner,
God forbid if you'd break up the square,
How you wished that you were not there!

But certain folks made you feel
That's okay—it's no big deal,
And Clarence, patient thru it all
In our book he sure stands tall.

He's seen us come, he's seen us go
And sometimes he's felt pretty low,
We've had our ups, we've had our downs,
But we're so grateful he taught us rounds.

He's opened doors for Louie and me;
I don't ever really see
How any of us can ever show
The gratitude we've come to know.

He's shown us fellowship, friendship, loving, caring,
All these things, always sharing.
And now I guess it's meant to be
The Clar-Adels become sweet memory.

Clarence, we'll always see you standing there
Calling—"all right—form your squares"
We love you Clarence, with all our heart.
It's not the end—just another start.

Clarence Freis passed away on December 1, 1991. The same dancer, Romaine, wrote:

In Remembrance of Clarence

I am not dead
I am there with you.
When you bow to your partner and your corner too.
I am there
When you make your feet go "whickety whack"
When you allemande left and you're on the right track.
I am there
When you give her a swing
And twirl and spin like everything.
I am there
When you square up with your pals,
And when you yellow rock those corner gals,
Then hug me too!
I am there.

BEN BLANKENHEIM began dancing in 1947. In 1949 he began instructing a group of friends in his basement at home. Following success with this group, in January of 1950 he accepted a calling assignment at Blessed Sacrament parish. In the fall of l950 Ben and Laura organized the Frontier Square Dance Club and he was instructor/caller for the group. In addition, Ben instructed classes for the Milwaukee Recreation Department for over three years. The Frontier Square Dance Club met twice monthly at Tony's Club, 3400 South Loomis Road, on Milwaukee's southwest side. Under Ben's direction, the group appeared in two public exhibitions held at Washington Park Temple of Music, sponsored by the Milwaukee County Recreation Department.

>─┤◆├─O─┤◆├─<

JOHNNY "RED VEST" TOTH
from information submitted by Louise Toth

Johnny Toth of South Milwaukee was a talented square dance caller for over 45 years. He was blessed with a beautiful singing voice and an ability to change moods with the music. He will be remembered for his smooth calling style, his commitment to new dancers and the promotion of square dancing in general, as well as his "trademark" Red Vest. Throughout his career, he taught thousands of people to square dance.

Johnny and Louise Toth

Johnny and his wife, Louise, were introduced to square dancing when another couple was needed to fill a square dance class. "We were 'dragged' in and were hooked," said Louise "and we never stopped enjoying the activity." There was a shortage of callers and it wasn't long before Johnny was encouraged to learn to call. Bert Rietz and Robert Stuart were influential in giving him his start. He pored over books and square dance records and participated in discussion groups, working diligently to develop the distinctive styling for which he was noted.

His primary work was done in the midwest, but he also called throughout the states and in Canada. He was caller for many local clubs including Ridge Runners, Circle 8, Kenosha Eagles, VIP's, '49ers and Swing Easy.

Time was also volunteered to South Milwaukee Middle School for square dance instruction. In the late 1950s Johnny pioneered camporees for square dancers who camped and also held square and round dance weekends at northern resorts with his partner of 25 years, Elmer Elias.

Membership in MACC, SDAW and Leaders' Council, charter membership in CALLERLAB and a lifetime membership in National Square Dance Campers' Association attest to his great support of square dancing.

His wife Louise was his greatest supporter, as were his three children, Chris, Jim, and Janine. "Johnny so enjoyed calling that he conveyed this joy to the dancers," Louise added. "In our forty-six years of square dance involvement there have been many memorable occasions, but two in particular stand out in my mind.

"One, when we knew Johnny was dying, we put together a memory book. Many of our dancers contributed to it."

"Two, Johnny's funeral—over 600 people paid tribute, most of them square dancers."

Upon Johnny's retirement from the Ladish Company after 40 years, the following letter was included in his retirement tribute:

Dear Johnny and Louise:

What a privilege to be asked to share in this celebration of your four score and more years of leadership in an activity that enriched the lives of so many whom we were able to touch. But greater still and even more important, were the countless numbers of wonderful people that touched ours.

You spent your life feeling the importance of the bond of love and respect between dancer and caller. To this day dancers past and present still consider their square dance years to be the happiest of their lives. How fortunate for us to have been the catalyst that made that possible.

I still can't get over the sheer mutual joy, the truly happy faces of the dancers and the loud enthusiastic applause at the end of each dance. More importantly, accepting the fact that they were not applauding us, but were celebrating with obvious joy their being a part of a cooperative, loving experience with the others in their square. The world truly needs that kind of release and fellowship more than ever before.

Weren't we blessed to have had leadership roles in an activity that filled to overflowing the cups of those who shared in the fellowship and joy we knew it offered.

Thank you Johnny and Louise for your support, encouragement, and more importantly, your love these many, many years.

Dale Wagner

Shortly after his retirement, Johnny Toth died—July 29, 1994. It is a tribute to Johnny that his wife, Louise has remained active in the square dance community and continues to play a leadership role. She is the Camping Chairman for the 1998 Wisconsin Square and Round Dance Convention.

>─┤◄▷─O─◁►┤─◄

GEORGE ZIEMANN began square dancing back in 1948-'49 about the time of the current upsurge in this recreational activity. He was an active member of the Milwaukee Area Callers group, the Wisconsin Square Dance Leaders' Council and the Square Dance Association of Wisconsin. He has held the offices of president, vice president and treasurer of SDAW and rarely missed any of its meetings.

George instructed beginners and intermediate classes at Custer High School under the auspices of the Milwaukee City Recreation Department. He was a member of "Pappy" Shaw's August classes at Colorado Springs every year since 1949 and also attended three of Herb Greggerson's Milwaukee classes.

An active caller in the Milwaukee area, George called for the Calico Square Dance Club at the Capitol Pladium and for the Burlington Square Dancers at Burlington, Wisconsin.

George Ziemann

>─┤◄▷─O─◁►┤─◄

BILL WILLIAMS of South Milwaukee started dancing in 1948 and decided to take up calling in 1949. He called for the Gorton Machine Tool Company in Racine, Wisconsin, and for several years for the Oklahoma Avenue Unity Lutheran Church Dancers. In addition he taught beginners and called for 4-H groups at the Junior State Fair. He was a member of the first, second, and fifth, Greggerson Milwaukee classes. He has taught for the Milwaukee School board and originated several dance figures including China Doll, the Miller's Daughter and others.

MARTHA CLARK, and her husband Fred, were active teachers, callers, and promoters, of fun with square dancing in Milwaukee for many years. Both were active in the Square Dance Association of Wisconsin, and Martha was an active member of the Milwaukee Area Callers' Council. She taught with the Milwaukee and Wauwatosa Recreation Departments, and led the dancing for the Martha Clark Golden Agers at the Wisconsin Social Center in addition to calling for clubs and organization parties and conducting private classes.

Martha Clark

Fred and Martha started dancing in February of 1948 and Martha took on her first calling duties in May 1949. They attended the "Pappy" Shaw classes in 1951, '52 and '54; Herb Greggerson's Milwaukee Ranch Dance classes from 1949-'50, and the Rocky Mountain Folk Dance Camp at Golden, Colorado, in 1950. Martha was active in the Wisconsin Square Dance Leaders' Council for over five years beginning in 1949 as treasurer and moving up to serve as secretary and then vice president of the group.

>─┤─◆>─○─<◆┤─<

JOHN EAGAN, a caller from Wautoma wrote about pioneering the square dance in Waushara county, for the May 1953 issue of *Fiddle and Squares*.

Square dancing in Waushara County (central and western areas) is a little more than two years old. After teaching several beginners classes, Marie and I have come to the conclusion that beginners have the most fun and that everyone would have the most fun if the overall dance level were held closer to the beginner level. Marie and I held open dances for about a year, and only last fall (1952) formed a club. After three classes the Waushara Starlight Promenaders now number twelve squares. From May until September we hold weekly dances in the open air pavilion on beautiful Silver Lake in Wautoma. When the weather drives us indoors the dances are held at the Wautoma, Plainfield, and

Hancock Community halls.

We have called dances and held classes in church basements, taverns, gymnasiums, schoolhouses, and town halls. In some of these places we have had to build fires in potbellied stoves and set up the P.A. system close by to keep warm. No trouble beating out the rhythm with your feet—it's a necessity. The stages in some of these buildings usually accommodate half a dozen children and a dog or two in addition to the caller. After the youngsters imitate their elders doing the Jesse Polka they fall asleep on chairs and couches and are tucked in with overcoats. They sleep peacefully to the hoedown music while their parents enjoy the rhythmic life of the square dance. This is the way it must have been years ago with whole families coming from afar to enjoy an evenings fun with their neighbors.

BOB DAWSON, of Milwaukee, took square dance lessons in the fall of 1950 under Howie Neher and that winter joined the Belles and Beaux Square Dance Club. Bob enjoyed square dancing so much, he decided to teach others. He started a set of two classes at the Northtown Club on Third and Center Streets and later began a series of open dances at the same hall. He joined the

Bob Dawson

Milwaukee Moose Club in September 1951, and organized beginner's classes on Sunday nights at the Moose Club. He also taught for the Social Center for two seasons and called for open dancing at Washington Park during the summer seasons of 1953 and 1954. Later he began advanced dancing at the Log Cabin, five miles west of Hwy 100 on North Avenue. Bob featured special parties; hayrides, Halloween costume dances, white elephant dances, auctions (polio benefits), Valentine and New Year's Eve events. One of his innovations was a square dance identification board. Each couple's photo was taken free of charge and mounted alphabetically to help the dancers get to know each other. Bob was a member of the Milwaukee Area Callers' Council, the Pioneer Round Dance Club, and Belles and Beaux Square Dance Club. He was the founder of *Here 'Tis,* Wisconsin's square dance magazine.

Unless otherwise stated, the caller profiles are condensed from Fiddle and Squares *magazine.*

CHAPTER 5

Peel Off
Area Associations

First couple out, balance and swing
Down the center and split the ring,
Lady goes east, gent goes west,
Swing with the one that you like best.
Swing 'em high and swing 'em low,
Turn 'em loose and watch 'em go.

SDAW—South East Area, Inc.

The Square Dance Association of Wisconsin-South East Area Inc., (SDAW-SEA) was established in 1961 to provide a central organization to coordinate the efforts of its member clubs, and as a liaison between the Square Dance Association of Wisconsin (SDAW) and the Wisconsin Square and Round Dance Convention Committee.

Each member dance club sends a delegate to the SDAW-SEA meetings, pays dues to the SEA association, and is allowed one vote on issues presented to the SEA.

The Milwaukee Area Callers' Council is a member of the SDAW-SEA, with all the rights and privileges of member dance clubs.

The SDAW-SEA appoints a delegate and alternate delegate to represent the area at SDAW meetings, and a delegate and alternate delegate to the Wisconsin Square and Round Dance Convention.

Every five years the Wisconsin Square and Round Dance Convention is held in the South East Area. Most of the chairpersons for that convention are chosen from among the South East Area dancers and callers. The other four areas send delegates to work on the convention in the pre-determined areas.

Every fifth quarter the South East Area hosts the SDAW Jamboree. This is an all-day activity consisting of educational meetings, lunch, SDAW meeting, and an afternoon square dance.

In addition, the SDAW-SEA provides the following services and activities.

Square Dance information phone number
Quarterly club calendar
Three year activity calendar
Promotion Committee for area lessons
Banner Program
Friendship Ring program
Leadership education
Spring Fling
Fall Frolic
Annual Christmas dinner dance

Milwaukee Area Callers' Council

The Milwaukee Area Callers' Council (MACC) began on April 15, 1951. For a number of years it operated very informally, being primarily interested in workshopping new round and square dance material and in promoting cooperation between callers.

Later it became more formal and a constitution and bylaws established the purposes of the organization:

1. To promote square and round dancing.

2. To promote good fellowship among the callers and leaders.

3. To provide for the free exchange of square and round dance activities of the callers and leaders as they may concern this organization as a whole.

4. To maintain a current directory of square and round dance callers and instructors.

5. To establish a code of ethics for the members.

6. To provide training, advice, and encouragement to members of Wisconsin Square Dance Leaders' Council and others as they may request it.

The MACC selects a delegate and an alternate to the Wisconsin Square Dance Leaders' and Callers' Council (WSDLCC). Other area caller councils do the same and these delegates operate as a state leaders' council to standardize the calling activity for the entire state.

>─┤◄►─O─◄►┤─◄

Elmer and Rosemary Elias

ELMER ELIAS, a co-organizer of the MACC, has been calling square dances and cuing rounds for over 51 years, beginning in 1947. The utility company where he was employed sponsored a ten lesson class, and since it was an activity that his wife Rosemary and he could participate in as a couple, they decided to give it a try. The instructor was Irv Kickbusch. He encouraged Elmer to call at the lessons. For instance, at lesson number three he would call what he had been taught at lesson two. At the end of lesson number ten Elmer was calling the whole course. It wasn't long before Elmer began calling for the EMBA square dance club and served as their club caller until he started to spend winters in Texas.

Elmer taught traditional, clogging, line dancing, contras and quadrilles, in

addition to square dancing. He originated several published round dances. His two favorite records are D&A Breakdown, and Scott's Hoedown. He is a past president of the Wisconsin Square Dance Leaders' Council (WSDLC) and co-organizer of the Milwaukee Area Callers' Council (MACC).

Elmer collaborated on the preparation of the *Windsor Book of Rounds*, and was director of two exhibition groups; The Folk Fair Dancers and the Roselle (black light) Dancers.

Although mostly retired from calling, Elmer remains active in square dance circles. He is a member of the Milwaukee Area Callers' Council, Texas Callers, LEGACY (board member), CALLERLAB, Lloyd Shaw Foundation, Wisconsin Square Dance Leaders' Council, and Wisconsin Round Dance Leaders' Council.

Asked what changes he had observed during his dance career he named three: Change in square and round dance attire, proliferation of figures in both square and rounds, and dancer "burn-out" from peer pressure. Elmer's philosophy stems from ten two letter words: *If it is to be it is up to me.*

>-!-+>-‹O›-‹+-!-‹

SDAW—South West Area (SDAW-SWA)
Submitted by South West Area Historians
Si and Marilyn Kittle

The following information is condensed from minutes taken at the South West Area-Square Dance Association of Wisconsin meetings. The first minutes available at the present time are from 1956. However, mention was made in these minutes of the 1951 edition of the Articles of Operation. In 1956 this organization was named the Madison Area Square Dance Leaders' Council. Mention was made of a Callers' Council in this area which met on a different date than the Leaders' Council. Representatives of the Callers' Council were invited to the Leaders' meeting to discuss square dance problems. The subject of joining the state SDAW was brought up in 1956, however this was not done until several years later.

There were 14 member clubs in this organization in 1957. That same year the Leaders and Callers started meeting on the same evening and the Callers' Council furnished a caller for dancing at each meeting.

In 1958 Round Dance lessons started in the area. A square dance directory listing the area clubs and dates of dancing started in 1959. A Jamboree was held in the Fall and Spring of 1961 and continues to the present.

The Madison area joined the State SDAW in 1962. In September 1962 the name of this organization was changed to the "South West Area Square Dance Association of Wisconsin." There were 21 clubs in membership in 1963. This year an area newsletter was started with the Callers' Council and Leaders' Council splitting the expense of printing. Promotion for square dancing in 1964 was through outdoor advertising pamphlets placed in hotels and motels in the area.

In 1966 the South West Area hosted the State Convention held in Whitewater. Total attendance was 5,254 with 175 camping units. In 1970 there were 19 callers in the South West Area Callers' Council.

The State Convention was held in Madison at the Coliseum in 1971. In 1972 the South West Area led in the number of clubs and callers in Wisconsin and in 1973 the membership was 28 clubs. The membership had been holding its own, but is slowly on the decline since that time, and presently has 14 clubs as members.

Since 1971 the State Convention has been held in Madison in 1976, 1981, 1986, l991, and 1996. It will be held in the South West Area again in the year 2001.

>―+◆>―O―<◆+―<

Wolf River Area Callers' Association
Submitted by Howie Fochs

I found this history of WRACA in a box of old minutes and sent a copy to Marion (Schneider) Mooney to see if it was correct, as she is the only charter member left that I know of. Marion called me and said it was just as she remembered.

Eleven callers of the Wolf River Area held a meeting on Sunday September 7, 1959, at the Orahula Ballroom, to organize a Caller Council for the area. Clint Forrest acted as temporary chairman and C. Florian Merbs as temporary secretary. The object was to learn the finer techniques of calling and to standardize the calls that were being used.

The area was discussed and mapped as follows: starting at Clintonville draw a line to Waupaca, to Wautoma, to Ripon, to Oshkosh, to Appleton, and back to Clintonville. Any caller having a club for which he calls regularly on the outer edge of this area will be accepted into this area group. The area was later established as counties of Waupaca, Outagamie, Winnebago, Waushara, Brown, and Calumet. In 1959 they decided to accept callers from adjacent counties for membership.

There were 16 callers in this area at the time. They were Harold Bammel from Waupaca, Robert Bickford from Oshkosh, Clarence Dorschner from Oshkosh, John Eagan from Wautoma, William Elliot from Clintonville, Arnold Evans from Appleton, Dorothy Evans from Appleton, Clinton Forrest from Poy Sippi, Kenneth Hooyman from Appleton, Herb Johnson from Oshkosh, Erwin Konrad from Oshkosh, Lyle Leatherman from Oshkosh,

C. Florian Merbs from Menasha, Irene Qually from Oshkosh, Edward Radke from Ripon, and Carlton Schneider from New London.

Of this group, 11 became charter members. They were Robert and Lorraine Bickford, Clarence and Enid Dorschner, John and Marie Eagan, William and Arlene Elliot, Clinton and Vi Forrest, Kenneth and Bertha Hooyman, Herb and Tilda Johnson, C. Florian and Lucille Merbs, Edward and Vera Radke, and Carlton and Marion Schneider.

A constitution and bylaws were discussed and later approved. The organization was called the Wolf River Area Callers' Association, or WRACA. The organization was incorporated in 1965.

On December 14, 1952, elections were held and Carlton Schneider was elected chairman, Herb Johnson, vice chairman, and C. Florian Merbs, secretary treasurer.

On February 7, 1954 the first issue of *Hoedown News* was printed by Lyle and Margaret Leatherman, and later taken over by WRACA and sent to the dancers by the callers.

CHAPTER 6

Grand Square
Wisconsin State Square and
Round Dance Conventions

You all join hands and circle, and make a great big ring.
Circle to Milwaukee, then make that Oshkosh swing.
Now all four couples separate, go round the outside track,
Pass right by your partner, but you meet her coming back.
You swing her when you meet her, it's twice around you know,
Then allemande left the corner and around the ring you go,
It's a grand old right and left boys, then the promenade begins.
Make a date with your pretty mate, it's Convention time again.

In 1959 members of the Wisconsin Square Dance Leaders' and Callers' Council formulated the idea of an official State Square Dance Convention. With the volunteer work of many callers, plus a financial loan from the Square Dance Association of Wisconsin, the first Wisconsin Square Dance Convention became a reality. It was held in Appleton with 1,700 dancers attending. A convention has been held each year since, except in 1979 when Wisconsin hosted the National Square Dance Convention in Milwaukee, attended by 22,170 dancers.

Shortly after the 1959 convention, the committee chairmen met to discuss the project. It was agreed that a Wisconsin Square Dance Convention Corporation should be incorporated (under state laws) to plan for future state conventions. A Board of Directors was elected by the group. Those elected would serve terms from one to five years, with one member retiring each year and the General Chairpersons of that year's convention taking a place on the board to serve for five years.

The second through sixth conventions were awarded to different areas on the basis of "bids" presented. After that, it was resolved that a fairer process would be to allot the conventions on a rotating basis. Now all areas know well in advance when the convention responsibility will be theirs.

Convention Booklet Cover.

The state of Wisconsin is divided into five areas for purposes of Caller/Leader and Dancer Associations and convention hosts. Each yearly convention is planned by a committee under the direction of the General Chair-man who is elected by the sponsoring area. Eight or nine chairmen are selected by the host area including a secretary and treasurer. A "dancer" chairman and "caller/leader" chairman are chosen by each of the other four area's caller/leader and dancer associations. These constitute the convention personnel. The Board of Directors of the Convention Corporation serves as a guiding hand to give help when needed and answer questions when they arise.

First Wisconsin Convention

The first official Wisconsin Square and Round Dance Convention was held in Appleton on August 28-30, 1959. John and Mildred Gardner were the convention chairmen.

Committee chairmen were Lyle and Margaret Leatherman for Registration and Housing; Carlton and Marion Schneider, Halls, Booths and Decorations; Herb and Tilda Johnson, Sound and After Parties; Jim and Pat Collins, Treasurer-Secretary; Will and Carol Ferderer, Workshops; Hug and Norman Hugdahl, Exhibitions; Mel and Loretta Schoeckert, Publicity; George and Carol Ziemann, Square Dancing; Ralph and Vi George, Publicity and Program; Art and Mary Weisensel, Panels; Lenny and Mabel Schwandt, Music; Ellz and Thelma Peckham, Round Dancing and Milt and Verna Thorp, Forum.

WESTPORT SQUARES: Dance on 1st & 3rd Fridays at the Westport Town Hall. Located just off County Trunk M. Time 8:30 to 11:30 p.m. Everyone is Welcome.

YORK CENTER SQUARES: Dance on the 2nd & 4th Sundays at the York Center Town Hall. Located on Hy 73 about six miles south of Columbus, Wis. Time 8:00 to 11:00 p.m. Everyone is Welcome.

Greetings To The 1st Wisconsin

ART & MARY WEISENSEL

Square Dance Convention

PYRAMID SQUARES: Dance on 1st & 3rd Saturdays at the Lake Mills Town Hall. Located in Lake Mills, Wis. on Hy 89. Time 8:30 to 11:30 p.m. Everyone is Welcome.

PARDEE SQUARES: Dance on 1st, 3rd, & 5th Wednesdays at the Marcellon School. Located just off Hy 22, 4 mil North of Pardeeville, Wis. Time 8:30 to 11:30 p.m. Everyone is Welcome.

15

Greetings to 1st State Convention.

The convention program booklet sold for 50 cents. The program printed on the inside of the front cover listed the events for each day but no times were scheduled. A combination of square and round dancing, workshops and exhibitions, panels and forums were the order of each day.

The exhibition groups were the Roselle Dancers, The Four Hits and their Mrs, and the Shootn' Stars, a Newark-Beloit 4-H team.

A style show was held on Saturday during the convention featuring clothes for clubs and conventions with Carol Ziemann as narrator. Prior to the 1950s ladies dresses were usually floor or ankle length, and cut in a full circle. By the mid-fifties skirts and dresses were getting shorter and petticoats a little fuller. The focus of that first style show was to combine suggestions for proper square dance costuming with the fashions. Here are some of the highlights from the original narration:

> *Fashions and clothes have been one of the most important factors in a woman's life for centuries and ladies of the*

square dance world are no different. There is a great deal of satisfaction in wearing something you have made for yourself.

Material for a dress may be most anything, but good wash and wear cottons and Nylon, Orlon or squaw materials that have a good body do excellently. Some body in the material helps the skirt to stand out and keep its freshness. Don't be a slave to the squaw type, they are expensive and not too much variety can be achieved to say nothing of the expense.

Watch the length; medium calf is a good rule and they look better too long rather than too short. Watch the sleeve pattern for action. Sleeves must have free up and down movement which can be added to a standard pattern by use of a gusset inserted underarm.

Nylon and cotton georgette dresses need little care once made properly. Lining the bodice with batiste or a cotton material to absorb moisture and be cooler also will give this material more body and longer life.

Petticoats add so much to a dress whether it be simple or extravagant. Some girls prefer several and this brings a variety of colors and kinds. Nylon nets are very popular but do not age well with the many washings they must stand. To renovate limp net petticoats there are many ways — Knox Gelatin — Epsom Salts — Perma Starch — commercial petticoat stiffener and I have heard some have used hair spray in an emergency. I have not been satisfied with any of these methods. Linit or other boiled starches work fine for a wearing or two. I have had a "busy day" success with Niagara Cold Water Starch, but made in an extra heavy solution.

Even though our dancing is full of twirls and turns let us not make a leg show out of it. It takes away the dignity of the dance. It is universally agreed that some type of cover-up is needed whether it is a knee length or the shorter type called "Sissy Britches". A pajama pattern can be used by simply cutting the legs knee length and adding a few ruffles.

Shoes — shy away from sandals and heel-less styles. They swish around on the foot and don't stay put. Ballet type are the most popular.

Tricks for shoes — Krylon, a special lacquer used in hobbies will renovate the color of the shoe. It comes in a spray can and is available in gold and silver too. These colors will cover any color that may already be on the shoes.

A novel idea to use for gathering material if you have the newer zigzag type of stitch on your machine is to zigzag over a piece of crochet thread and then draw the thread for the desired fullness.

Store your slips, pulled through plastic garment bags, on a shelf or under the bed.

Many changes in square dance clothes will be seen at the style show, such as the permanently pleated dresses that are machine washable. There are many early American prints and gingham with a variety of different styles and necklines. There is a breaking away from three tiers and puffed sleeves are returning. Men seem to be selecting shirts that are wash and wear with white being the most popular.

⤜⊶⊶⦿⊷⊷⤛

Overview
by Agnes Thurner

We've come a long way since that first convention. We now start off on Thursday with a Trail's End dance for early convention arrivals, hosted by the local area or one or more of its clubs. This is not part of the actual convention so there is a separate charge to attend this dance. Friday morning the real excitement begins. Final sound checks are being made, retail shops and Showcase of Ideas are setting up, campers are looking for their area, the fashion show chairperson wants to get into the theater to do the stage set-up, exhibition dancers are searching for an area where they can rehearse—a lot of little details need attending to. At the same time callers and dancers are arriving with a myriad of questions. The registration area becomes a bottleneck. If you are preregistered for the convention you can get in and out quickly but if you waited until arrival to register it takes time to complete the registration forms and receive your dance ribbons.

The General Chairpersons and Assistant Chairpersons are run pretty ragged. Some last-minute changes are inevitable. This all adds to the excitement of being a part of this major extravaganza. For some chairpersons the duties are all but over; publicity is something that must begin over a year ahead of time and is generally in place before the big event. The person in charge of the Souvenir Program Booklet must have it ready to stuff into convention packets well ahead of the actual day. The Showcase of Ideas, Fashion Show, and Special Events Chairpersons have already put a lot of work and thought into their projects and at this point are on tenterhooks praying that everything goes as planned.

Then it's all over; the dancers, callers, and retail sales people pack up and go home, the chairmen break down their table set-ups, and Showcase of Ideas displays are re-loaded into the convention trailer. For the chairpersons it's still not the end. There are final reports to be written, a postmortem meeting to evaluate the weekend and determine what could or should have been done differently. The convention treasurer still has final bills to pay before it can be determined if the convention came out in the black or the red. And for the General Chairmen, it won't be over for five more years.

That's how long they continue to serve on the Convention Board, as advisors to upcoming convention chairpersons.

Is it all worth it? You bet. Becoming involved in this kind of square dance leadership is one of the most stimulating, educational, challenging things you can do for yourself. It's second only to...you guessed it...SQUARE DANCING!

>—⊢◄►•O•◄►⊢—<

Left Allemande in Dairyland
28th National Square Dance Convention, by Vera Schreiner

At the February 1975 SDAW meeting Don and Vera Chestnut were elected l979 National Convention Chairmen elect, and if the bid from Wisconsin was accepted as the winning bid at the National Convention in Kansas City, Kansas, in 1975, a National Square Dance Convention would be held in Milwaukee, Wisconsin, June 28-30, 1979, with Don and Vera Chestnut as General Chairmen. Bids are awarded four years in advance, and there is a definite format set forth by the National Executive Committee when presenting a bid. WISCONSIN WON THE BID! Alice in Dairyland helped cheer the crowd!

National Convention Book Cover.

From that time on, everything is history! What a great convention it was. There were 22,170 dancers in attendance, 4,824 from Wisconsin. Even with the gas crisis (shortage) that evolved in May of 1979, and ended the weekend of the Convention, service stations in the immediate area did a booming business on Sunday, June 30th!

Immediately after the February 1975 SDAW meeting, plans started taking shape for the Bid Book, which had to be in the hands of the National Executive Committee 90 days prior to the June 1975 National Convention, and for the formal bid, which is presented at the Bid Session at the National Convention. Patrick J. Lucey was Governor of the State of Wisconsin and Henry W. Maier was Mayor of Milwaukee.

The convention was held at MECCA (the Milwaukee Exposition Convention Center and Arena) complex in Milwaukee which included the Auditorium and Arena. All three buildings were connected by an Astro-walk over Kilbourn Avenue, therefore the Convention was classified as being all under one roof.

4,025 hotel rooms were blocked in Milwaukee county, and 2,000 rooms in the suburbs, plus other available housing equaling 10,000 possible rooms.

State Fair Park was reserved for campers—2,000 spots plus private and county campgrounds were used.

A Wisconsin Square and Round Dance Convention was not held in 1979 as dancers throughout the state supported the National event.

Highlights of the 1979 Convention

Registration fees were $8 in advance per person, $10 per person after 5/1/79, $28 for a four-day campground fee.

Letter from Mayor Maier.

Saturday June 30th a 180 pound wheel of Wisconsin Swiss Cheese, courtesy of Green County, the Swiss Cheese Capital of the USA, and the wonderful Swiss cheese makers from Monroe, was on display. Free samples were handed out as long as they lasted, which wasn't long!

West Kilbourn Avenue was closed between North 4th and North 6th Street, Thursday, June 28th and Friday, June 29th—6 p.m. to 11:30 p.m., and Saturday, June 30th from 8:00 a.m. to 1:00 a.m. Sunday, July 1st. Dancers could walk across the street between the three buildings if not using the Astro-walk.

Cookbook—3,000 1st order, 3 months later ordered 1,850 more, and 3 months later ordered 1,700 more. No books were left and many more could have been sold. Cost was only $4.50 each. It took a lot of persuasion to get the original copy of a placemat from ADA—American Dairy Association—to use as the cookbook cover.

Style Show—held in the Arena on Saturday afternoon "Wonderful Win-some Wisconsin" was an all Dairyland theme, including life-size cows as props. The floor of the arena was done in green carpeting in the shape of the state of Wisconsin. Music for the event had to be approved by the Musicians Union. Only one organist was chosen, and he was the Brewers' baseball official organist.

Education Program—"Smooth and Uniform Dancing" was the theme of the entire program. All clinics, panels, and seminars followed this theme. New events were: Roots of Square, Round and Contra dancing, How to Plan a Regional Festival, Dance Basics for Kids, Organization Leadership Seminar—divided between club, area, and state, and What is Roundalab?

Exhibitions— enjoyment for everyone in attendance.

Parade of States—Saturday evening—Vera Chestnut sang the Anthem.

Exhibitors—174 booths were sold and a waiting list established.

"Gemütlichkeit"—Turner Hall— German dinner Saturday evening, June 30th, by reservation was sold out.

Dancers from Boise, Idaho, hitch-hiked to the convention.

A Japanese couple spent their honeymoon at the convention. They had met at a square dance function four years earlier.

Belt buckles, pendants, and earrings commemorating the convention were for sale.

Convention caterers set up a bar outside MECCA on the sidewalk hoping to sell beer. You cannot sell alcoholic beverages at a national square dance convention. It didn't work!

Large working clocks in each hall were made by the Assistant Services Chairpersons, Ted and Dennette Laczkowski.

Wonderful Winsome Wisconsin— Fashion Show.

WONDERFUL
WINSOME
WISCONSIN

A
T
R
A
V
E
L
O
G
U
E

O
F

FASHIONS
FORTUNES &
FUN

Presented by
In The Arena
Doors Open 12:15

Your Style Show Committee
Saturday 1:00 p.m. til 3:00 p.m.
All Seats Free

>─◆>─◦─<◆─◦─<

Al and Vera Schreiner have worn many hats during their square dance careers. For many years prior to the National Convention in 1979, Vera and her first husband, Don Chestnut, were actively involved in square dance leadership in Wisconsin. They were members of the Verona Square Dance Club in Madison from 1963 until it dissolved in 1985. During that time they held all the club offices and most committee chairmanships, some more than once. They chaired the Mid-America Square Dance Jubilee held at the World Dairy expo in Madison for the 13 years it was in existence and were chairmen of the 13th Wisconsin Square and

Round Dance Convention held in Madison in 1971. They were assistant advisors to the Detroit, Michigan, National Square Dance Convention in 1962.

Al and Harriet Schreiner, housing chairmen for the 1979 National Square Dance Convention in Milwaukee, were charter members of West Allis Grand Squares (WAGS) and held various offices in that club. Al and Harriet were assistant chairmen of the 24th Wisconsin Square and Round Dance Convention held in Whitewater in 1983.

Don Chestnut passed away in 1984, and Harriet Schreiner in 1985. In 1986, Vera Chestnut and Al Schreiner were married.

Don and Vera Chestnut

Together, Vera and Al have held multiple offices in several clubs including Boots and Slippers Square Dance Club (disbanded after 27 years in operation) and EMBA, where they are still active members. They are past president of the Square Dance Association of Wisconsin and currently are Contact Secretary for the association. Vera became executive secretary for LEGACY International in 1983, and now holds this position jointly with Al. They served two terms as publicity chairmen for ECCO and participated in the 1987 state convention in Eau Claire, as chairmen of an educational panel. Vera was on the Here 'Tis staff from 1984 to 1987 as editor of the Cook's Nook column.

This is just a brief outline of the square dance activities Al and Vera have been involved in throughout their many years of dancing. They have played an important leadership role in the square dance community and contributed greatly to the history of square dancing in Wisconsin.

Al and Vera Schreiner

Wisconsin's Square Dance Flag

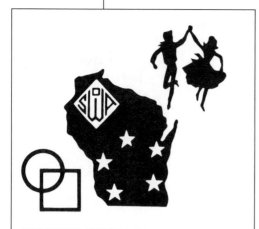

WISCONSIN OFFICIAL SQUARE DANCE FLAG

Wisconsin Square Dance Flag.

Wisconsin is the only State that boasts it's own square dance flag. The idea of a state flag came up in February 1971 when Bill and Gwen Wild of Monroe decided that something different was needed to promote square dancing in Wisconsin. The flag was introduced at the 1979 National Square and Round Dance Convention held in Milwaukee.

Gwen Wild's design was selected from several that were submitted. The flag was dedicated at a special ceremony on August 21, 1971. Mr. Charles Smith, the State Treasurer, was on hand to unveil the flag, which is copyrighted. Our flag is in the Library of Congress and the National Archives in Washington D.C. On November 16, 1971 the Wisconsin Square Dance Flag Foundation received its incorporation papers. The flag is displayed at all state square dance functions.

The flag depicts a green map of Wisconsin representing the rich hills and countryside of our state. Five white stars on the map represent the five areas of the SDAW. The SDAW acronym shown in a diamond is the logo of our association. The overlapping square and circle symbolize how square and round dancers work together; and red dancing figures complete the design.

The flag is available as antenna flags, bumper stickers, and inside window decals. The Foundation is currently looking into larger flags that might be flown from a flagpole or porch. To date, over 8,000 antenna flags have been sold in the state.

Gwen and Bill Wild

The incorporation papers provide for the distribution of profits from the sale of the flags to be used solely for the promotion of square and round dancing in Wisconsin. The "Where to Dance in Wisconsin" brochure is an annual project of the Flag Foundation. The incorporation agreement further provides that in the event the Foundation disbands, all remaining monies will go to the SDAW. If the SDAW does not exist the monies then go to the State Historical Society. There are representatives of the Flag Foundation in all areas of the state.

Convention Memories
by Agnes Thurner

I got my feet wet as assistant publicity chairperson at the 29th Whitewater Convention in 1988, working with Joanne and Jerry Morrison. I was publicity director for the Swingin' Singles Squares at the time, and was surprised to receive a phone call from Joanne Morrison. She introduced herself, and then "out of the blue" asked me if I had ever been called "Mike". I admitted that had once been my nickname. Joanne said she recognized my voice as being one of her coworkers at a local savings and loan in the early '70s. I remembered her well and we had a good time reminiscing and catching up.

Joanne and Jerry Morrison

Joanne explained that she had taken lessons with Swingin' Singles Squares. While in lessons she met Jerry Morrison, who became her square dance "angel", and later her husband. Joanne went on to tell me that she and Jerry were publicity chairpersons for the convention in Whitewater and were looking for someone to assist them.

Jerry and Joanne were very enthusiastic and took their responsibilities seriously. We had a good time publicizing the "Whitewater Express", as the convention was called. The Morrison's had developed a "Road Show" and they took the exhibit around to various clubs, to the National Convention and conventions in neighboring states. Jerry and Joanne were good leaders and it proved to be a perfect way for me to "learn the ropes". The Morrison's went on to become General Chairpersons for the 34th Wisconsin Square and Round Dance Convention held at MECCA in Milwaukee.

Aggi Wegner (Thurner) modeling in 1989 Fashion Show.

The 1988 Fashion Show, was called The Fashion Station in keeping with the train theme, and I made my square dance modeling debut wearing a dress I crafted especially for the convention. That experience was very helpful to me when, in 1990, I chaired the Fashion Show at the 31st Wisconsin Square and Round Dance Convention in Oshkosh.

"Singing in the Rain" dance sequence. L to R — Faye Goocher, John Chaffee, Doris and Jim Wetzel, Mary Ann and Flash Gordon.

The theme for the 31st convention was Slide Down the Rainbow to UW-O (University of Wisconsin-Oshkosh), and to me it suggested a Wizard of Oz theme. The result was "Fashion Wizardry in the land of Ahhs". The show incorporated a skit featuring Dorothy (Linda Sanchez-Reid) and her three pals (who had become square dancers); the Scarecrow (Sid Sampson), the Tin Man ("Flash" Gordon) and the Cowardly Lion (Joe Bott). Other characters were Tricia Chartier, Chris Tiefert, and myself as three wicked witches; Lucy Mattson as the Good Witch, Cecil Turner (narrator) as the Wizard of OZkosh, and Lynn Majchrzak as Tinker Bell. Dorothy, her three friends and the fashion models were all following the "Yellow Rock Road" looking for the end of the rainbow. Dorothy was hoping to find the pot of gold so she could save Auntie Em's farm—the models were looking for the square dance convention. It turned out to be a challenging production.

We were fortunate to recruit Tom Thaney, theatrical director at Brookfield East High School, to help us coach the "actors" and with his guidance constructed a very ambitious stage set. Jim Dundon, stage manager, produced the "rocks" used to border the "yellow rock road", and with backdrops borrowed from Brookfield East we were able to create the fantasy world of OZkosh. The stage at the Frederic March Theater was so huge that it took two truckloads of bushes and greenery (courtesy of Stein's Garden Center in Oshkosh) and a number of borrowed artificial Christmas trees to help complete the set.

I was also blessed with an enthusiastic committee of helpers: Vic Doers created artwork for flyers, buttons, and program cover,

Claire Dundon sewed costumes, Phyllis Pionkoski and Ike Kleitz managed the dressing rooms, Greg and Joan Polly arranged lunch for the models, Pat Wolf made the model's corsages, and Roger Erdman lent his electrical know-how. Many others helped behind the scenes and onstage, including Fay Goocher, Maryann Gordon, John Chaffee, and the Siegmann Family Singers.

During the 1990 convention I reported to Karen and Ellery Gulbrand, assistant General Chairpersons. The Gulbrand's have been active in the SDAW and on convention committees for many years, as well as in their local area association. In 1995 they were named General Chairpersons for the 36th Wisconsin Square and Round Dance Convention and I was privileged to work with them once again, as my husband Max and I were chairpersons for a new chairmanship—the Showcase of Ideas.

We used a Memory Lane theme for the showcase which is intended to give clubs, and associations from Wisconsin and other states an opportunity to display square

Karen and Ellery Gulbrand

dance promotion ideas and histories. The SDAW display boards, featuring convention memorabilia, were part of previous Wisconsin conventions and are now given a permanent place in the Showcase of Ideas. The chairmanship was a truly educational experience and strengthened my interest in Wisconsin's square dance history.

>─┤◄>─·O·─<├─┤─◄

Exhibitions and Demonstrations

The Special Events programming is an exciting part of every convention, especially for those performing. The exhibition teams start rehearsing new steps, and sewing costumes, many months before the event, and look forward to presenting their routines. Many trained exhibition groups have appeared at state and national conventions as well as for the general public.

The American Heritage Dancers began in 1964 as the Folk Fair Dancers, an exhibition group under the direction of Elmer and Rosemary Elias. They appeared regularly in Milwaukee's Holiday

*Early
American
Dancers.*

Folk Fair wearing traditional square dance attire. For the ladies this meant dresses with long sleeves, floor-length skirts with hoops, and ankle-length pettipants. The men's attire was usually dark pants with a plaid shirt and string tie. The group also danced the traditional dance figures, rather than those associated with Modern Western Square Dancing. The Heritage Dancers also performed at several Wisconsin Square and Round Dance Conventions.

Jerry and Jan Kachelmeier took over leadership of the Folk Fair Dancers sometime after 1983 and in 1985 Dwayne Olson

*American
Heritage
Dancers.*

became director of the group. Dwayne made few changes in the dance format.

He wanted to maintain a bit of the past and blend it with a bit of the present. At the Holiday Folk Fair, in the International Showcase, the dancers still appear in traditional square dance attire, but are now dancing more modern choreography. In the Beer Garden at the Folk Fair they wear either modern square dance attire, or red, white, and blue costumes in keeping with their patriotic name.

The American Heritage Dancers participate in the *Milwaukee Journal Sentinel* Rose Festival every June, and give performances at area nursing homes and other interested organizations on request. The group hosts a reception for new Americans at swearing-in ceremonies once or twice a year and sponsors fund-raising dances for various charities and to promote and perpetuate square dancing as our American Heritage. In 1998 they will perform at the Wisconsin State Square and Round Dance Convention in Racine, in both the Special Events program on Saturday evening and in the Fashion Show.

Verona Squares, Inc. was formed in 1956 with the help of caller Milt Thorp and his wife Verna. Their largest beginners class was made up of ten squares, with many experienced dancers turning out to workshop with the new dancers. The club kept growing and in 1968 was incorporated. Milt Thorp was the regular club caller for one dance a month and a guest caller was hired for the second dance. Several special events were scheduled each year; an open house to introduce square dancing to anyone interested, a graduation party, a special Halloween Dance, a Christmas party, and an

Verona Squares.

annual picnic in July. The new dancers were included in the Halloween and Christmas parties even though they hadn't yet graduated.

The Verona Square's formed an exhibition group, directed by Milt and Verna Thorp. The purpose of the group was to exhibit Western Style Square Dancing. Exhibitions were put on every year at nursing homes and other institutions. They appeared at the 1972 convention in La Crosse where they introduced a special number using a Polka Style Clog Step. They also appeared at the Heidi Festival in New Glarus and in special Centennial events. Verona Squares disbanded in 1985.

Other popular exhibition groups included the Wolf River Rollers, headed by Herb Johnson. The members of the group did a black light routine on roller skates. The Roselle Dancers from Milwaukee organized by Elmer Elias, also performed under black light.

There were a number of teen exhibition groups that performed over the years. The Jamboree Juniors from Oshkosh, the Crosstrails Exhibition Square from the Madison area, and the Teen Twirlers danced at the seventh state convention in 1965. The T-P Teens, ages 11 to 17, started as a 4-H group and appeared at the 1975 convention. The Whirling Wheels, a pre-teen group and the Stardusters, ages 6 through 18 were organized by Dwayne Olson. The Stardusters danced at the 1981 convention as well as the Harvest Festival, the Greendale Village Days Parade, and the holiday Folk Fair in Milwaukee.

The Promenaders, was a group of teenagers who did modern square dancing in a double square (eight couples to a square instead of four). They danced to standard figures and also some advanced figures which made their dancing smooth and rhythmic. Another youth group was the Family Squares. Both groups were directed by Steve and Marilyn Wettstein. Caller Jim Burss was a member of these exhibition groups for nine years, dancing

Promenaders.

at state conventions, Holiday Folk Fairs, nursing homes, churches, and lodges.

Jim's parents, Russ and D-D Burss started square dancing in 1969. D-D said that Russ was sure he was not going to like square dancing but she had been after him to try it and he finally consented to go "just this once". "It was a bitter cold January day and the last chance to get into Ken Johnson's lessons," said D-D. "It was one week too late for Dale Wagner's class and besides, Todd Post on 92nd and Beloit in Milwaukee was much closer to home than Calhoun Hall."

Family Squares — Jimmie Burss (first row, 3rd from right), Teena (back row, 3rd from right)

"The next Sunday—you guessed it—Russ was the first one ready to go. Our daughter Michelle was ten so she took lessons along with us. Our other daughter, Teena, started the next year. Poor Jimmie had to sit there with his coloring books through two years of lessons. He was only four but Steve Wettstein let Jim begin lessons at age six. By then, Jimmie was already calling. When he was five-years old, Dale Wagner stood him on up a bar stool so he could call. When Ken Johnson would ask Jim what he was going to be when he grew up, he would answer, an artist, and a square dance caller."

D-D recalled that at the age of 14, Jim graduated his first class of eight

Jim Burss

members, all youngsters. After that calling became secondary to other interests. Then in 1986 Jim's Dad, Russ, who had been calling for about 12 years, developed cancer. On the first night of lessons with 16 couples ready to learn, Russ completely lost his voice. Jim agreed to fill in until his Dad was better, but that never happened. After Russ died, in 1986, Jimmie kept on calling for Swinging Stars, a club started by Russ in 1978. Since then he has been busy teaching mainstream classes, doing private parties, and calling for various clubs.

In 1990 Jim, with Vern Weisensel a caller from the Madison area, graduated a total of three squares of young people and teamed their groups, called The Future of Square Dancing, for an exhibition at the state square dance convention in Oshkosh. Jim is very interested in square dance youth. He offers classes for age six and up and organized a club called Swinging Families, for parents and their children. In 1995 Jim married Deanna Weisensel, Vern and Billie Weisensel's daughter. Their first child, a boy, was born in 1998. With callers on both sides of the family, Little Joe should be ready to call square dances by the year 2003.

Some unusual exhibition groups included the Midnight Squares, a group of blind dancers led by Warren Berquam. They appeared at the 1982 Convention. That same year Warren Berquam presented the Perfect Squares, whose 12 members danced in wheelchairs. The goal of both groups was to perform in Hawaii in the coming year.

The Wisconsin Square Wheelers was an exhibition group founded originally by caller, Bob Lewis, as the Dell City Wheelers. Records indicate that Judy Wilson, another Milwaukee area caller, worked with them briefly before Bill Webster took over in the late 1980s.

The Perfect Squares.

Bill graduated from Art Radoll's square dance class and took round dance lessons from Mary Edge. He joined Dudes and Dolls and was a member there for over ten years. He couldn't learn fast enough—he took plus lessons from Harry Lind in '78, was a charter member of the Busy Bee's in Burlington, and the Checkmates in Wind Lake. He belonged to the Swingin' Singles, R Squares and the Moose 49ers. In 1986 Bill became involved with Eric Tangman's caller's class when his fiancé, Jean Lorenz, volunteered them to dance with the group. He attended the workshop for 14 months, followed by one year of apprenticeship with Johnny Toth. He made his calling debut at the Moose 49ers in July of 1988, and shortly afterward became club caller for R Squares and instructor for Ridge Runners in Racine. Webster served two terms as secretary of the MACC.

Bill Webster

Under Bill Webster's tutelage the Wheelchair Dancers worked up a routine incorporating both mainstream and plus calls. Bill didn't stint on his calling. He used standard calls in the same tempo used for "stand-up" dancers. Eventually "stand-up" dancers were brought into the exhibition team to show that wheelchair dancers could hold their own with anyone on the square dance floor. The Square Wheelers were always well received at local and state exhibitions and conventions.

In 1990 the National Square Dance Convention Board invited seven different handicapped clubs to perform in Memphis. Due to financial difficulties, one by one they were forced to drop out. Bill Webster appealed to the Wisconsin callers and dancers for financial help. Many individuals and clubs made donations and many clubs held special fund-raising dances. Enough funds were raised to enable the Wisconsin Square Wheelers to purchase new costumes and to transport the dancers and their equipment safely to Memphis.

In June of 1990 the Wisconsin Square Wheelers gave ten performances and received twenty-one standing ovations at the Memphis convention. A reporter from TNN was present resulting in television coverage on the Nashville network. After their outstanding performances at the convention inquiries were received from all over the country from other square dance clubs wanting to know how to form their own wheelchair dance group.

Tragically, Bill Webster died in a freak accident in 1991, while on a Florida fishing trip with his father. He was 43 years old. The square dance world lost a good friend and an accomplished caller. Without their strong leader the Square Wheelers lost their motivation. The group is disbanded but some of their members still make their way onto the square dance floor where they are always warmly welcomed.

G & L Dancers.

The D & L Dancers were the brainchild of square dance caller, Dwayne Olson and round dance cuer, Lorelei Hempe. They thought about how much the two dance types go together and came up with an exhibition group that dances squares and rounds simultaneously to the same music. The group started in October of 1986 and appeared for the first time in the 1987 convention in Eau Claire. In 1989 Gordy Ziemann took over as caller leader and the name of the group was changed to the G & L Dancers. They will be performing for their 12th straight state convention in Racine in 1998.

Clog dancing is another popular dance form seen at conventions, parades, city and state functions, and folk fairs. To help you better understand this art form, Laurie Johnson of Spencer, Wisconsin, has written a history of clogging.

Clogging is a traditional folk dance that originated in the mountains of Virginia, South Carolina, North Carolina, Georgia, Kentucky, and Tennessee. It is a mixture of the dances of the people who settled in those mountains, such as English, Polish, German Dutch, Scotch-Irish, Cherokee, and African. The dance would vary from community to community depending on which influence was the strongest. The Cherokee Indians, for example, who were native to the Southeast mountains were very friendly to the white mountain settlers from Great Britain. The people observed and shared each others culture. Cloggers picked up some of the steps from their Indian neighbors and incorporated them into their dances. The buck step, where the dancer brings the knee up very high, comes directly from a Cherokee ceremonial dance. The foot stomp, also a characteristic of Clog dancing, was a gift from Black Americans who traced their dance patterns back to Africa.

Very little written material can be found on either the exact history of clogging or the clogging steps. This is due to the fact that the people in the Appalachian Mountains were very much an oral people, passing the clogging steps and dances from one generation to another. It is only within recent years that books on clogging have been published.

There are many clogging definitions: Hoedown, Mountain Style, Buck and Wing, Jig, Flat Foot, and Precision; but basically there are only two types of clogging: Precision, which is exactness in rhythm, timing, step changes, and coordination, and Hoedown, which is freestyle.

Clogging is not limited to a particular age group. In the mountain region where the dance developed, children are clogging by age five. It's not unusual to see people in their seventies dancing at mountain festivals.

In the traditional version, no two people dance alike. Each creates individual steps. Clogging is "what each person feels inside". It's handed down from one generation to the next.

Working people wore industrial clogs, or wooden shoes, from whence clogging gets its name. The heavy shoes provided a good clear beat and the dance developed along rhythmic rather than musical lines. The cloggers in England refined the form, holding competitions and giving prizes for the dancers with the best skills. The modern clogger has forsaken the wooden clogs of his ancestors in favor of sensible tap shoes...usually securely tied or strapped. Traditionally, clogging relied mainly on a fiddle and banjo for music, but clogging routines can be adapted to the latest country-western or popular music.

Anyone who has ever clogged knows how much fun it is, but they might not know how healthy it is. Clogging is a form of dance that meets all the criteria of "total exercise", stretching, toning, posture/coordination, circulation/energy, and stress reduction.

Clogging involves the use of all of the large muscles of the body. Any activity that uses the large muscles and is done smoothly and continuously is very effective for toning and firming the muscles. Clogging aids in burning up excess fat and also trains the heart and lungs to work more efficiently.

If you are serious about using clogging as a way to shape up, or as a way to stay in shape, you can look forward to a reduction in body fat, a decreased risk of heart attack, stroke, and high blood pressure. You will notice an increased energy level and you will have more stamina. Clogging can greatly reduce your level of stress.

A true folk art, clogging allows individuals, couples, and groups to develop endless dance variations based upon a few easily learned steps.

If there is one word to describe clog dancing, it is "FUN"!

Laurie did clog dancing in the Wisconsin Rapids area prior to her marriage to Clifford Johnson. She and Clifford own the Golden Pheasant Game Farm in Spencer where they raise and sell pheasants, rheas, and other exotic birds worldwide. The Johnson's have three children. Laurie says she misses dancing and hopes one day to resume square dancing and clogging.

The Calico Country Cloggers had its beginnings at the '81 State Square and Round Dance Convention. As of 1983 the club had graduated approximately 160 cloggers, and had over 50 members ranging in age from seven to sixty-plus. They performed at numerous conventions and exhibitions including a Muscular Dystrophy Telethon, beginner square dance jamborees, shopping centers, and folk and country fairs.

The Cripple Creek Cloggers of Madison were organized in 1982 with 15 members They soon grew to a membership of over 75, ranging from age four to over sixty-five years old. Their exhibition routines were performed in lines, duets, and mountain figures. In addition to clogging, the club did some square dancing, and a variety of lines dances and mixers. They performed at nursing homes, parades, festivals, churches, schools, and for other special events. They were featured at the 1984 Wisconsin Square and Round Dance convention in Stevens Point.

Calico Country Cloggers.

Teresa Olson-Alioto who helped form the Cream City Cloggers and the Milwaukee Clogging Company, started square dancing at the age of seven with a youth square dance exhibition team that did a lot of traveling. They performed at local events, state, and national square dance conventions, and the Holiday Folk Fair.

As a child attending square dance conventions down south, Teresa saw a youth clogging group perform. At the time, clogging had not yet reached Wisconsin. She started taking lessons when they became available and was put on an exhibition team. In 1987 she became a charter member of the Cream City Cloggers. This group of energetic adults named the club after the cream-colored bricks found in the Milwaukee area. They have performed in numerous cities for a variety of functions including fairs, festivals, society and club meetings, celebrations, and many parades and fund-raisers. In January 1998 they completed a performance tour of Paris, France, and London, England. They range in age from eighteen years old and up. Not all of the dancers perform; some like to meet once a week for the social and exercise benefits. This is an adult group geared toward fun and relaxation.

Teresa soon became a Certified Clogging Instructor (CCI) and the main instructor for the Cream City Cloggers. In April of 1996 she formed a new group, The Milwaukee Clogging Company, and opened a studio located at 6301 West Greenfield Avenue in West Allis, Wisconsin. This clogging team was formed to provide the best of clogging for young people. The age range of the group begins at seven and goes through age twenty-four. This is a very enthusiastic group of dancers. Many of them have been performing for several years. They have clogged throughout Wisconsin and across the United States, recently completing a European Clogging Tour. They have won several awards for their performances.

Teresa has taught at state and international conventions and teaches clogging at the University of Wisconsin-Milwaukee campus. When she isn't square dancing, she serves as director of the Youth and Adult American Cloggers for the International Institute of Wisconsin. Her clogging affiliations and memberships include Clogging Leaders Association of Wisconsin, Clogging Association of Wisconsin, CLOG National Clogging Organization, National Clogging and Hoe-Down Council, and the International Institute of Wisconsin. Other talented, certified instructors on the clogging team are Julie Olson, Brooke Heebsh, Kelly Heebsh, and Tiffany Ulbing.

As soon as dancers graduate from a beginners class they are encouraged to "get out" and dance as much as they can. This helps them to develop confidence and reinforces the square dance calls. However, one of the first things a new dancer learns after graduation is that the Do-Si-Do is not done back to back, it is a partner swing; and when weaving the ring, they don't just pass by their partner, they pat hands and do a hip bump, or grab hands, rear back and kick. Although these little gimmicks add variety and fun to the dance they are inappropriate at a public dance demonstration. Square dance clubs are often called upon to demonstrate square dancing at nursing homes, shopping malls, schools, and for parades and civic festivals. The club members are usually not part of a trained group. When dancing for the public, whether as an exhibition team or an informal demonstration by a club, dancers are always instructed by the caller to "dance the way you were taught."

CHAPTER 7

Go Red Hot
Square Dancing At Its Peak
1950-1980

Had an old cow as black as silk,
Old black cow who gave white milk,
We churned butter most everyday,
And all that silly old cow could say
Was A..a..a..allemande left!

What is a Caller?
Harold Silvers, Neenah, Wisconsin

A mike, some records
An amplifier too,
A stand, some cords
And real broad view.

For equipment alone
A Caller won't make.
He's really there
For the dancer's sake.

So a Caller is Dancers
One Square or more,
Precision and goofs
And F-U-N galore.

A friend to have
Sometimes a teacher.
If the occasion arises
He's even a Preacher.

A program, a method,
A way of life.
Caller is plural
To include a wife!!

＞—！—◆〉—○—〈◆—！—＜

In the 1950s square dancing became the "in" thing to do throughout the state of Wisconsin. The number of callers and square dance clubs increased and dancers and callers were in demand for demonstrations and exhibitions. Dance hall owners went out of their way to accommodate the square dance clientele and you could find a square dance going on somewhere just about every night of the week. The tremendous interest in square dance activity continued throughout the seventies and into the eighties. This chapter recounts the history of just a few of the callers and clubs that were active during those years.

＞—！—◆〉—○—〈◆—！—＜

BILL KERSEY

Square dancing was just becoming popular in the Milwaukee area when Bill Kersey came home from the service in 1946. At the insistence of his wife, Betty, and some friends, he agreed to go square dancing. "You should have seen us," said Bill. "We were the best dressed folks on the floor. The ladies were all togged out in matching dresses and the men wore fancy shirts—pink, with black trim and red roses. The problem was, we couldn't square dance. Joe Lewis, an out-of-state caller was in town. He used to accompany himself on the accordion. He'd say allemande left and before he got to the next call we were lost. We left, and went on to take lessons.

In those days you only had to learn about ten calls and you were dancing. We went to a lot of dances and every so often the caller would have me up to call one. I finally started to call in earnest in the mid-fifties, and I called for 35 years.

"I called for various clubs. The OK Squares, Fun Dance Squares, the Squarenaders. I called whatever the dancers wanted. I called for Marquette University for 25 years and always called for fun. I didn't expect to get new dancers from the university students, they were only at school for a few years and then were off somewhere else. I always tried to learn and

Bill and Betty Kersey

understand what I was teaching. Callers Alex Brabender, Howie Reoch, Del Langlois, and Andy Anderson were some of my pupils.

"There are too many levels in square dancing today, too many steps to learn. You don't need all that new stuff to have fun. As one caller used to say 'any darn fool can get up and stop a floor, but it takes a real caller to keep the dancers moving.' I used to practice, practice, practice—sometimes all night before a dance. It takes a lot of work to be a caller, and if you expect to make money at it, forget it."

In 1968 Bill and Betty Kersey were assistant General Chairmen for the 10th Wisconsin Square Dance Convention held in Waukesha High School. At that time Bill had been calling for about ten years, and twice was chairman of the MACC. About that same time Bill began writing a weekly column for the *Metro-News*. The column called Squarely Yours, covered SEA square dance activities, lesson and convention information.

When Bob Dawson stopped publishing the *Here 'Tis* in about 1970, the MACC took it over. Bill and Betty Kersey were appointed to edit the magazine, and did so for about five years until Elmer Elias became the publisher.

Bill Kersey is also remembered for his balloon artistry. He always brought a supply of balloons to the dances and kids and adults alike were delighted by his imaginative creations.

Bill stopped calling in 1993. He says he learned a lot about people in his 35 years of calling. Although he had a full time job as superintendent of a machine shop, he never treated his square dance calling as "just a hobby". He was a dedicated caller and square dance advocate.

>─┤◄►─·─O─·─◄►┤─<

HARRY AND BARBARA JASHINSKY, who were round dance cuers, had their first brush with round dancing with Howie and Hildegard Bernard in the fall of 1950 at the Paragon Club in West Allis. Later Harry and Barbara joined the Pioneer Round Dance Club, organized by Bill Barr. Harry began teaching the class in 1951, when the Barrs moved to California. They also taught round dancing at the Wisconsin Avenue Social Center on 27th and Wisconsin Avenue, and for the city recreation department.

The Jashinsky's attended the College of the Pacific Folk Dance Camp, in Stockton, California, for three years running. By popular demand from their dancers they formed a club of their own in 1953, the International Folk and Round Dance Club.

>─┤◄►─·─O─·─◄►┤─<

IRV PASCH—La Crosse, Wisconsin
Here 'Tis—1958

When Irv started square dance calling in 1952, it wasn't exactly new to him, as he'd had a little experience in calling as a young lad at his home near Ladysmith, Wisconsin. The urge to call again came to him when a small group of enthusiastic dancers inveigled him to call a basement session. Irv developed an excellent calling style and soon had a large following of dancers. He called for the Coulee Region Promenaders of La Crosse and the Hilltop Whirlers of Cashton, Wisconsin. He occasionally did guest calling for a Sparta group and in the summer called for the local 4-H club.

Irv was an active member of the Southeastern Minnesota Caller's Clinic and called at the Minnesota Federation Festival dances. He and his charming wife, Pearl, attended square dance camps at LaVeta, Colorado, and Asilomar, California. These square dance vacations gave him a great deal of teaching and calling knowledge and a host of new friends.

Irv owned a welding shop and after a hard day at work would come home for a quick lunch and shower, then was off to a square dance, sometimes a bit weary. As soon as the dancers were gathered on the floor, laughing and having fun, he warmed up his favorite record "Hashin' the Breaks", and all signs of weariness would disappear. He was called "Irv Pasch, King of Hash" in his area.

Pearl was a faithful worker behind the scenes, keeping the records, corresponding and helping with the new round dances. She was Irv's greatest critic and faithful supporter.

Following Dad's Footsteps

Dennis Leatherman has 23 years of calling and instructing experience under his belt. It all started way back in 1953 when, during 5th grade, his classmates at Oaklawn School in Oshkosh wanted to do a Square Dance Program and his dad couldn't get off of work during the school day. He learned to call and teach the "Jesse Polka Square," "Hurry, Hurry, Hurry," and a couple of other dances, then shared what his dad taught him with his classmates.

His real start came about 20 years later at Zaragoza Air Base, Spain. In 1975 Dennis mentioned to some friends that he loved to square dance. They responded that they did also and together they decided to try to do something for America's Bicentennial and Zaragoza's Bimillennium. They did, and the Zaragoza Promenaders, and Dennis' career was launched.

His mentors were his parents, Lyle and Margaret Leatherman. They taught Dennis to square dance during Summer Recreation Programs at Riverside Park in Neenah and Pierce Park in Appleton. He learned about calling as he listened to his dad practice, read the *Sets in Order* and *American Squares* magazines, attended square dances and "filled" in with Mom, and as they attended SDAW Jamborees and WSDLCC Worksprees all over the state. Dennis wanted to follow in Dad's footsteps.

Dennis and his wife, Karlene, have been active members of CALLERLAB, LEGACY, the Overseas Dancer Association, ECCO, WSRDCC, WSDL-CC, SDAW, WRADA, and WRACA. They were editors of *Hoedown News* (WRACA) and owner/editors of *Here 'Tis* (SDAW).

Lyle and Margaret Leatherman

Dennis reported that one of the big changes he has seen in square dancing is the increase in the amount of material that has to be taught during lessons, and the decrease in the fun people are having at those lessons.

Dennis feels very strongly that if square dancing, as we know it today, is to continue into the next millennium, we need to get fun back into our lessons and dances. "We need to do more with less...more fun, with less figures," he said. "We need to back CALLERLAB and the ACA as they try to slow down the rush to plus. We need to look at our Canadian, European, and Australian counterparts to find out how they continue to grow and thrive with programs that are at the Basic and Mainstream levels and we need to promote the Community Dance Program."

Dennis went on to say that a caller today needs to develop patience, flexibility, and skill in order to become a Master

Craftsman of Square Dancing...taking a few reliable, comfortable, and well-honed tools; knowing precisely when, where, and how long to apply them; taking care to do things right the first time, and every time; and finally ending with the true Masterpiece, a dance floor filled with happy square dancers.

Dennis and Karlene's motto for Classic Country Dancing is:

> *The smooth blending of line, couple, mixer,*
> *and square dancing fun.*
> *Anyone can share our fun—young or not—*
> *solo or not—dancer or not.*

Our Square Dance Life
by Howie Reoch

I have been a square dance caller and cuer for over 27 years and a proud member of the Milwaukee Area Callers' Council (MACC); and since Beverly and I spend our winters in Arkansas I

have for the past 15 years been a member of the Arkansas State Square Dance Federation.

Buzz Kaczmarek, Bill Kennedy, Jim Noonan, Chet Walker (deceased), and myself were what "we" refer to as the class of '69. Sponsors were Johnny Toth and Alex Brabender, MACC, and CALLERLAB members.

On my way to becoming a caller I had a memorable first trip to Peaceful Valley, Colorado. Dale Wagner, Bert Rietz, and Art Radoll of Wisconsin were staff leaders. Although I didn't get to meet "Pappy" Shaw or Henry Ford, I did have the pleasure of talking

Howie and Beverly Reoch

with Bob Osgood, Ed Gilmore, and Ralph Page, noted square dance callers of that era.

How did it all begin? I was working second-shift at Continental Can Company when someone suggested that square dancing was a good get-away activity for a mother of two. That's how Beverly and her cousin Harold Lehner came to take square dance lessons at Nicolet High School in 1955. Bert Rietz, a teacher at Nicolet, was the instructor. The rest, as they say, is history.

Soon Beverly and I were taking lessons with Bill Kersey. These were held at Granville School and cost us the huge sum of $15 for sixteen lessons. There were 55 couples in Bill Kersey's class.

Thirty-some Continental Can Company employees, Alex and

Gen Brabender included, became involved in one-night stand type dances on Sundays at Hamm's Tavern on Green Bay Avenue in Milwaukee. Hamm's is now a historic landmark, operating as the Silverspring House.

At age ten, our son Craig, began lessons with Alex Brabender in his Mequon basement. Three years later daughter Cheryl turned ten and followed suit, taking her lessons from Steve Wettstein (Wettstein's Promenaders). Unfortunately, neither of our children continued in the square dance activity, and our five grandchildren don't seem to be interested.

In 1957 we became charter members and corresponding secretary of the Squarenaders. We danced at Norbie Baker's Hall. Bill Kersey was the caller. Later Squarenaders become OK Squares and Circle D with Otto Kenyon and Del Langlois calling.

We became very interested in round dancing and were active with the original Roundabouts throughout 1970-1980.

We assisted many callers doing exhibitions, providing limousine (taxi) service, helping with snacks and skits, and advertising duties. You might say we were all-around square dance ambassadors.

Bev and I joined the National Square Dance Campers' Association, Inc. in fall of 1961 and are badgeholders to this day. We have been active in the association here in Wisconsin, as well as nationally and internationally.

During our square dance career we attended a total of 35 Wisconsin State Conventions, 11 National Square Dance Conventions, and 12 Arkansas Square Dance Federation Festivals. We have square danced in Maine, Florida, Alaska, Hawaii, and California, as well as Europe. In Germany we even danced on the wine keg atop of Ol' Heidelberg.

There were so many outstanding moments during our square dance life that it would take a large book to tell of them all. The people, music, scenery on our travels, the friendship of dancers country-wide have kept us interested and involved all these many years. We are grateful for all the wonderful people we've met because of this great square dance activity. Enuf Said!

Squarely in His grace,
Howard and Beverly Reoch

Jack and Lolly Gaver
Dousman, Wisconsin

It was always easy to find Jack and Lolly Gaver's home, you just had to look for the square dance couple on the mailbox.

The Gavers started square dancing in 1960, graduating from a class held in the community center in Dousman. After dancing for a few years, Jack began calling. It was too much then, as they were trying to get their kids raised so they dropped out for awhile. Thirteen years later, the Dousman Derby Dancers were still going fine, and still giving lessons so they took them again. They graduated in 1978. Jack went back to calling then and called for ten years.

Jack felt that a caller needed his own club to back him, so the Gavers started the Hartland Hoedowners, a group that is still going strong. He also taught a small class at the University Lake School. Since a caller's wife doesn't have much to do at a dance, Lolly Gaver decided to be a round cuer.

An activity they both enjoyed calling for was the annual Girl Scout/Father Square Dancing Day which attracted more than 200 people. Jack Gaver retired as a teacher from Lad Lake. Lolly was a retired librarian, and made all her own dresses. The couple was active in the square dance activity until the early 1990s. Jack passed away March 7, 1992.

>––!‹›–•–O–•‹›–!‹

Bob Holup
Wausau, Wisconsin

"Bob Holup retired last week, but don't worry square dancers. He only quit to spend more time as a caller." That was the opening paragraph of an article by Dewey Pfister printed in the *Wausau Daily News*. He was announcing Bob Holup's retirement after 31 years as Wausau's Building Inspector.

Bob and Pauline Holup

Thousands who swung their partners to Holup's square dance calls up to seven nights a week may not have realized he had a daytime job. Builders knew the other Robert M. Holup. A construction carpenter-foreman and son of an Antigo contractor, Holup settled in Wausau because his wife, Pauline, was a Wausau native. His long career included service to fellow building inspectors. He was a founder and first president of the Northeast Building Inspectors Association and the 1962 president of the Wisconsin Building Inspectors.

Bob's square dance calling career started when he filled in one night for Arnie Meilahn of Wausau. He went right out and sold his prized possession, a deer rifle, and bought a calling machine. He hauled his public address system and records in a motor home or his big Cadillac. Bob said he bought cars for their trunk size and used to put on 25,000 miles a year, just calling. He called in over 13 states and 5 countries. Holup was the club caller for the Merry 8's in Wausau until 1995, when he resigned his calling duties due to illness.

>─┤─◆>─·O─·<◆·┤─<

Howard and May Donna Gilmore
Rio, Wisconsin

Howard and May Donna Gilmore began square dancing in their youth in 4-H and other rural recreational programs and were involved in modern club dancing for over thirty years. In 1962 Howard began his calling career. He and May Donna were club caller and taw for the Markesan Wheels, Ripon Twirlers, Westfield Jolly Squares, and Hampden Hoedowners. Their new dancer classes, workshops and one-night stands included contras as well as traditional dances.

Howard and May Donna Gilmore

The Gilmores fulfilled many leadership roles in the area caller and dancer councils, in the SDAW and WSDLCC. Conventions are another area where they served; as General Chairman in 1975, Board of Directors for seven years, and as chairmen of various committees. They were Contra Dance Vice-Chairmen for the 28th National Convention in Milwaukee. Howard and May Donna were members of LEGACY, CALLERLAB, CONTRALAB, the Lloyd Shaw Foundation, and the National Square Dance Campers' Association.

As SDAW Historian they were responsible for maintenance and storage of state square dance memorabilia and displays of square dance history at national and state conventions. May Donna was an accomplished writer and Howard was a prominent church soloist who often performed at Welsh Singing Festivals, weddings, and funerals.

May Donna passed away on March 1, 1992, and Howard died on July 16, 1996.

>─┤─◆>─·O─·<◆·┤─<

Dave and Nancy Hussey
Appleton, Wisconsin

Here 'Tis Caller of the Month—Spring 1979

Dave and Nancy became active in square dancing when they took lessons in 1971 from Brad Landry. Dave had an edge on Nancy when they started. He had some prior experience at La Crosse University where he majored in Physical Education and had to teach square dancing in high school Physical Education Classes. At that time he did a little calling but the activity was scheduled for only short segments each year and the next year he would have to start all over again. For this reason he had little chance to progress with his calling.

After graduating from Brad's class Dave got a taste of calling in front of "real live" adult dancers. Brad, Lyle Leatherman, and several other Wolf River Area callers were a great source of help and encouragement. They would invite Dave to call a tip at their dances and the dancers actually stayed on the floor, which always amazed both Dave and Nancy. They attended two of Cal Golden's caller colleges and Dave also learned a lot about calling from his brother Bob, who was a caller in central Illinois.

Dave and Nancy Hussey

Dave called for three clubs: the Sovereign-Aders in Winneconne, The Twin City Squares in Marinette, and the Inter-Level Squares in Appleton. He gave several workshops at Wisconsin Teacher Conventions and also did guest calling. Besides calling, he officiated at high school football and basketball games around the state.

Dave graduated from UW-La Crosse in 1960 (the year he and Nancy were married) and in 1962 he earned his M.A. Degree at Eastern Illinois University. He taught at Xavier High School in Appleton until 1966. In May of '66 the family left for Somalia, Africa. Dave was hired as Director of Health and Physical Education at the National Teacher Education Center by US-Aid in the State Department. When he and Nancy returned in 1968, Dave went back to Xavier for one year and then taught in the Appleton public schools until 1976 when he became principal of Xavier High School.

Dave Hussey passed away unexpectedly on December 23, 1993 at age 57. Dave was an active long-time member of the Wolf River Area Callers' Association.

Pat and Bob Kelm
by Pat Kelm

Bob and I began square dancing March 17, 1972 with Clarence Freis and the Clar-Adel Dancers. A few years later I found I was singing the calls along with Clarence while I was dancing. I knew then I wanted to be a caller. Clarence encouraged me, and as soon as I was ready had me call guest tips. When I started a club he would always come and critique (in private) when necessary.

I called for several clubs over the years beginning in 1976-1977. They were: Shirts & Skirts (1978-1988), Square Generations (1991-1996), OK Swingers, a plus club (1988-1997), and Jacks 'N Jills, Cleveland, WI, a mainstream club. Dale Bashaw and Joe Loberger were the callers for the Jacks 'N Jills before me. When Bob and I moved up north in the summer of 1997, Kevin Jochims took over. I was, also, club teacher and cuer for the Kettle Squares in Plymouth for many years.

Pat and Bob Kelm

We've seen many changes during our square dance career. When Bob and I first started Flutterwheel was one of the new moves sweeping the country. There were fewer moves to learn and we danced a year before going to some workshops for more mainstream moves. The quarterly selections which we learned along the way became most of the Plus list. Callers used to teach and call round dances, line dancing, and mixers also, during a dance.

What changes or improvements would I like to see? I'd like the friendliness currently seen among dancers and callers to continue. I'd like to see the clubs sponsor some "basic" dances, especially in the summer months when the "snow birds" come north, and to keep the newer dancers active. I'd like to change the term "basic" and include more variety in dances such as lines, mixers, contra, along with rounds and squares. I'd like to see more emphasis on dancing to the music; stepping to the beat, dancing with the phrase.

We used to dance every tip and every round dance in an evening. I used to stay up all night the evening before the state convention sewing on square dance costumes. One year at an after party I fell asleep momentarily while dancing in a square—the other two couples were active.

My philosophy? Smile, be friendly, be gentle, dance to the music, and above all, laugh and have fun. That's what square dancing is all about.

Why We Square Dance
by *Margaret Leatherman, Menasha, Wisconsin*

Be there a man with soul so dead
Who never to his taw has said,
"Get out your Square Dance dress and shawl,
There's a dance tonight at the Square Dance Hall."

Know you this man, then why not say,
"Come along, Joe with us today,
Bring Kate along and soon you'll know
Why a Square Dance is the place to go!"

It creates new friendships, renews the old.
For we're all as one in the square dance fold.
Regardless of creed, position, or race,
We all go to dance in the very same place.

It's the fun we have, and the people we meet.
The smiles we share as we walk down the street.
Our worries seem less, and our life more gay,
"A Square Dance!! —- Perfect end of a busy day!"

The Hodag Twirlers
Rhinelander, Wisconsin

This history of the Hodag Twirlers is taken from articles appearing in the Here 'Tis *1980 spring issue, and information provided by Judy Hogan.*

Early in 1951 the Hodag Clam Diggers was organized. Members danced to records under the leadership of Clarence Wine (a teacher) and Charles Russell (a barber). By 1954 lessons were offered to attract more dancers to the renamed Hodag Square Dance Club and they were having real callers.

In 1959 Rhinelander celebrated its Diamond Jubilee and the club members danced in the big parade. Then there was no dancing in the area for awhile and dancers had to travel fifty miles and more to find a square dance. Through the efforts of Bob Fease, who operated Fease's Shady Rest Lodge, dancing was restored to the area in 1960. Fease opened the lodge to square dancers and many square dance weekends were held there. A new club was formed known as the Shady Squares with Leroy Hitzke doing the calling.

Late in 1963 the club was renamed Belles and Beaus and danced in the Rhinelander area again. In 1968 the club became the Hodag Twirlers. The Hodag is Rhinelander's mascot and the name

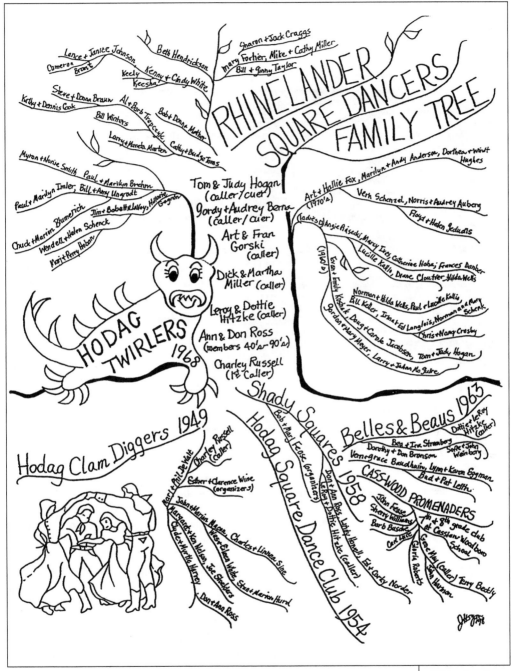

Rhinelander Square Dancers family tree.

is applied to many organizations there. In February of 1979 Ann and Don Ross of Rhinelander were made honorary members of the Hodag Twirlers. They were the only charter members still active in the club at that time.

In 1972 Art Gorski became the full time club caller. He and his taw, Fran, worked very hard to keep square and round dancing alive and well in the northwoods.

Art and Fran were indoctrinated into square dancing in Chicago, through a caller named John Pearson. After ten years of prodding by Pearson, Art finally joined his class. A few weeks later they joined a second class taught by Ralph Gladding. Art was left handed, and Fran had never danced, so they needed the extra practice. A few months later Pearson asked the Gorski's to join his round dance class. Now they were going three nights a week.

Fran and Art Gorski

They were having a problem putting the round dancing all together so Art purchased John Pearson's old equipment so they could practice in their basement. Things began to come easier. Art, being musically inclined, caught on very fast and one day he asked Fran to get the neighborhood kids together so he could teach them how to square dance. Fran spread the word and soon they had three squares, ages seven through fourteen. The kids did so well, and enjoyed it so much, they invited their parents to come and watch. After seeing how well the children were doing, they also joined the class. It was such a large group that Art and Fran had to get a hall. About this time, Art formed a three-piece band and called to live music but he had to disband the group and go to records as the expense was too great. The children were grasping the steps sooner than the parents, so the parents wanted to dance on a separate night. Early in 1963 both groups graduated. It was then the Flying Squares and the Polka Dot Teen Club were born.

In 1966 the Gorski's joined a group of dancers from the Boots and Slippers Club in Milwaukee for a Fun Night on the Milwaukee clipper. They danced all night on the 90-mile trip to Michigan and back. They met some of the Belles and Beaus from Rhinelander, and after hearing Art call, they asked him to call at their annual Snowmobile Dance in January. He accepted and was asked to call again in 1968 and to become the club caller. Since Art loved to fish and wanted to get out of the city, he accepted.

Later Art formed two other clubs, the Eagle Chain Squares, and the Lakeland Promenaders, and also taught dancing at Nicolet College. Art spent the last 20 years of his life in Rhinelander with his wife Fran. Art passed away on February 15, 1986, at age 69.

After his death, Judy and Tom Hogan became caller/cuer for the club. Judy enjoys working with groups and clubs who are interested in doing folk dances such as a Virginia Reel type dance. When the Hodag Twirlers get together, Judy does the cuing and Tom calls the squares for the mainstream and plus level dancers.

The M-T Saddles
Ozaukee County, Wisconsin

September 1963 was the beginning of the M-T Saddles Square Dance Club. Harry Schopp was the caller/teacher. Most of the couples who attended these first lessons at the Grand Avenue School in Thiensville were from the Thiensville-Mequon area. This helped solve the problem of a name for the club. The group incorporated the first initials of both communities into the club's name. The badge selected for the members pictured an empty saddle with the initials MT. The first class was graduated in June of 1964. Scotty's at Five Corners near Cedarburg was chosen as their dance site and the second and fourth Friday of each month became "Square Dance" time.

The interest in square dancing grew and people from outlying areas joined the group. In addition to regular dancing at Scotty's, exhibitions were staged at Thiensville Firemen's Picnic, Northwest Carnival and other local events to stimulate the spectator interest in square dancing.

For several years members provided entertainment at the Lasata Home near Cedarburg. Residents in wheelchairs joined in the dancing fun. Special treats were barn dances and an

Harry Schopp

evening of dancing at the Cedarburg Firehouse. A bi-centennial exhibition at Circle B highlighted the 1976 activities.

When Scotty's was no longer available the club moved to Thiensville Gardens for a short duration. In 1972 the large hall at beautiful Circle B on Highway 60 between Cedarburg and Grafton became available to them. In the summer of 1976, after four years at this hall, the 10,000th dancer received a pass for a year's free dancing. In 1978 there were 21 member couples. Harry Schopp was the club caller/cuer until the club ceased dancing in 1986.

M-T Saddles Ad

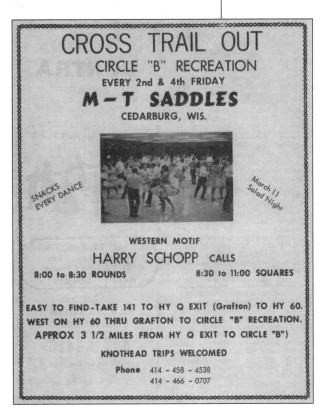

CROSS TRAIL OUT
CIRCLE "B" RECREATION
EVERY 2nd & 4th FRIDAY
M-T SADDLES
CEDARBURG, WIS.

SNACKS EVERY DANCE

March 11 Salad Night

WESTERN MOTIF
HARRY SCHOPP CALLS
8:00 to 8:30 ROUNDS   8:30 to 11:00 SQUARES

EASY TO FIND-TAKE 141 TO HY Q EXIT (Grafton) TO HY 60.
WEST ON HY 60 THRU GRAFTON TO CIRCLE "B" RECREATION.
APPROX 3 1/2 MILES FROM HY Q EXIT TO CIRCLE "B")

KNOTHEAD TRIPS WELCOMED

Phone 414 - 458 - 4538
         414 - 466 - 0707

"R" Squares
Milwaukee, Wisconsin
From a 1975 Report provided by Greg and Joan Polly

The history of the "R" Squares dates back to 1961 when four couples attended Ernie Randall's first beginners' class in Milwaukee. They, and five other couples from the second class, started the "R" Squares in March of 1962, dancing at the Mill Inn. The first presidents of the club were Doc and Gerene Reiser. Thirteen couples graduated on the first anniversary of the club in 1963. The "R" Squares were incorporated with the State of Wisconsin as a non-profit organization on August 9, 1966.

Ernie Randall was the regular caller of the "R" Squares until his death in 1971. After that, the club hired various callers from the area and throughout the state.

The "R" Squares were a very active club in the SDAW-SEA and club delegates served seven terms as officers of the SEA. Members of the club served as committee chairpersons at the state convention five times.

The "R" Squares sponsored beginner classes starting every September. The instructors were Jim and Bette Noonan.

There were four major club functions each year: first quarter, club dinner; second quarter, picnic; third quarter, hayride or knot head trip; and fourth quarter, a gala New Year's Eve party.

The "R" Squares dances were held at Venture Inn, 3945 North 35th Street and the Orchard Inn located one-half mile north of the Starlight Theater on Hwy. 145. The officers of the "R" Squares welcomed anyone seeking fun in square dancing to join them on the first and third Friday of each month. The club ceased operation in 1988. Eric Tess and Donna Barth were the last recorded presidents, Greg and Joan Polly were vice president.

"R" Squares.

CLUB OF THE MONTH

R

NOVEMBER 21 1975

Happy Twirlers of La Crosse
Prepared by Sue and Skip Comeau

The Happy Twirlers were organized in 1961. The club danced from 8:00-10:30p.m. in the Presbyterian Church basement each Wednesday night. During the summer months the club met alternate weeks in various parks, dancing at the plus level.

Norm and Jennie Indvick were the first club callers and round dance leaders. George White followed and Les LaLone is presently calling for the club, with the support of his wife, Jan.

The club has always been dancer-run and from the start has featured guest callers and round dance cuers, both area and national.

The Happy Twirlers sponsored a weekend of dances at the La Crosse Oktoberfest from its inception in 1961, staffed by national and area callers and cuers. Starting in 1962 an annual Spring Fling weekend was also sponsored with similar format and staffing. These events brought thousands of square dancers to La Crosse and one Oktoberfest attracted dancers from 18 states and 5 Canadian Provinces.

One club was responsible for these two annual events, plus other traveling callers, hence the trademark "Square Dance Capitol of the World" was registered.

Sue and Skip Comeau

The club has helped to host three State Conventions, and many of the members were on the Education Committee for the National Convention held in Milwaukee in 1979. Once again, after 12 years, the club helped host the 1992 and 1997 Wisconsin State Convention, as well as many SDAW Jamborees between 1990 and 1997.

Since 1992 the club has been doing an exhibition dance at the annual Riverfest, held on the 4th of July, our largest promotional dance to create interest in square dancing and recruit new members.

In 1995 our club spawned a new caller who has been registered, and three others now in training, including a woman.

It is the year 1998 and the Happy Twirlers still dance every Wednesday night, 8:00-10:00 p.m. and alternate weeks in summer at the YMCA in La Crosse. Lessons begin every fall in September on the same night, beginning at 6:30 p.m.

Circle 'n Star Halloween Dance.

Circle 'n Star

Circle 'n Star square dance club was established January 19, 1959. The purpose of the club was to increase the general knowledge of square dancing and to promote a wider friendship among its members. Harold Phannenstill was the original club caller and instructor.

In 1965, Gene Dreyfus became the club caller and taught the beginners as well. The round dances were taught by Glen and Elaine Dolmer. In 1967 Earl Thompson became the club caller. Doug and Virginia Miller took over the round dances.

In 1971, on the 12th anniversary of Circle 'n Star, the members began a traveling door program. Every year on the anniversary dance, it came home and then started out again with the couple who lived farthest away.

In 1976, Bob Wilson took over as club caller until 1988 when the club disbanded. Mary Edge had taken over the round dance cuing from 1977 to 1988.

The club enjoyed a banquet at the end of each season as well as a club picnic in the summertime. During their annual Halloween dance the club would hold bake sales and raffles to raise money. Circle 'n Star would also charter a bus to transport its members to national conventions where a good time was enjoyed by all and where many new friends were made.

The Westport Squares
Submitted by R. Lecheler

The Westport Square Dance Club was started at St. Mary's of the Lake Church at Westport, Wisconsin. Election of officers was held and five ladies were nominated for the offices of President, Secretary-Treasurer and Food Chairman. The one who received the most votes became President, the second most votes was Secretary-Treasurer, and third place became Food Chairman. For quite a few years women were the officers (and did all the work).

Name tags were voted down as not being necessary because the members all knew each other. Their first dance held on June 25, 1955 was attended by 23 couples. Art Weisensel was the caller and his fee was $15. The dance fee was $1 per couple. It was collected in the square during a tip by the head couple leading to the right and collecting from each couple.

They graduated their first beginners class on April 11, 1956.

It is not clear when the club moved into the Westport Town Hall, but in July 1955 they purchased screen hinges, springs and screens. They must have been working on the hall. In September they paid 8 cents for toilet paper. They wouldn't have had to buy that if they had been dancing at the church. In October they paid for light, wiring, and a broom. They must have moved in about then. For about the first five years after they began dancing at the hall there were outhouses and a pot belly stove in the corner that had to be tended to.

Westport Squares "club house" is an old cheese factory that was moved to its

Art and Mary Weisensel

present site in 1902 and converted to a Town Hall. It served as the Town Hall for voting and town meetings from that time until the new Town Hall Administration Building was built in 1984. Voting is still held in the old Town Hall. The hall was without central heat or plumbing until it was remodeled and the garage was added in 1960.

At a meeting in 1958 there was a big discussion on how to attract new dancers and how to keep them dancing. Things haven't changed a whole lot. They're still having the same discussion.

The treasury was small, always well under $100. They dealt in pennies for years. A Gift Exchange at Christmas was limited to 50 cents. They voted in 1958, after much discussion, to donate $1 to the Empty Stocking Club. Get Well cards cost either 13 cents or 18 cents including postage. There is an unsigned IOU that says "We owe the club 9 beers and 3 pops." In 1958 the club bought a refrigerator for $5 from Lodi Valley Squares and then paid $5 to have it repaired. I think it lasted until about 1989 when it was replaced.

Even with their tight budget the members always gave Mary Weisensel a corsage or flowers on her birthday. Don Niva and his wife Joan, were still signing in as dancers in 1958 and then in 1959 as a caller and taw. And at that time the club was paying the Town of Westport $30 every six months for hall rent.

In 1960 the Club lost $47.20, checkbook balance zero. They have risen several times from the ashes. In 1965 the dance admission was raised to $1.25 per couple.

January 1966 marked the first annual dinner held at Waunakee American Legion Hall. The dinner (chicken and ham) and the dance was $6 per couple. Mixed drinks were 45 cents and beer was 15 cents.

In 1967 the beer price was raised from 15 cents to 20 cents a bottle at the hall and pop went from 10 cents to 15 cents. That year the club held a Table Dance. For a $1.50 a couple could buy a lunch table for the Town Hall. A card table was given away as a door prize.

In 1970 the club members volunteered to paint the hall.

In 1973 the callers fee was raised to $25 for Art Weisensel but not for guest callers. The dance fee was raised to $1.50 per couple.

While Art was club caller it was voted that there would be no more than four guest callers a year and only when Art couldn't make it. If Art had to cancel more than four times the dance itself would be canceled.

Art Weisensel was Club Caller until his death July 28, 1975. Will Ferderer then started calling on the third and fifth Fridays but was not named club caller until 1979. He was club caller for three years and since then the club has been using guest callers.

In 1976 Larry Endres remodeled the hall with paneling, cupboards, signs, etc. at his own expense.

When beer was stocked in the refrigerator all the beer and beer cases had to be removed from the Town Hall during elections. Somewhere along the line in the '80s square dancers stopped drinking beer during the dance so they stopped stocking it.

Westport Squares celebrated their 40th anniversary in 1995. They are facing the same problems as all clubs, how to attract and retain new dancers. Costs are escalating and with the lower number of dancers in the area attendance at dances is generally down, even for name callers. They feel that their banner stealing activities have helped immensely in that area. They've been fortunate to be able to stay in the same hall all these years at a reasonable rent. They're holding their own and looking forward to many more years of dancing enjoyment at Westport Town Hall.

The Swingin' Singles Squares

Material for this article was provided by Larry Guse, Joyce Donnell, Louise Erler, Jim Layman, and early issues of the Swingin' Singles Newstip.

For many years modern square dancing was enjoyed by couples in the United States and many parts of the world. Here in the Milwaukee area it was limited to mostly married couples. This was changed when in the fall of 1973 a group of single adults called the Greenfield Avenue Single Adults hired a local square dance caller, Loren Shaw for mostly "one-night stand square dances." These square dances were held in the basement of the First Presbyterian Church on 60th and National in Milwaukee on the last Saturday of each month.

In the summer of 1974 the Shaws went to a National Square Dance Convention. There they saw groups of single adults who were members of Single Square Dancers USA and Bachelor and Bachelorettes clubs. Such clubs had started on the west coast and were spreading across the country.

In the fall of 1974 Loren, and his wife Carroll, with two angel square dancers, Jodie Ryback and Larry Guse (a recent graduate of Greendale Village Squares dance class), began teaching a group of about 100 single adults how to square

Loren and Carroll Shaw

dance. Many of the students were members of the Greenfield Avenue Single Adults Club. The late Ione Quinby Griggs, in her advice column in the *Milwaukee Journal Green Sheet*, provided much support for this group.

The ratio of ladies to men was about three to one. Several of the ladies rotated dancing on the left side of the couple to provide a chance for all ladies to dance. In the spring of 1975, the 20 single adults who completed the 30 weeks of lessons, (8 men and 12 women), along with Ryback and Guse, gave birth to the Swingin' Single Squares.

The first slate of officers was: Shirley Winklemann, president, Shirley Ryback, secretary, and Russell Hints, treasurer. Loren Shaw was retained as club caller with a dance scheduled the third Wednesday of each month. The club moved to the N&B Hall.

Swingin' Single Squares grew to the point that it expanded lessons to two nights; Tuesdays and Thursdays. Some students attended both lessons. Along with the Wednesday dances which had gone to the second and fourth Wednesdays, the schedule became too much for one caller. Eventually the club hired Randy Tans, Jim Noonan, John McKinnon, Dwayne Olson, and our current teacher, Eric Tangman.

The *Newstip* of November 1980 reported a membership of 140. In 1981 The Red Carpet Bowlero at 117th and Burleigh became the club's new home. It was about this time that a different local caller was booked for each dance. Jerry Haag was the first national caller retained to call for the Swingin' Single Squares. The event was on July 7, 1982.

Loren Shaw died in 1986 but he lived to see the Swingin' Single Squares grow to become the largest club in Wisconsin. His wife Carroll now resides in Albuquerque, New Mexico, and continues to correspond with some of the charter members.

Swingin' Single Squares hosted the "Solo Hall" at the National Square Dance Convention here in Milwaukee in 1979, as well as an after party at each Wisconsin State Square Dance Convention since then. Single Square Dancers USA Dance-a-Rama 1986, a national singles square dance convention was hosted by Swingin' Single Squares at the Red Carpet Hotel on South Howell Avenue. The main hall was carpeted, so prior to the convention the Swingin' Singles banded together to lay a wood floor over the carpeting. Singles from all over the United States attended the event.

Four charter members, Joyce Donnell, Louise Erler, Larry Guse, and Ginny Lucky are currently active members of Swingin' Single Squares and have held various offices and angeled for lessons. Club members have been involved in all phases of square dancing assuming many leadership positions in the SDAW-SEA over the years. A number of the Swingin' Single club members belong to exhibition groups and the club encourages members to participate in promotional events and other activities to help support the square dance community.

Swingin' Single Squares can be credited with providing singles an enjoyable outlet for their energies, their need for mental stimulation, and thirst for healthy socialization. They also generously support other SEA clubs by regularly attending their dances. Former and current members of Swingin' Single Squares continue to dance with mainstream, plus, advanced, and challenge clubs throughout the state.

In addition to regular club dances, Swingin' Singles sponsors many special dances and social events throughout the year, including a New Year's Eve dance, Christmas dinner dance, a Halloween "Nite Owl" dance, Sadie Hawkin's Dance, plus knot head trips, picnics, corn roasts and a number of "singles only" activities.

The Swingin' Single Square Dance club is a member of Single Square Dancers, U.S.A, a national organization for single square dancers.

The Square Benders Square Dance Club

It would be difficult to tell how the Square Benders originated without talking about the role Alex and Gen Brabender played in the formation of the club. Alex and Gen took beginners lessons from Bill and Betty Kersey in 1958. That was the beginning of a long and beautiful relationship with the world of square dancing. The Brabenders had been square dancers for four years at the time Alex decided to start calling. In 1963 Alex and Gen Brabender began by holding open dances in a small tavern hall in the little Village of Decada and later in Fredonia, Wisconsin. An official club was organized and dances were started at Big John's Hall in Fredonia in 1965.

During this time Alex and Gen held beginners classes each year. In 1965, a group of 12 couples decided to form their own club, and a meeting was held to select a name. "Square Benders" seemed a natural choice given that Alex and Gen Brabender were Caller and taw. Vic Doers was asked to design a club badge, officers were elected and the club was off and dancing.

Square Benders show off their new banner.

The next home for the Square Benders was the Black Wheel in Cedarburg (1978). New classes of dancers were graduated each year and the club grew. As the number of members and guests increased, the size of the hall was no longer adequate. Another new address for the club was found at Circle B in Cedarburg in 1982. Another "new home" was found in 1990 at the Northwest Senior Center in Milwaukee. Although Square Benders has changed halls several times, they still dance on the first and third Wednesday at the Northwest Senior Center on 76th and Good Hope Road in Milwaukee.

Over the years many special dances were held for the pleasure of all Wisconsin dancers. "Shindig in the Barn" held at the Tetzlaff farm in Grafton, the annual corn roast, annual brat night, many New Year's Eve dances, and every year an Anniversary dance for the club.

The club members changed as over the years new members joined and some drifted away. Some of the early members are still listed on the club roster; Chet and Claire Anderson, Bob and Gerri

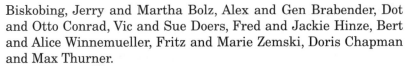

Biskobing, Jerry and Martha Bolz, Alex and Gen Brabender, Dot and Otto Conrad, Vic and Sue Doers, Fred and Jackie Hinze, Bert and Alice Winnemueller, Fritz and Marie Zemski, Doris Chapman and Max Thurner.

Square Benders celebrated their 25th anniversary on November 7, 1990, and on November 20, 1991, Alex Brabender announced his retirement from calling at a special celebration dance. Although he and Gen retired from calling they haven't retired from the club and are still active members and leaders.

So the dance goes on. The club was struggling in 1996 to keep the club fiscally afloat and considered dropping one of their monthly dances. Eric Tangman, an excellent caller and teacher came to the rescue. Eric offered to call at one dance each month, encouraging the Square Bender officers to keep the club dance on the first and third Wednesday of each month. The results have been good. Eric had an excellent following especially among the Swingin' Singles and they turn out in force to dance to Eric's calling. The club is growing again. For the past two years Square Benders has combined with Swingin' Singles to hold beginner lessons with Eric teaching. Both clubs send "angels" to help the new dancers and many of them choose to join the Square Benders after graduation.

The club is also improving financially, and attendance has increased. The dance fees and membership dues were increased but this was done in keeping with other local dances.

The club looks for opportunities to promote square dancing. They participate in parades, exhibitions at hospitals, nursing homes, and senior centers and other club activities to promote good fellowship through square dancing.

T-P Taws & Paws
Submitted by Doris Palmen

The club started lessons in September 1977 in Antioch, Illinois. Ted Palmen was the original caller-instructor. Lessons were held at an Antioch Bank.

The first dance was held in March, 1978, at the Legion Hall in Antioch. Jerry Packman and Betty Drafz did rounds for a year or so.

After a couple of years the club moved to Lake Shangrila in Kenosha County. We were a mainstream club to begin with. After moving to Lake Shangrila we alternated tips with mainstream and plus and danced first, third and fifth Fridays. Fifth Fridays were later dropped.

One Friday a month the Homeowner's Association of Lake Shangrila sponsored a Fish and Steak Fry in the hall basement. Most of the dancers always came early and really enjoyed having dinner before the dances.

The club rounds were now being cued by Doris Palmen. The hall had a great wood floor for dancing even through it had a hump in it.

The club later moved to Kenosha and has danced in a number of different halls. In September 1996 the club changed the first dance of the month to first Thursdays in order to be able to visit clubs that danced on first Fridays. We now dance on the first Thursdays at the Somers Town Hall, behind the Fire Station, in Kenosha County on Highway E. The third Friday dances are held in Kenosha at St. John's Lutheran Church on 7th Avenue.

The only original members left are Ruth O'Neill of Antioch, Illinois, and Ted and Doris Palmen, the club cuer/caller instructors.

Doris and Ted Palmen

The club has been trying to put FUN back into dancing and not be so serious. We do fun things like Jackson Steal, and badge dances. Apple Munchers, Siamese dance, crazy hat dance, Luau's, with a pole dance, and Venus dance are some of the things we have been doing. Dancers always enjoy our Glow Worm, Hobo and duet nights. Years ago, when the club was young, we danced next to the railroad tracks. One night we had a Hobo Dance and all the dancers left the squares when a train came by to wave at the engineer, leaving Ted standing calling to an empty floor.

We have a Christmas dinner party with our new dancers, and have done the "candle-lighting ceremony" for graduations for many years.

We hold our square and round dance lessons at nursing homes. It gives us a place for lessons and entertains the residents at the same time. We also promote square dancing by participating in the Kenosha County Fair. We participate in the SDAW-SEA banner program and serve refreshments at all dances. We are now dancing the Mainstream program with one plus tip at each dance. Besides rounds, mostly Phase II, we do some line dances and sometimes a mixer or contra.

We celebrated our 20th anniversary with a Cake Walk in March 1998.

Rounds are still done by Doris Palmen and Ted Palmen is still the club caller-instructor. We do have various guest callers during the year.

Ted and Doris Palmen learned to square dance with the Swingin' Swedes in Zion, Illinois, and graduated in February 1971. Their enthusiasm for the activity rubbed off on their children who were members of the Paris Swingin' Livewires 4-H Club. Ted was volunteered to teach the group. The first class of two squares graduated in February 1972. As more 4-H'ers entered into the spirit of the dance, the group became known as the T-P Teens, named for Ted Palmen, and in 1975 they put on an exhibition at the State Square Dance Convention in Madison.

Ted and Doris attended Callers' College at Promenade Hall in Indiana, and callers' seminars at National conventions. Ted was instructor for the Paddock Lake Squares, the Swingin' Swedes, and the Shirts & Skirts youth club at Great Lakes, Illinois. In 1977 Ted and Doris started T-P Camp 'n Dance outings at Spring Grove, Illinois, and at Bark River in Jefferson, Wisconsin. The group became known as the T-P Trailers.

The Palmen's are active in the MACC and live in Bristol, Wisconsin.

>—I—‹›—O—‹›—I—<

Diamond Squares
by Art and Helen Anhalt

Diamond Squares of DeForest started in August 1978 when four couples, Elvin and June Myklebust, Art and Helen Anhalt, Connie and Lorraine Hendrickson, Del and Jan Brock, put on an exhibition in the DeForest park with Don Niva calling. The club was incorporated and the first dance was held May 12, 1979, at the DeForest High School cafeteria. The club has been dancing ever since, with many activities.

Fun on the Farm was started to have operating money. It continued for ten years through rain, heat, and cold, with lots of fun, hayrides, many new friends, and hours and hours of dancing.

New Year's Eve at Holiday Inn Southeast in Madison was the highlight of the year. A midnight brunch was served by the members, and those that still had energy danced until 3 a.m. People came from other states to be with friends, and most took advantage of special room rates and stayed over.

Diamond Squares club members are easily recognized at special activities by their club outfits. Women wear skirts with alternating red and white panels, each with a Diamond Squares emblem trimmed with sequins. Men have vests of reversible red and white with the club emblem and sequins.

One night we boarded the Col-Sac Ferry near Merrimac. Equipped with a caller and music we danced while the ferry made trips back and forth. Luckily there weren't that many cars on the ferry. The operator called his boss and said, "You won't believe what's going on."

We've danced in many places—deep down in Mammoth Cave, the Capitol at Washington D.C., the largest number of squares in one place at Seattle, Washington, parking lots in Canada, Madison's Monona Terrace, swimming pools, barns, cold park shelters, and weddings.

One unforgettable experience happened at a festival in Chicago. We could see the hotel from the highway as we drove into the city, but had a hard time getting to it. When we finally arrived we found that the hotel was actually a residence for senior citizens. Our rooms were, well we won't say, but we had to chase a pigeon out of one. The pool was unusable. After the initial shock we settled in. Going to and from the ballroom we held doors open and shared elevators with senior citizens, some in wheelchairs and walkers. The style show was well attended by the senior residents. The weekend turned out to be very rewarding to us, and we're sure the elderly enjoyed our company.

Another unforgettable experience happened at one state convention. Caller Gene Knutson kept saying, "If you can't do it, do push-ups." On cue, the next time he said it, our square dropped to the floor and did push-ups. The whole room stopped dancing to watch.

Square dancing is all about traveling, fun, meeting new people, and lots of dancing. We hope this never changes.

Country Swingers

Delores and Maynard Laufenberg

A meeting was held on October 3, 1967, for the square dancers of the Huilsberg area (Huilsberg, Rubicon, Neosho, Hartford, Hustisford, etc.) to find out if a club could be organized in the vicinity. Mrs. John Lemerond was asked to be the moderator.

A club was indeed formed with the decision to have dances on the first and third Tuesday of each month. Dues were to be $1.50 per year, with a $1.25 donation at the dances. Dancers were to bring sandwiches and snacks to the dances. Officers for the first year were: President, Roland and Marge Heuer; Secretary, John and Catherine Lemerond; and Treasurer, Len and Ruth Siegmann. Club members also immediately voted to join the Square Dance Association of Wisconsin—South East Area (SDAW-SEA).

At the organizational meeting, much discussion was held on a name for the club. A suggestion was made that names and club pin designs be solicited until the first dance. Then the club members in attendance would vote on the names proposed, with a prize being awarded to the submitter of the winning name. About 10 to 12 names were suggested. These were drawn up on paper and posted on a bulletin board at the first dance. "Country Swingers" and "Whirlaround" were tied, so another vote was taken to split the tie, with "Country Swingers" being chosen. Marge Skudlarcyzk of Campbellsport had suggested the name and won the prize. Pins and banners for the banner stealing program were then designed, with square dancers on a swing representing the club name.

Delores Laufenberg was asked to be the club caller. Her fee was to be one-half of the admission donations, but no more than $15 and no less than $5. Guest callers were to be hired for special dances. The proprietor of the Hall (Lisko's) agreed to allow the club to use the hall for free when they didn't need heat, and for $5 when they did. They would also be charged for electricity "if they used a lot of it for special dances."

Country Swingers held regular and special dances at Lisko's Hall in Huilsberg for 30 years until their last club dance in October 1997 with 21 squares in attendance, live music, and a potluck supper. Delores Laufenberg and Len Siegmann were the callers. The whole celebration was joyous and filled with fun and memories. It was a great ending to a great club.

Ruth and Len Siegmann

Dudes and Dolls Square Dance Club
Racine County
Submitted by Mary Edge

The Dudes and Dolls Square Dance Club began in 1958 when four couples from Sturtevant were attending square dance classes with the Fox River Melody Squares in Waterford. They wanted square dancing closer to their homes, so they asked the caller, Art Radoll of South Milwaukee to start classes in the Village Hall in Sturtevant. They mailed three-cent postcards to all their friends asking them to try square dancing. The first lesson was held on Wednesday, September 10, 1958, and three months later Dick and Arlene Hansen were elected the first presidents. Five names were suggested for the club and Dudes and Dolls was chosen.

The Dudes and Dolls danced at the Sturtevant Village Hall for 14 years. In 1979 the club moved to the Yorkville United Methodist Church and danced there for 13 years. From 1985-1991 the dances were held at Drought School at the corner of Highway 45 and Seven Mile Road. 1991-1993 found the club dancing at the Raymond School. In 1999 they moved to their present location at the Raymond Town Hall.

During its 40 years, the club has had three club callers. Art and Marge Radoll called for the Dudes and Dolls until Art retired on June 13, 1987. On September 27, 1975, Roger and Mary Edge started their career as Round Dance Cuers for the Club. Jerry and Ceil Wenglewski called for the club from September 19, 1987, until June

Dudes and Dolls Poster.

10, 1995. On September 9, 1995, Jimmie and Deanna Burss became the club callers.

The club has always been known for their hospitality, friendliness, and for great food. The Sausage and Kraut night and the Barn Dance are annual events and are always well attended.

⟫—┥—◆⟩—○—⟨◆—┝—⟪

The Tale of Loyal Circle 8's
by Nathan and June Noeldner

In the spring of 1960
A great idea was born,
An ad was put in the local newspaper
A Square Dance club to form.

Classes started at the High School gym
And little did we know
The fun we'd have, the friends we'd make
Learning to 'do-si-do'.

Twenty-two couples at our first dance
Gave encouragement and support.
We named the club 'Loyal Circle 8's'
From then on, we went forth.

Freddie Justman was our caller,
Stayed with us through thick and thin.
Places to dance changed several times
But we kept going, never gave in.

Our club did some crazy things
To earn extra pins and banners.
Did some traveling, and some stealing,
Never forgot their manners.

The club sponsored Johnny LeClair
Who came from Wyoming to call.
Dancers met at the Silver Dome Ballroom
A great time was had by all.

Clyde Tanglefoot was introduced;
A traveling dummy from La Crosse.
We brought him home, he traveled on
A club pin was added by us.

Camping, picnics, parties and floats.
Anniversaries, conventions and more.
All made for happy memories
Friends got together, fun galore.

Patty Justman, our caller's wife
Helped teach the allemande left.
Her friendly ways helped us all
We learned and passed the test.

When Freddie decided to leave us
We needed a caller to take his place.
Milton Ystad filled our need
It was a big job to face.

Bonnie also became a friend
Milton's wife and helper.
She came along most of the time
A club member, very dapper.

Milton now is semi-retired
Some new callers fill his shoes.
It's hard to keep the club alive
"Determination" is the word to choose.

Dances are not held weekly
Like dances of years gone by,
The officers keep it going
With determination—they try.

The dancers have happy memories
That cannot be taken away.
We are so glad for the fun we had
And the friends we have today.

Hartland Hoedowners
by Ann Dow

May of 1981 was the time of the first dance of the Hartland
Hoedowners, at Lincoln School in Hartland, Wisconsin. Jack and
Lolly Gaver were the club callers. Jack called squares and Lolly
cued rounds.

The club outfits were red bandanna prints with black and
white accents. One of the first activities was the production of club
identification.

At first we had a red hoe, and later a club banner. Fresh doughnuts, fried at the dance, became one of the popular refreshments of dancers.

The death of Jack Gaver left a void in the Hartland Hoedowners, but the club is still active. Hartland Hoedowners now dance at University Lake School outside of Hartland.

>─┼─◆>─┼─○─◆>─┼─◆

Kettle Moraine Squares
by Lloyd and Joyce Gatzke

The Kettle Moraine Squares formed in November of 1981 by Dan and Paula Siegmann, as a caller run club. The first "niter" was held on November 20 at Badger Middle School in West Bend with 40 couples in attendance. The next fall eight couples started a lesson program and the beginners graduated on April 17, 1983. In July of 1984 the dance location was moved to Wolf's Hall in Allenton and this has been the club's home ever since.

Dan decided to give up calling and cuing in March of 1985 so he could spend more time with his family. At this time the members elected officers and became a member run club. Judy "Hot Pepper" Wilson became our club caller until she retired in May 1987.

Again our club was fortunate. Gordy and Mary Ann Ziemann took over the duties of club caller and cuer. We dance mainstream on the first and third Friday of each month. A guest caller is scheduled for the third Friday. Fifty-four dancers make up the membership of the club; ages are ten through eighty-plus. We have several special dances each year. Most popular are our Kielbasa night and a Thanks for New Dancers night. 1998 marked the ninth annual Thanks for New Dancers night. The dance is to honor our new graduates and includes a dinner of roast turkey, salads, and angel food cakes. The dance held at Kettle Moraine Bowl in Slinger cost $5.50 per person.

Kettle Moraine Squares owns a float and participates in area parades and performs various exhibitions in the West Bend Area. The club also volunteers for the Adopt-a-Highway program.

Lloyd and Joyce Gatzke are president of the Kettle Moraine Squares, and are very active in the square dance community. They are past president of the SDAW-SEA, and are the 1998 delegates to the state SDAW. They are assistant chairpersons-facilities for the 39th Wisconsin Square and Round Dance Convention in Racine, Wisconsin, July 17-19, 1998.

Paddock Lake Squares
Submitted by Gladys Elda Bishop

The Paddock Lake Squares was formed in the 1970s for the purpose of enjoying square dancing. Initially the club met at Westosha Central High School on Highway 50 at Paddock Lake in Kenosha County. Elmer Williams was club caller and Ted Palmen, instructor. The Paddock Hooker Lake Clubhouse was the scene of many of the dances and lessons. Club callers through the years also included Harry Lind, Paul Baumann, and Mike Krautkramer. The club members most often exchanged visits with Circle 'n Star, Allemande Club, Dudes and Dolls, T-P Taws & Paws, Ridge Runners, Circle 8 in the Kenosha and Racine areas, and Buoys and Belles in Waukegan, Illinois.

The club gave exhibitions at schools, county fairs, nursing homes, and special community events. The annual dinner dance was held in the spring of the year, and provided an opportunity to conduct club business.

The Paddock Lake Square Dance Club ceased to exist by the fall of 1992 due to a small number of active members, and the financial difficulty of making ends meet, to pay the caller and the rental of facilities.

><del>+<del>+O+<del>+<del>

Shadow Viners Round Dance Club
Submitted by Mary Edge

The Shadow Viner's Round Dance Club held their first dance in September of 1987. That first year the dances were held at Veteran's Park on South 6th Street in Milwaukee. The next year the Club moved to the Classic Lanes in Oak Creek and danced at that location for two years. The next move was to Willow-O-Way in Grant Park in South Milwaukee. Dances were held in that location for four years. We all remember the dark drive to get there. September of 1994 found the Club moving to its present location. Dances are held on the first and third Wednesdays at the Grobschmidt Senior Center in South Milwaukee.

Roger and Mary Edge are the cuers for the Club, which is a caller run club. Two party nights are held each year. One is the Christmas Party when everyone brings finger food to share. The other is the "End of the Season" ice cream social on the third Wednesday in May. Roger brings the ice cream and everyone else brings the toppings. Some yummy creations result. When the Edges are in town, a pig roast and picnic is held at their home sometime during the summer.

Dancing goes from 7-9 p.m. A typical evening consists of four segments. Six dances are included in each segment. The first two dances are Phase III and the last four are Phase II. Between the second and third segment there is a 15 minute teach. There is considerable emphasis on the Classics and new material, but old favorites are also included. Requests are always in order.

At first the membership consisted of mostly people from the South Milwaukee and Cudahy area, but as the Club has grown so has the membership area. We now have dancers coming from as far away as Waukesha and Brookfield.

Fun and fellowship are emphasized as members share their birthdays and anniversaries with each other. Many times members bring treats to share. Get Well cards are sent to those who are unable to dance with us. Everyone is made to feel welcome.

>─!─◆>─○─<◆─!─<

History of the NorJen Dancers
La Crosse, Wisconsin
Prepared by Sue and Skip Comeau—1998

The club started in 1971. Norm Invick and his wife Jennie were the clubs first round dance leaders (1971-1977) and the club was named in their honor. They danced at the Presbyterian Church in La Crosse on Friday nights.

Following Norm's death, Fritz Parins and wife Lou became the round cuers for the club (1977-1996). The club danced in the base-

Fritz and Lou Parins

ment of their home for the first three years after they took over. In 1980 the club moved to the Chinchilla Bar on Green Island due to the increase in members. The dances were held every Friday night.

Fritz recruited new dancers from the Happy Twirlers and other area square dance clubs. These lessons were on Monday nights in the same location from 7:30-9:30 p.m. When the club dancers started decreasing the lessons were moved to Friday nights, from 6:30-8:00 followed by the regular club dance from 8:00-9:30 p.m.

A spring and fall annual round dance was hosted by Fritz and Lou for ten years on a Sunday at the Moose Lodge in La Crosse. Cuers and their clubs in the area were invited to attend and the cuers participated in the program. The special treat at these two annual dances was Lou's homemade candy of about ten varieties. These dances were very well attended and a good time for all.

Fritz was a very dedicated teacher and cuer, who also supported the state associations. Following his death in 1996, Tim
Manning, with the support of his wife Charlotte, became the present club caller.

>─┼─◆〉─◆─O─〈◆─┼─≺

Grand Squares
Madison, Wisconsin
Information compiled by Royal and Joan Gibson

Founded in 1974, this club became one of the largest in the
South West Area of the SDAW. The club boasted more than 50 dues
paying couples and several singles. In the face of declining interest
in square dancing nationwide, the club remained strong.

They were fortunate in having Jim Underwood as the original
club caller. Jim was with the club for just over ten years and was
one of the strongest "draws" in the area.
His dances were always well attended.
On Jim's retirement a new caller, Jim
Gates, became his successor. The club
also had one of the best round dance
cuer-couples in the midwest, Bob and Lu
Paull. The Paulls were club members as
well as cuer-teachers.

Grand Squares had a unique election
structure. In addition to the usual president, vice-president, secretary and treasurer, a couple was chosen as President-
Elect. Persons in that position served as
liaison with the area SDAW, made all the
caller/cuer contacts and did the hiring.
This provided continuity of leadership as
the incumbents proceeded into the presi-
dency. The method took a considerable
burden off the current presidential cou-

*Lou and Bob
Paull*

ple and other officers who, in other clubs, parceled those responsibilities among themselves.

The years 1992 through '94 saw a gradual decline in dance
attendance although the club membership held steady. Activities
other than square dancing began to take precedence in peoples
lives.

During 1995 the club started to have serious financial problems due to declining attendance and increased costs. Attendance
declined to four squares or less—they needed at least five squares
to break even. Enlisting officers became a problem. The older members felt they had already had their turn at being officers, and the
few younger members were too busy with their private lives.

At the annual meeting in 1995 dissolution of the club was discussed. Officers, however, were elected, dues were increased, and an increase in admission was instituted. The club continued to struggle and at the annual meeting in 1996 a motion was proposed to disband. Some last minute volunteers for club officers kept the club going for yet another year.

A special membership meeting was called in 1997. A lack of funds, and no further volunteers for officer positions prompted a vote to disband the club as of December 31, 1997.

The demise of the club was caused by the same problems that seem to plague many other area clubs; lack of attendance, increased costs, lack of affordable dance locations, lack of volunteer officers, and a decreased interest in square dancing by the general public.

>─┼─◆>─○─<◆─┼─<

Here 'Tis square dance magazine had a regular column called "The Spotlight Shines on" in which a caller, cuer, club or dancer was spotlighted. As a rule, dancers were seldom in the limelight, although many of them deserved recognition. Following are biographies of just a few "Dancers of the Month".

Art and Dorothy Wegner
Milwaukee, Wisconsin—Winter 1977-78 issue.

Until 1948 Art was a bowling enthusiast, but that year Art and Dottie decided to replace his bowling activity with square dancing.

They attended a beginners class instructed by Bill and Dolly Barr. After graduation they joined the Q-T Square Dance Club.

Square dancing took second place to participation in their children's activities, and in 1955 they took a second set of beginners lessons from Jim and Pat Collins. In 1955 they started round dance lessons with the Eliases and in March of 1961 Elmer invited them to join the Roselle Exhibition Dance group. Art and Dorothy traveled with the group to Texas, Florida, Canada, Nebraska, Michigan, and many other places doing black light exhibitions. They participated in the International Folk Fair for 15 years.

During their dance career the Wegners were active in all phases of square and round dance activity. They served as vice-president of the EMBA Square Dance Club, were on the registration committee for the 1964 Wauwatosa convention and the 1968 Waukesha convention. They were assistant general chairmen for the 19th state convention at MECCA in Milwaukee. They assisted the bid committee and participated in the bid for the 1979 National Convention.

Art and Dottie taught round dancing to teenagers in the

Milwaukee square dance program, and Dottie wrote the Cook's Nook for the Wisconsin Squares and Rounds *Here 'Tis* for several years.

><!◦>•○•<◦!><

Brownie and Regena Brown
—Fall 1978

Square dancing became a way of life for the Browns, who took beginners lessons in 1950. The class was taught by Carol and Margaret Carlson of Rockford, Illinois, callers for the Janesville Swingin' Squares.

Brownie and Regina served as treasurers for their club, and organized dinner dances and helped plan the special dance when their club celebrated 30 years of dancing in September of '75. They were delegate and treasurer to the SDAW-SWA and worked on several committees. They were alternate delegates to the state SDAW and Director of Programs for the 28th National Convention in Milwaukee in 1979.

Brownie worked for the Janesville Fire Department for over 30 years and was the Red Cross First Aid Chairman for 15 years. During that time he taught first aid and lifesaving to several hundred people. The Browns were members of their church council and Regena served as part time receptionist in the church rectory.

><!◦>•○•<◦!><

Win and Jo Ann Erlandson
—Winter 1978-'79

Win and Jo Ann Erlandson

Win and Jo Ann started their square dance activities in 1962. In the spring of 1963 they joined the Whirl-A-Ways Club in Green Bay. Brad Landry was the club caller. The Erlandsons served as officers for the Whirl-A-Ways and were club delegates and past president of the Wolf River Area Dancer's Association-WRADA.

In 1965 their participation was extended to include the chairmanship of the 7th Wisconsin Square and Round Dance Convention, held in Green Bay. They served on the convention board of directors for five years and were Assistant General Chairmen of the 28th

National Square Dance Convention held in Milwaukee in 1979.

Win was employed by Wisconsin Physician's Service as a group sales representative and Jo Ann worked part-time as a psychiatric nurse at St. Vincent Hospital in Green Bay. The Erlandsons believed their lives were enriched by the many friends they acquired through their square dance activities.

>-+◆>-◦-<+-<

Jim and Jeanette Conner
—Spring 1979

Friends tell that it took Jeanette about three years to convince Jim they should take up square dancing. This accomplished they joined the beginners group of the Janesville Swingin' Squares. Ray Quade was the caller/teacher. They graduated in April of 1960. From then on if anyone said "let's go square dancing" they were ready and eager to go.

Not satisfied to participate just as dancers, the Conners extended themselves into other areas of the activity. In 1962-63 they were president of the Janesville Swingin' Squares. They served as secretary for three state conventions, and participated as representatives and secretary for the SDAW-SWA. They were secretary to the publicity chairman for the 1979 National Convention and in conjunction with those duties attended the Oklahoma National Convention to help promote the National Convention in Wisconsin.

CHAPTER 8

Explode the Wave
National Organizations

All jump up and never come down,
Turn your honey around and around,
'Til the hollow of your foot
Makes a hole in the ground.

A Caller's Life For Me
by Aggi Thurner

I used to love to square dance; it was a lot of fun.
Challenging, good exercise, good friends rolled into one.
I graduated mainstream, then plus became my goal.
Advanced and challenge were a snap cause I was on a roll.

I squeezed round dancing in between and mastered
    every move.
From hover through Varsouvienne I stayed right in the groove.
But I needed more fulfillment; my dance goals now attained.
I looked to square dance calling as being foreordained.

I took some caller lessons and practiced day and night.
I bought some new equipment so the sound would be just right.
I taught a few new dancers not much to brag about,
So I worked even harder to get my message out.

Soon the phone began to ring, and though I'm not a grumbler;
Just how did all those old age homes get hold of
    my phone number?
At last I am a caller. I knew I'd make the grade,
But somehow I always figured that I'd wind up getting paid.

I joined the local callers' league and the National order too.
But I could never get ahead - there was always something new.
"Don't use that call, it's obsolete, here's one we recommend.
There's a caller meeting Monday; it's one you must attend."

No I no longer square dance, cause I'm no longer free.
I lost control to CALLERLAB and the MACC.
I used to love to square dance and in considering,
If I could do it over. . .I'd do the same darn thing!

There are countless National square dance organizations. Following are articles about some that have made an impact on Wisconsin's square dance environment.

CALLERLAB

Before square dancing became a specialized activity callers simply taught themselves how to call. They learned by trial and error. They traded calls among themselves and helped young callers to learn to call. Some of these callers were looked up to as leaders in their area, but in some areas this experienced leadership was missing and as new callers came into the field, they lacked the opportunity of the experienced guidance. These were the areas that often lost the square dance activity.

In 1961 *Sets in Order* inaugurated the Square Dance Hall of Fame as a means of honoring leaders who had left their mark on the world of square dancing. Over the following decade a number of outstanding individuals were added to the list. Anyone looking at these names would recognize them as representing the ultimate composite of square dance leadership at the time. Any single one of these men might not alone be able to capture the respect of all callers, but, with all Hall of Fame members working together, they presented a "body of knowledge" that a great percentage of callers could respect and follow. Their backgrounds and accomplishments formed an impressive foundation for square dance caller/leadership.

Invitations were mailed to fifteen members of the Square Dance Hall of Fame to attend a meeting in February 1971, as guests of the *Sets in Order* American Square Dance Society. Eleven of those invited were able to attend: Marshall Flippo, Ed Gilmore, Lee Helsel, Bruce Johnson, Arnie Kronenberger, Frank Lane, Joe Lewis, Bob Osgood, Bob Page, Dave Taylor, and Bob VanAntwerp. When the meeting, held at the Asilomar Conference Grounds in California, concluded, the group enthusiastically and unanimously signed an eight point charter and began planning for the future. That was the start of CALLERLAB (The International Association of Square Dance Callers).

CALLERLAB is an association of currently active square dance callers which has been established to assist the members both professionally and personally in all aspects of their involvement in the square dance activity. This association makes possible, thru communication, the coordinated application of the skill and the experience of both the square dance activity and the calling profession.

Membership, which is on a personal invitation basis, requires that potential members be actively engaged in calling on the average of at least once each week for a period of the three most recent years; that he or she be personally nominated for membership by a present member. In addition, all members subscribe to the CALLERLAB Code of Ethics.

What Does CALLERLAB DO?

CALLERLAB, an international organization of over 3,000 square dance callers, held its first convention in 1974. However, the roots of CALLERLAB go back to the mid-1960s. CALLERLAB people have been working in many ways to help square dancing since then. Following is a list of CALLERLAB accomplishments:

- More than 20 years ago, CALLERLAB members developed dance programs that have been accepted worldwide. These dance programs let you go anywhere in the world and dance.
- CALLERLAB members documented and negotiated an international agreement on the definition of all the calls we use. For the first time ever, calls were taught the same way in California as they were in New England—or old England, Germany, and everywhere else.
- CALLERLAB has printed and published thousands of pages of publications to help callers and dancers. These publications are used by dancers and callers everywhere, including the members of other square dance organizations.
- CALLERLAB members are featured in nearly all of the calling slots at the National Square Dance Convention and conduct the caller training sessions at these same conventions.
- CALLERLAB has established a Caller-Coach program to improve caller skills and thereby better serve dancers. CALLERLAB also provides a broad range of caller training sessions at its annual convention.
- When BMI & ASCAP threatened clubs in the U.S. with license fees for every dance, CALLERLAB and ROUNDALAB working together negotiated a new form of licensing so that dance leaders could take over this obligation from the clubs.

CALLERLAB—
The International Association of Square Dance Callers
829 3rd Ave SE. Suite 285.
Rochester, Minnesota 55904-7312

This history of CALLERLAB was partially compiled from an account created by Lee Helsel, Arnie Kronenberger, Bob Osgood, and Bob VanAntwerp, founding members of the organization. Additional information came from documents in the SDAW leadership manuals.

"OK men! Once again -- and this time with emphasis."

ROUNDALAB
—The International Association of Round Dance Teachers, Inc.

ROUNDALAB is a professional teachers organization open to all who are actively teaching round dancing, at any level, anywhere in the world. It was formed to promote, protect, and perpetuate the general round dance movement as a compliment to the overall square dance picture. It is the organization of choice for round dance teachers who wish to bring full professional competency, accreditation, standards, ethics, and recognition to the round dance instructorship field.

ROUNDALAB is an organization of all round dance teachers who are honestly dedicated to the preservation and enhancement of round dancing as a distinctive form of dance, similar to, but uniquely different from folk dancing and ballroom dancing.

ROUNDALAB is the only international organization whose membership is limited to those actively engaged in the teaching of round dancing. It is the only organization where all who teach round dancing on a regular basis can work together to improve the round dance teaching profession with no outside or irrelevant influences.

ROUNDALAB was organized under the sponsorship of LEGACY and has been recognized as the organization which speaks for the round dance teaching profession by CALLERLAB and many local and area square and/or round dance organizations. It is incorporated as a non-profit professional society.

The primary purpose is to make round dancing more enjoyable for the dancer, worldwide and at all levels.

⪼┄⟡┄○┄⟡┄⪻

LEGACY

LEGACY is defined as "a leadership and communication resource center." It is a non-profit international assembly of "trustees" representing all facets of square dancing, including dancers, callers, cuers, suppliers, publishers, and special interest groups.

The LEGACY idea was conceived in 1973 by three editors/publishers of nationally known magazines: Charlie Baldwin, *The New England Caller*; Stan Burdick, *American Square Dance*; Bob Osgood, *Square Dancing (Sets in Order)*. They envisioned a service-leadership organization and development of better communication among the many facets of the square dance activity.

Since its inception in 1973, LEGACY trustees have expressed concern over rough dancing, non-descriptive calls, lack of standardization of calls, too many new movements, teaching programs, competition, use of alcohol, styling, dress code, ethics, recruitment/retention of dancers, and social aspects of dancing.

LEGACY has been instrumental in encouraging the development of leadership training at the local and state level. It is composed of trustees and affiliates. Trustees meet every two years in varying locations to exchange ideas and formulate proposals and guidelines for the welfare of the overall square dance activity.

Trustees are individuals who have been dancing for at least five years or served at least three years as an accomplished leader. To become a trustee, the individual must be nominated by an existing trustee and attend a biennial convention. This convention is held in May in odd years, beginning on the Thursday following Mother's Day and continuing for three days. These trustees represent one or more of the component groups—dancers, callers, cuers, suppliers, publishers, record companies, foundations, special interest groups, and organizations of dancers, callers, round dance teachers/leaders, and conventions. Many of the trustees have been involved in the activity for over twenty years. All trustees pay their own expenses.

Affiliate memberships are available to individuals and organizations who would like to receive reports of LEGACY and other information, have the opportunity to express their ideas, and contribute to the purpose of LEGACY without being asked to serve on committees or attend meetings.

Among LEGACY'S achievements are a worldwide dancer survey for general guidance and information, and encouragement of leadership programs on the local and state level. The questionnaire surveys were designed to ask square dancers to express their feelings about certain aspects of square dancing and related activities. From the many comments and excellent return rate, it is obvious that the dancers want to be heard. The results are tabulated, put on computer and distributed to all publications and organizations. LEGACY plans to continue conducting this survey as deemed necessary.

LEGACY was the catalyst for the formation of the National Association of Square and Round Dance Suppliers (NASRDS) and the International Association of Round Dance Teachers, Inc. (ROUNDALAB).

The organization maintains a Hot Line to anyone in the activity who feels the need of communication within the square dance world.

LEGACY encourages the adoption of September as Square Dance Month. Dancers may choose the particular dates best suited for local programs and climate. A promotional kit with a theme, ideas, and suggestions is available through LEGACY at a nominal cost.

Working with the National Square Dance Convention Committee, the LEGACY Education Committee conducts dancer leadership seminars at National Conventions. Also encourages local leadership programs (Mini Legacies) and its trustees stand ready to assist in their development worldwide. Mini-Legacies bring local leaders together for learning and sharing, the end result of which is the enhancement of area square dancing.

➤─┼─◄►─◆─O─◆─◄►┼─◄

ECCO

ECCO is Wisconsin's mini-LEGACY. The acronym stands for Education, Communication, Club, Organization. It was formed in 1979 by Wisconsin LEGACY Trustees. The object of this group was to help perpetrate square dancing in the Wisconsin area by conducting mini-legacies. Like LEGACY, ECCO, through its seminars, attempts to provide square dance clubs, organizations, callers, and leaders with leadership training. These seminars are conducted approximately every eighteen months and rotate among the five areas of the state.

By continuing to act as a visionary organization, coordinating and promoting helpful programs, never controlling, but assisting as needed, LEGACY IS A VALUABLE RESOURCE CENTER upon which dancers in any facet of the activity may draw.

➤─┼─◄►─◆─O─◆─◄►┼─◄

History of the National Square Dance Campers' Association, Inc.
Compiled by Alex and Mona Vetter (first NSDCA historians)
Submitted by Dick and Marilyn Lenz of Little Chute

The National Square Dance Campers' Association—a growing organization. Square dancing or camping—Which came first? Square dancing and campers have enjoyed both activities for a good half century or longer. The nucleus of the National Square Dancers and Campers had its beginning in the late '50s when a group of callers and families of the Wolf River Area Callers' Association (WRACA) began a series of weekend meetings for callers. These camp outs were sort of "Caller Retreats" where callers would talk shop and discuss square dance techniques, local, state, and national trends. Camping fitted very well into this form of recreation as it provided an opportunity of closeness and comradeship through potluck suppers, campfires, and dancing.

Square dance clubs in some areas had been having weekend gatherings, as dancing in a campground was inexpensive and at times free, except for the use of campgrounds and facilities. Needless to say, word got around to some campers that a group of callers at their retreat didn't mind having visitors come to their workshops.

It seemed only natural that these groups of callers and dancers

Square dance campers gather at La Crosse Oktoberfest in 1974.

would foresee the great possibilities in merging into partnership. In 1958 it was decided to hold a combined camporee of callers and dancers at Shawano Lake, Wisconsin. This proved to be so successful that Shawano Lake was scheduled for camporees in 1959 and again in 1960. Attendance began to mushroom.

To further gain recognition, the minutes of the 1961 WRACA meeting approved a motion to organize a committee to study samples of pins.

The group consisted of Clarence and Enid Dorschner and Herb and Tilda Johnson. By the end of 1961 a badge designed by Jim and Mitzie Bero was approved. Within a short time, 68 badges had been ordered with some badges going to out-of-state dancers. 1964 was

the year when NSDCA was incorporated as a non-profit, non-stock organization, and the badge design was registered in Wisconsin. It is impossible to list all persons who played an important part in this beginning, but a few names stand out at this time. In addition to names listed in the previous paragraph, there were: Brad and Bernie Landry, Carlton and Marion Schneider, Lloyd and Carol Siewers, Lyle and Margaret Leatherman, Dick and Betty Vanderpool, Glen and Pat Nicklaus and Bert and Fern Hill.

Growth and interest in the organization became quite evident after the 1964 Camporee at Bear Lake, Manawa, Wisconsin. In March of 1965 a group of 17 families in New Jersey met and the Garden State Square Dance Campers came into existence. They applied for membership to NSDCA, were accepted and became Chapter 001 of NSDCA. This was followed quite rapidly by more chapters being formed in Wisconsin, Michigan, Illinois, Ohio, and Iowa. (Chapter 002, Pine Tree was the first Wisconsin chapter to form.) Chapters were forming so quickly that the charter members of NSDCA could do no better than become Pioneer Chapter 010, the tenth chapter to form.

It soon became apparent that area campgrounds no longer had the space nor the facilities to accommodate the increased attendance that had gone above the modest 15 to 20 squares. A committee began searching for locations that could host a larger group of callers, dancers, and family campers. An invitation by the Black Hawk Cross Trailers, Chapter 014 of Illinois was accepted and became the camporee spot at Pacatonica, Illinois. This was at the Winnebago County Fair Grounds with adequate buildings and halls to house the many activities in addition to Square Dancing. Pacatonica was our home for 1969 and 1970. Other areas offered services of county and state fairgrounds plus a few large recreation areas that could furnish guests with showers, water, electricity, etc. NSDCA went to places such as Monroe, Michigan; Spencer, Iowa; Bowling Green, Kentucky; Bloomsburg, Pennsylvania; Des Moines, Iowa; Elkhorn, Wisconsin; Elkhart, Indiana; Huron, South Dakota; York, Pennsylvania; etc, etc.

A whole new panorama of growth and changes was emerging within the organization from its early beginning, namely: 1. Camping equipment was changing from tent and tent trailers to self-contained travel trailers and motor homes. 2. Square dancing levels needed additional halls to meet many needs. (The 1980 Camporee in Elkhart, Indiana, used four large halls for Mainstream, Mainstream plus quarterly selections, Plus 1 and 2, Teen dancing, round dancing and family dancing including the tiny tots.) Incidentally the 1980 Camporee had a roster of 35 registered callers and 9 round dance leaders. 3. Teenage participation was growing. The 1980 NSDCA Camporee had a total of 300 young people who came along with their parents. Forty of the 61 chapters represented had at least one youth along.

Over the years the attendance has grown from a small gathering with a few callers in 1958 to a total of 432 families composed of 864 adults, and 300 youths of all ages for a total of 1,164. This was the final count at the KOA campground in Elkhart, Indiana, in 1980.

It is commendable that the callers and dancers of the original nucleus had the foresight to see the enormous potential in organizing NSDCA.

Sources of Information: Minutes of NSDCA Board of Directors Meetings, NSDCA Times *issues, personal contact with people actively engaged in the early formation of NSDCA, personal attendance at some of the early formation meetings.*

>⊷⊶○⊷⊶<

The Overseas Dancer Association

At the 1961 European Association of American Square Dance Clubs (EAASDC) round-up in West Germany, a suggestion was made that the dancers get together for a reunion after they returned to the United States and Canada. The friendships made while overseas were so important it was felt they should not be lost, but rather renewed and revitalized from time-to-time. As a result, the first Annual Reunion of Overseas Dancers was held in Amarillo, Texas, in August of 1963, with 44 dancers and 11 callers.

OSDA, as an association was born at the 1970 Florida reunion in Springer Isle. Its sole function is to provide an annual reunion. Its officers, except for the president, are permanent until voted out or until they resign. The General Chairman of the upcoming reunion is always the President. Permanent (unpaid) officers are treasurer, newsletter editor and membership chairman, historian/photographer, executive secretary and publicity chairman, and the executive board which consists of all past, present, and known future presidents and present permanent officers of OSDA.

To be eligible for membership a person must have learned to dance overseas, or have been, or be a member of an overseas club. Dancing overseas while on vacation or as a member of a tour group does not qualify. Overseas is defined as any place outside the United States and Canada, and any place within the United States and Canada currently or previously designated as a foreign tour area by either government.

A newsletter is published periodically to keep members informed of plans for reunions and to maintain contact among members. OSDA members reside in 39 of the 50 states; 4 of the 12 Canadian provinces; and 14 overseas countries.

The 1998 annual reunion of the OSDA will be held right here in Oshkosh, Wisconsin. The last time it was held in Wisconsin was ten years ago, in the Madison area. Nancy and John Merkt and

Gladys and Martin Bishop are Co-General Chairmen of the event.

Nancy Callaway Merkt of Madison remembers how she became eligible for membership in the association.

The year was 1962. My girlfriend convinced me to attend a square dance at the Truax Field Service Club, and to join the USO to participate in USO activities. At the Service Club I met Don Callaway who suggested I join him for lessons at the NCO Club. The Service Club had to start over every couple weeks because of new people attending. Don had been square dancing for five years. He knew if I attended the full set of lessons I would enjoy square dancing as much as he did. He was correct in that assumption. The lessons were taught by Milt Thorp, who was the caller for the USAF Contrails Squares club at Truax Field.

THE OVERSEAS DANCER ASSOCIATION

WELCOMES ALL AREA DANCERS
TO THEIR OPEN

REUNION TRAIL END DANCE

WEDNESDAY AUGUST 5, 1998 7:30 - 10:30 PM

FOR YOUR SQUARE DANCING PLEASURE . . . 8:00 PM

JOHN KALTENTHALER
POCONO PINES, PENNSYLVANIA
DENNIS LEATHERMAN
OSHKOSH WISCONSIN

FOR YOUR ROUND DANCING PLEASURE . . . 7:30 PM

LYNN SANDSTROM
LAKEWOOD, NEW JERSEY

DONATION: $6.00/COUPLE

Oshkosh Hilton & Convention Center
One North Main Street
Oshkosh, Wisconsin
920-232-3043

INFORMATION
JOHN & NANCY MERKT
1217 JUNIPER AVE
MADISON WI 53714
608-244-7218

Overseas Dancer Association Annual Reunion Poster – 1998.

Milt will always hold a special place in my heart because he brought Don and me together, through dancing, to enjoy many years of fun. He also gave me the opportunity to meet many, many friends over the past 35 years. Don and I were married in 1964 and in 1965 we were transferred to Germany with the military.

While in Europe we joined a club in Germany and danced in many locations. We were in Germany from 1965-1968 and had an opportunity to dance in Berlin with the Dancing Bears club. The Berlin Wall was still up. The tour of East Germany was something I will never forget. I don't think we American's really appreciated what we had in this country until we came out of Checkpoint Charlie and realized just how special our freedom was. We received a badge for dancing behind the Iron Curtain and were given another badge for dancing on a wine barrel in a castle at a summer jamboree dance in Wiesbaden, Germany.

From Germany we were transferred to Ft. Meade, Maryland. In 1968 we joined the Boots 'n Bows square dance club at Ft. Meade. Jocko Manning was the club caller and also the general chairman for the Lucky Seventh 1969 OSDA Reunion in Annapolis, Maryland. Jocko asked Don and me to join the OSDA and help him with the reunion, which we gladly did. It was a wonderful experience with dancers from all over the world.

In 1987 OSDA celebrated its 25th anniversary, and we went to Denver, Colorado, to participate. 1988 was a working year for our family. Susan, Karen, Christine, Don, and I were the General Chairpersons for this reunion. It was a lot of work but so satisfying to show our friends from all over the world our great state of Wisconsin, and especially the Madison area. Friday is always our tour day, and we had two busloads going to New Glarus for a tour of the Swiss Miss factory and a lunch at the New Glarus Hotel. Swiss Miss was left very green by all the material purchased for square dance clothes.

In January 1992, Don passed away after ten months in a nursing home. He sure enjoyed square dancing all over the USA and Europe. Later in 1992 I attended the reunion in Portland, Oregon. There I met another wonderful person and on November 21, 1992, John Merkt and I were married in the assembly chambers of our state capitol. Four-hundred people were present for our ceremony and reception. John was quickly accepted by my home club, the Diamond Squares, and when we attended the 1993 reunion in Huntsville, Alabama, the OSDA group made him feel welcome. 1994 took us to San Antonio, Texas, and in 1995 to Keene, New Hampshire. Last year (1997) we attended the reunion in Ogden, Utah.

That brings us to 1998. This is going to be a busy year. Gladys and Martin Bishop and John and I, are Co-General Chairmen for the reunion. For the second time in ten years it will be held in our state. Former Assembly Speaker David Prosser suggested we bring the group back for Wisconsin's sesquicentennial year. We bid for it and were successful. So four and one-half years after submitting our bid we look forward to welcoming all our friends to the Oshkosh Hilton in Oshkosh, Wisconsin.

I think what I like most about square dancing is the opportunity I had to meet new people from all over the world through the OSDA reunions. After twenty-two OSDA reunions and many happy years of dancing with Diamond Squares, Verona Squares, Boots and Slippers, Ocean Waves, Boots 'n Bows, Cross Trails Jr., and USAF Contrails Squares clubs, I can only hope the young dancers of today will enjoy the square dance activity as much as I have.

Gladys Bishop of Pell Lake, also has fond memories of the overseas dancers:

In 1965 Gladys Steil left her home in Grosse Pointe, Michigan, to become a civilian teacher for the Department of Defense Overseas Dependents Schools at Clark Air Force Base, Philippines. The opportunity to square dance with the Pampanga Promenaders provided a wonderful leisure-time activity. As an elementary student Gladys had learned to square and round dance with classmates at the home of Mrs. Paul Franseth. That group continued to meet from fifth grade through twelfth grade with caller Decco Deck taking over during the high school years.

From 1966 through 1971 Gladys served as a first grade teacher at Lindsey Air Station in Wiesbaden, Germany. She also held membership in the Kuntry Kuzins Square Dance Club, the Gay Squares Square Dance Club, the Mainz Masters Square Dance Club, and the Fancy Pants Round Dance Club. She met Steve Voltz at the dances. They became engaged in Germany, and were married in Detroit, Michigan. They lived in Silver Lake, Wisconsin, and became members of the Paddock Lake Squares, and the Happy Rounders Round Dance Club. Gladys continued to square and round dance following their divorce.

Dancing overseas in the Philippines and Germany as a member of an overseas club enabled Gladys to qualify for membership in the OSDA.

Bob and Liz Wilson had been active in square dancing in Spain, so they also qualified for membership in the organization.

In 1980 Gladys Voltz attended the 18th annual reunion of Overseas Dancers in Wagoner, Oklahoma, with square dance caller, Bob Wilson, his taw, Liz, and Liz' s mother, Edith Russell. They had asked Gladys to help with registrations for the 19th OSDA Reunion in Zion Park, Illinois. The dancing was a lot of fun with square dance callers and cuers from all over the world, but most of all it was the genuine caring of the people that sparked friendships that have continued to this day.

It was in Zion, Illinois, where Gladys first met Don and Nancy Callaway, and their daughters Sue, Karen, and Chrissy. In 1983 Gladys married Martin Bishop, whom she met at Limber Timbers Square Dances in Elkhorn, Wisconsin. Later they would team up to help host two OSDA Reunions in Wisconsin. The Callaways made a bid for the 1988 reunion to be in Madison, at which time the square dancers were delighted to visit the Swiss Miss embroidery fabric factory. By the next reunion evidence of Swiss Miss fabrics could be seen whirling around the dance floor. After Don Callaway died, Nancy married John Merkt, together they made a bid to have the 36th OSDA Reunion in Madison, but later Oshkosh was chosen as the site. John and Nancy Merkt, and Martin and Gladys Bishop were happy to co-host the 1998 reunion in Wisconsin, during the state's sesquicentennial celebration, the 150th anniversary of Wisconsin's statehood.

The official motto of the OSDA "Friendship Is Square Dancing's Greatest Reward" has certainly proven true.

The Lloyd Shaw Foundation

The Lloyd Shaw Foundation is incorporated as a non-profit organization and is governed by a board of directors elected by the general membership. The men and women who serve as directors represent a great range of talents and include a number of internationally known dance leaders.

Membership in the Lloyd Shaw Foundation is open to anyone who wishes to join. Members come from all parts of the United States and from many other countries. Many are dance leaders, many are active dancers, but many are also those who do not dance (or no longer dance). All of them, whether dancers or non-dancers, believe in the value of preserving and disseminating our great American dance heritage.

Members receive a subscription to *The American Dance Circle*, the Foundation's quarterly magazine, which is filled with articles about dance and dance history, discounts on Foundation books and recordings, and reduced rates to attend Foundation events. The Foundation has the following membership categories: ...individual ($20) ...couple ($30) ...supporting ($35) ...sustaining ($50) ...patron ($100) ...life ($1000).

The foundation is eager to involve a wide range of dancers in its activities and is particularly interested in helping promising young people develop dance leadership skills. Those who cannot meet the full costs of a Lloyd Shaw Foundation Workshop, Dance Leadership Seminar or Dance Week are invited to apply for scholarship aid.

The Lloyd Shaw Foundation welcomes your support and your questions. To become a member or to obtain additional information, please contact:

Enid Cocke, President
Lloyd Shaw Foundation
2924 Hickory Court
Manhattan, KS 66503
(913)539-6306
ecocke@ksu.edu

CHAPTER 9

Take a Little Peek
Memories, Reminiscence, and Poetry

First couple out to the couple on the right
Take a little peek.
Back to the center and swing your sweet.
Out to the side and peek once more.
Back to the center and swing all four.
Take your partner on to the next,
Take a little peek.
Back to the center and swing your sweet.
Out to the side and swing once more.
Back to the center and swing all four.

Looking Back

The following rules applied to square dancing over 100 years ago. Read them and discover how much "progress" we have made since then.

Admittance 50 cents, refreshments included.

The music is to consist of a fiddle, a pipe or tabor, a hurdy-gurdy. No chorus is to be sung until the dance is over.

No lady to dance in black stockings, nor have her elbows bare.

Every lady to come with a handkerchief with name marked.

To prevent spitting, no gentleman will chew tobacco or smoke.

No whispering allowed. If anyone should be found to make insidious remarks about anyone's dancing, he or she will be put out of the room.

No gentleman will appear with a cravat (tie) that has been worn more than a week or a fortnight.

Long beards are forbidden, as they would be very disagreeable if a gentleman should happen to put his cheek alongside a lady's.

Those ladies who have not white stockings and black morocco shoes will not be admitted under any pretense whatever. Two old ladies to examine all who enter.

No gentleman shall squeeze his partner's hand nor look earnestly upon her; and furthermore he must not pick up her handkerchief, provided it were to fall. The first denotes he loves her, the second he wishes to kiss her and the last that she make a sign for both.

For distinction sake, the master of ceremonies is to wear a red coat, buff small clothes, green shoes and furtout. (Anyone know what a furtout might be?)

Reprinted from The New England Square Dance Caller
—June 1985

Her Grandpa Was a Caller!

Christine Schmidt of West Bend passed on this interesting tidbit. It seems that in the early 1900s, her grandfather, Henry Burgraff, and his three brothers, Ed, John, and Ervin, manufactured violins out of cigar boxes. The four boys, then in their teens, learned to play and went on the road with their novel instruments. They soon became well-known, in and around their hometown in North Dakota, for their unique talent. Henry called for local square dances, weddings, and other occasions, with his three brothers as backup.

Ed Burgraff later moved to Duluth where he joined the Duluth Symphony Orchestra and played with the group most of his adult life.

Henry moved to Superior, Wisconsin, and took a job as a round-house foreman for the railroad. But he didn't forget his square dance background. He continued to call for dances in the Superior area for many years. Henry passed away in 1986.

>—+—‹›—•—O—‹›—+—‹

A Square Move
by Norma DeBoer

Moving to Oshkosh was something I did not care to do. Compared to Madison, where there was always something going on, Oshkosh seemed sort of square. There was nothing I could do about the necessity to move, so I decided to make the best of it.

How I missed the friends we had left in the Madison area. The monthly potluck card parties and church activities had produced a number of acquaintances, who later became good friends. In Oshkosh I knew not one person, but here was where we would now live.

My husband had been transferred from the Madison office to Oshkosh. We had found an older house to buy which needed a lot of redecorating. Whole-heartedly I delved into that project. Still I continued to miss our friends in Madison.

On returning home from work one day my husband stated, "A man I work with is a square dance caller and has invited us to come and take lessons."

Norma and Stan DeBoer

"Square dancing? Who would ever want to square dance?" I answered. However, it would be a change from housework, so might as well try it.

Our first lesson was at Shoreview Lanes in September and we joined the 16 other couples who were also there to learn square dancing. What fun! Everyone was in a jolly mood. We do-si-doed, swung our partners, promenaded, all to the beat and rhythm of the music. We listened to Herb, our caller, and attempted to remember all he was teaching us. If we missed a call, no one cared. We laughed and went on to the next call. Gone were the concerns and worries of the day. Here was relaxation, lots of exercise, and fun with a group of folks who were having as good a time as we were.

Needless to say, we kept on with our lessons and graduated to join the Timber Toppers Square Dance Club the following April.

Seven years later as we were deciding to retire, my husband

asked, "Where would you like to live during our retirement? Madison, Tomah, Black River Falls, (places we had previously lived) or Oshkosh?"

"Oshkosh!" No second thoughts there. The move to Oshkosh and learning to square dance had changed the tone of our lives. From sedentary card playing to fun-filled evenings of dancing with a host of wonderful friends.

Yes, Oshkosh was square. But squares filled with fun and friendship.

In 1970 Stanley and Norma DeBoer moved from the Madison area to Oshkosh. Stanley worked for the Department of Natural Resources and became acquainted with Herb Johnson who also worked for the DNR. Herb, and his wife, Tilda, persuaded the DeBoers to try square dancing. As they were total strangers in the area they decided this might be a good way to make friends and also have a fun time dancing. They thoroughly enjoyed the classes and graduated in 1971 with a host of new friends.

The DeBoers went on to become club president for the Timber Toppers for two terms, secretary for two terms, Wolf River Association delegates for two terms. Round dancing was accepted as another challenge. In 1979 they served as Directors of Chaperones for the national convention in Milwaukee and were Assistant General Chairmen of Facilities for the 21st Wisconsin Square and Round Dance Convention in 1980. In 1985 they were named General Chairpersons for the 26th Wisconsin Square and Round Dance Convention, held in Oshkosh.

Stanley and Norma were ardent campers all their lives and this led to an active membership in the National Square Dance Campers' Association where they served a four year term as vice president on the National Board of Directors.

>–I–◆>–O–◆–I–≺

Reminiscence of a Square Dance Brat
by Ann Ratajczyk Buck

My father and mother were Paul and Mary Ratajczyk. My dad was a caller in the Milwaukee area when he was felled by a double aneurysm in 1948. Mom helped teach the dances and acted as hostess.

Growing up during that era was the best childhood any child could hope for. For three years my dad had no other job but square dance calling. I was able to be with my parents some of the time when they were teaching, calling, or demonstrating. In the '40s the square dancers not only got together to dance, but there were many family get-togethers, picnics, skating parties, and tobogganing parties. What fun we kids all had! I still treasure Polish Christmas egg

ornaments that my mother purchased at the Holiday Folk Fair in the '40s, when they were there to dance.

On one occasion in August of 1952, my parents had decided to take a trip to Door County. For some reason we left early in the morning after my dad had called at the Log Cabin the night before. His equipment was still in the car. When we got over to Washington Island my mother, Mary, and the hotel owner, Mrs. Stelter, struck up a conversation because of their mutual interest in rosemaling. That led to talk of square dancing and the fact that Paul was a caller and his equipment was in the trunk. Mrs. Stelter got very excited and said, "Why don't we have a square dance tomorrow night." She got on the party line and the news of the square dance spread. A square dance was held the next night at a community center which looked more like an abandoned store or school.

Several fishermen were staying at the hotel. Their wives had been left at home. The fishermen were finagled into coming to the square dance. Because of the lack of single women, my mother and I were kept busy dancing all night with the fishermen. Some of them even danced with each other.

These are only a few of the memories I cherish from my childhood, as the daughter of an early square dance caller. There are many more, from watching my mother spend a whole day starching and ironing the skirt of her pioneer-style square dance dress, which was the fashion then, to my lifelong interest in Western history. That was mainly due to "Pappy" Shaw. After a week of calling and dancing lessons with "Pappy" in Colorado Springs, there would be a family picnic at Palmer Park on the bluffs east of the city. After dinner, "Pappy" perched himself on the furthest outcropping and

Ann Buck (left front) poses with mannequins (some are real) at the 1995 Showcase of Ideas. They are modeling outfits from her mother's collection of square dance costumes.

with the sun setting over Pike's Peak, would tell the history of Colorado and that area in particular. Those times were the best any child could hope for.

>─┤◆>─○─<◆├─<

Fun in the Fifties
by Leona Klemp

In 1950 my husband Oscar, and I learned to square dance at Waubeka Fire Hall. Les Riebau was the caller. Later we were square dance "angels" at Turner Hall in Fillmore with caller Byron Held and his wife. We helped the new dancers do the right steps. We also square danced at the Legion Hall in Fredonia for a short time, and then at Hiltgen Hall in Fredonia. We danced at our first big Jamboree in Jackson, Wisconsin, and once danced at the West Bend High School. We danced at Lake Ellen for quite awhile—Byron Held was the caller there too. We danced in Cascade for a long time; a few times in an old hall and then at St. Mary's Church Hall. We often went to Plymouth with another couple where we danced at Lyson Hall. It was a nice place—the hall was upstairs

Square dancers pose for a picture at Waubeka Fireman's Hall, circa 1950—Leona Klemp is furthest left—second row from front. Also pictured are the Stagemans, Grules, Eggerts, Fromans, Arndts, Tancks, Blocks, Nosters, Rollingers, Retzers, Eisentraurts, Paulus', Neuens, Wagners, Muelbergs, Eichens, Stadlers, Dobberphuls, Huira', Voeks', Ribaus, Miss Xenia Meyer, Mrs. Hattie Schulz, Barney Solms and "Chessie".

Taken at a dance at the Mermac Hotel — West Bend, Wisconsin — Mr. and Mrs. Retzer, Mr. and Mrs. Leroy Arndt, Mr. and Mrs. Froman, Mr. and Mrs. Miller, Mr. and Mrs. Merlin Degnitz, Mr. and Mrs. Grule, Mr. and Mrs. Oscar Klemp, Mr. and Mrs. Saueressig, Mr. and Mrs. Witte. (Leona Klemp is second row, center.)

Dancing at Waubeka Fireman's Hall, circa 1950 — Pictured are Mr. and Mrs. Jack Paulus, Mr. and Mrs. Andy Eggert, Mr. and Mrs. Emil Neuens, Mr. and Mrs. Oscar Klemp (farthest right).

over a tavern. The caller was from Sheboygan and he always drew a big crowd. We went square dancing three to four times a week.

I remember going to Sheboygan for a two-day 50th wedding anniversary for a caller from there. Square dancers came from all over. On Saturday we were given a big dinner and on Sunday we went to a different hall, and again were treated to a big meal.

Another time we went to the Howard Grove High School for a big square dance. It was on a Sunday afternoon and many square dancers attended.

I made all my own square dance dresses, long ones with big bottoms. We danced until the mid-'60s when circumstances forced us to stop.

Leona now lives with her daughter and son-in-law (George and Evie Tetzlaff) in Grafton. The Octagon barn, owned by the Tetzlaff family and the scene of many a square dance shindig, is right across the road. Leona still enjoys cooking and helping around the house. Although she hasn't danced in many years, and doesn't recall all the details, she will always remember the fun.

><del>+++++++O+++++</del><

How I Became Involved In Square Dancing
by Elizabeth (Betsy) Isenberg

While a 7th grade student at Brown Street School (20th and Brown Streets) in Milwaukee, we had a teacher by the name of Herman Fink. Mr. Fink had been hospitalized during and following World War II, with injuries. Some nurses at the hospital decided that the best therapy would be square dancing, since they knew it "exercised" mind, body, and soul. When he returned to teaching, he thought it would be good to teach his grade schoolers the fine art of square dancing. I was lucky to be a part of the first grade school class in Milwaukee to put on exhibitions for T.V.

"The Square Dance Jamboree" and "Tuesday Night Square Dance," as well as for the Milwaukee area Parent-Teacher Association meetings. Needless to say, we had a great time. (We also had to make our own dresses, or blouses and skirts. The boys could buy their shirts.) I have enjoyed square dancing at various times since, but it wasn't until I was widowed, that I really went to lessons again at Swingin' Singles with Dwayne Olson; then I joined Lariat and Lace with Lew Snyder. When Ted and I had been married a couple years, I mentioned square dancing, and he "swung" right in. We both took lessons with Eric Tangman in Swingin' Single classes, graduated and then joined Square Benders. We love the friends we have made, the exercise we get, and all the fun we have square dancing!

><del>+++++++O+++++</del><

"ALL JOIN HANDS"

CERTIFICATE OF PROFICIENCY

-IN-

SQUARE DANCE

THE ART OF ... CALLING

IS

AWARDED TO

Ida Tjepkema

For supreme effort in completing the
prescribed course of study in square dance
leadership - this day of *Feb 12* in the
year of *1951*.

DeVerne Mathison
DeVerne Mathison, Sq. D.
Prof. of Square Dance

Square dancing was part of the curriculum at Wood County Normal School when Ida Tjepkema earned her square dance teaching certificate in 1951. Ida called for private home parties, for the PTA and Port Edwards' scout group as well as the school Phy. Ed. class.

The Floral Organdy Dress Speaks
(A Tribute To My Dance-Loving Parents)
by Judy Berg Hogan, February 1998

I am so old that my memory grows dim, but I'll try to tell the dance story of the Bergs and Hogans. Lorraine and Frank Berg were raised in the Milwaukee ballrooms of the '20s and '30s, where dancing with friends from DeMolay and other young people's groups was among their favorite social activity. Moving from the city to the country community of Menomonee Falls, they took a little class in square dancing and began a lifelong hobby that only stopped when Frank had a major stroke in the late '80s. They danced with many of Wisconsin's early callers: Bert Reitz, Dale Wagner, Johnny Toth, Howie Reoch, Art Weisensel, Bill Kersey; loving the dancing, the friendships, and the wonderful fun they all had.

Lorraine must have purchased me for a special square dance party in the late '40s or early '50s. Finances were always tight, so I must have been a party dress greatly on sale. She added a bit of black rickrack trim to add a square dance flavor.

My next memory is that of being revived and worn by Judy, Lorraine's 7th grade daughter, for her very first school dance. There were no physical education specialists in the Menomonee Falls school system in the mid-'50s, but Judy's 7th grade teacher loved to dance and throughout the school year she taught polkas, schottisches, and other dances to her students. It was an evening of magic. Judy returned home from her flute lesson in Milwaukee and I was waiting for her. Her mom curled her hair and swept it into an up-do. She was even allowed to wear a bit of lipstick. She put me on and together we looked like a southern belle ready for the ball. Judy looked in the mirror and hoped it would be an unforgettable evening and so it was! Never having been to a real dance party she was amazed to be invited to dance every dance. She wondered in her most secret thoughts what the future might hold.

I must have been put away for a very long time. Judy grew up. Her parents continued to square dance and were instrumental in the formation of the Falls Promenaders Square Dance Club. They had many wonderful dance friends. Dancing continued to be their major social activity and their dance friends became family friends. They all enjoyed family picnics and parties as well as get-togethers at each others homes after the dances. Those were the days! Dance until 10 or 11; return to someones house for incredibly wonderful sweet desserts in front of a cozy fire; play cards until 2 or 3 a.m.

Judy and her sister Sherry had learned a bit of square and circle dances in the Girl Scouts (6th-8th grade), but it was not until the late '50s between Judy's junior and senior years of high school that they took a 10-week square dance course at the Mitchell Park open-air pavilion with Milwaukee teens, that they learned to square dance in earnest. Their teacher, Art Steckmesser was also the caller for the Shirts and Flirts a teen exhibition group whose show piece was a double square grand square done to 'The Alabama Jubilee'. Judy's dance life began to really take off. She and her sister danced with their parents; mom shared dad with anyone else who was available. The whole family attended the 2nd Wisconsin State Square Dance Convention held in Whitewater. Judy, Sherry, and some of their teen friends decided to try the hot hash hall where Scott Lamster's dad was calling. Squares formed all around them, and, taking the needle off the record he proclaimed, "If someone doesn't dance with these kids, I'm not going to call!" So people joined them and they had a great time. Back home on Wednesday nights they danced on the asphalt parking lot of the rather new Mayfair shopping center, wearing out several pairs of ballet slippers before switching to sneakers. There was no dating, just lots of dancing. Bob Vircks was Judy's frequent partner and their dance friendship continued through part of her freshman college year. They corresponded (he was at MIT and she was at Oshkosh State College) until Christmas. She expected to meet him at a Christmas dance she and her parents attended at Calhoun Hall with Dale Wagner calling but he did not come. Life goes on….

She discovered that her college math professor, Mr. Fine and his wife were square dancers and got them to take her with them to some Timber Toppers dances. Wheel and Deal and other card deck movements such as Shuffle the Deck and Acey Deucy were all the rage. Getting to the dance was tricky as professors did not fraternize with students, so Mr. Fine would wait in his car and his wife would call for Judy at Webster Hall (her dorm).

Judy dreamed of going to Colorado in the summer between her junior and senior years to work at Peaceful Valley, a ranch where Dale Wagner spent his summers calling, but she and her parents could not afford to send her there. Happily, her college roommate, Gloria Desch was from Rhinelander where Judy, her family, and their square dance friends had spent a couple of wonderful vacations and they recalled visiting Fease's Resort where square dances were held on Saturday nights. Riding a train home with Gloria during semester break she met the Feases and got hired as a waitress for the next summer. It was great: hard work, sun and water, entertainment for the guests, and best of all twice a week square dancing. One night for the guests of the resort, and the other night for the weekly dances for area square dancers. The following summer, Judy again worked for the Feases and her boyfriend, Tom Hogan, spent the summer working at the Northernaire as the golf pro, visiting Judy whenever he could, often on Saturday nights. He soon tired of watching her flipping her skirts out on the dance floor, and so one night they threw him into a square. With a little extra help from Bob Holup, caller for the guest night square dances and the patience of local dancers on Saturday nights when Leroy Hitzke was calling, he learned to dance without actually taking any lessons. He remembers Swing Thru as the most difficult call to learn.

Judy returned to school for an extra year and did her practice teaching in Green Bay while Tom taught in Oconto. Meeting on Wednesday nights to dance at the Whirl-A-Ways helped ease the culture shock she experienced going from the university setting to the public schools. They married in 1965, dancing near Atlantic City, New Jersey, while going to school and honeymooning that summer. The newlyweds were glad to feel so welcomed in a strange place.

Settling in Menominee, Michigan, square dancing was, as it still is, their major couple activity. They danced with some of the same dancers and callers as they had in Green Bay; Brad Landry and his twin sons-in-law, Vern and Jim Bero. They even danced their first contra dance with the legendary Ed Gilmore. Those were some crazy times, mostly good. Both teaching full time, sometimes Judy had quite a struggle to drag Tom out to dance after an exhausting week at school. There were hunting stew dances where some of the hunters spent the day cooking (a sip of booze for the cook and one for the pot). Those men did not dance too well that night. New Year's Eve dancing in that group was not so great because of excessive drinking. It is probably good for the activity that people seldom put drinking and square dancing together nowadays.

When Tom and Judy moved to Rhinelander in '69, local square dancers welcomed them. Ann and Don Ross became lifelong dance friends and encouraged them in all of their dance pursuits. When their first child arrived they stopped dancing for three years and were pleasantly surprised to find that review lessons were not even needed, though some new movements had come on the scene such as Flutter Wheel. Caller Art Gorski and his wife Fran had moved to town from Chicago and they were a major influence in the expansion for northwoods square dancing, changing Rhinelanders club name to Hodag Twirlers and forming the Lakeland Promenaders (Minocqua, Woodruff) and the Eagle Chain Squares (Eagle River).

By the '70s northern square dancing was starting to experience major competition from snowmobiling as well as other factors: more women in the workplace, expanded sports activities, television, etc.

Tom and Judy became active club members. Judy's parents continued to square and round dance. Sometimes they got together to dance. In the summer of 1981 Judy and her parents came in from a day trip and found Tom sitting on the living room floor playing square dance records on an ancient calliphone sound system he had just purchased from the widow of retired caller, Howard Thrap. Ostensibly the set had been purchased because Judy was trying to teach the girl scouts (shades of her own youth) a little square dancing. Lorraine looked at Judy and said, "Someday he is going to be a caller."

In 1983 Judy applied for and received a scholarship to attend the Minnesota Callers' School with Warren Berquam. The whole family, Tom, Judy, Heather (13 years old), and Steve (10 years old), went. Steve learned to call "The Devil Went Down to Georgia" (singing call) for the occasion even though he did not even know how to square dance! Heather just put up with it all. Mom learning to be a caller was definitely not cool. Tom learned as much as or more than Judy and began to do rhythm studies and choreographic research. They both caught the dance leadership bug, attended the Wisconsin Caller's Workspree in 1984 and began running down the path to becoming callers, teachers, and choreographers. Tom pursued mainstream and plus, while Judy discovered a career path in one-night stands and line dance (the old style non-country western).

For Judy the promotion of the love of dance in churches, schools, camps, resorts; anywhere she could drag people off chairs and get them dancing was a challenge she accepted with great joy. She brought a background of not only square dancing but also training in ballroom, tap, ballet, and Middle Eastern dance, to enhance her repertoire of movement, and she gladly spent many hours doing the research and practice necessary to make her skills saleable. She has traveled hundreds of miles all over the northwoods sharing that knowledge.

Choreography became Tom's focus. He did his research late at night often after doing homework for his math teaching day job. For him the scientific study style was like dessert after a tough day with the Jr. High students.

They tried to get a casual square dance group going, calling it The Rainbow Squares, and though a few people became interested and later took mainstream lessons, it never had adequate community support and lasted under a year. When Art Gorski retired from calling in the late '80s Tom accepted the opportunity to call for the

Hodag Twirlers parade float.

Eagle Chain Squares, which by then was a tiny group that could only dance in the summer when enough tourists increased the local dance population. Soon after that Gordy Berna stepped aside as Hodag Twirlers caller so Tom could call more often. He's been the club's caller/teacher ever since. As he has grown in skill he has increased his service to the Wisconsin square dance community through leadership at state conventions, and local and state caller associations.

In the early '90s Judy added round dance cuing and teaching to her repertoire due to a local need in that area. Returning to part-time math teaching, she stopped teaching line dance.

But what happened to me all these years? I was pretty much ignored and forgotten. Lorraine made many beautiful square dance outfits replacing me. Judy was also making her square dance outfits often stitching the hems as she ran out the door to a dance!

Suddenly while contemplating the occasion of their 25th wedding anniversary Judy remembered me! They decided to hire Bob Wild and Bob Paul (caller-cuer) to celebrate with their friends. She revived me once again for this very special occasion. I was thrilled to be part of it all, to again relive the splendor of the dance.

After the dance, I was lovingly folded and packed into a special box labeled for square dance memories.

Judy and Tom are dancing and calling still. Having learned that danger lurks when one turns a hobby into a profession, Judy has trimmed her calling schedule severely and now seeks to dance more than she calls, trying to maintain a delicate balance while continuing to share her knowledge and skills wherever possible. Tom is doing a bit more guest calling statewide, and is looking forward to teaching more classes when he retires from public school math teaching this spring.

From the '40s when Judy and her sister watched the long hoop-skirted dancers swirl around gym floors while perched on the highest bleachers, to the sophisticated modern western styles of the '90s, square dancing has been and continues to be a great addition to life.

As for me, I lie quietly in wait for another magical day when a historian or perhaps even a grandchild will again take me out and we will dance!

>─┤◆>─○─<◆├─<

Square Dancing Keeps Me Young!
by Phil Koch

Phil Koch is a recycled square dancer. The first time around he and his wife Marguerite square danced with the likes of Mel Schoeckert, Doc Newland, Bob Dawson, and Dale Wagner. They were active square dancers for about 15 years, from 1949 to 1965.

At that time Mel Schoeckert was teaching square dancing at Wauwatosa East High School, Doc Newland was holding dances in his basement, Bob Dawsons' dances were at the Moose Club on Jackson Street, and Dale Wagner held court at Calhoun Hall. "There were no square dance clubs when we first started dancing ...the callers did everything," Phil said.

Phil and Marguerite also learned to round dance. "Rounds weren't being cued then—the dancers memorized all the choreography for songs like 'Salty Dog Rag' and 'Old Monterrey'. When we heard the music we knew the steps," said Phil. "Dale Wagner was a real good caller—he was fast; he called a lot of arches and ladies duck under."

Phil worked at the same place throughout his work career but for different companies. He started out with Reiss Coal in Sheboygan. They were bought out by North American Coal Corporation, later sold to Great Lakes Coal and Dock Company, and sold again to Industrial Fuel Company. Phil retired from Great Lakes Coal and Dock Company at age 62, but worked another eight years as a sales manager for Industrial Fuel, retiring from there at age 70.

Phil Koch is Baby New Year—Swingin' Singles party 1995.

Phil did his best to pass on his passion for square dancing to his son Phillip. Phillip and his wife Donna square danced for about two years but family commitments caused them to move on to other activities.

Marguerite passed away in 1990, and in 1991 at the urging of friends from Dousman Derby Dancers, Phil joined Jim Noonan's beginners class graduating for the second time in 1992. "Jim is a good caller—very thorough," said Phil.

After graduation he continued going to Jim's

workshops and also joined the Swinging Stars. Jimmie Burss, the Swinging Stars caller, had helped out at the class. When other class members joined the club Phil followed the crowd. From 1993 to 1994 he was president of Swinging Stars. He joined Swingin' Singles in 1994 and served as special events chairman for two years, and as lesson coordinator for the 1996 and 1997 classes. He plays Marryin' Sam at the annual Sadie Hawkins Day dance, and Baby New Year at the New Year's Eve dances.

Since he graduated from square dance lessons in 1992, Phil has never missed a National Singles Convention or a Wisconsin State Convention. He also attended National Square Dance Conventions in St. Louis and San Antonio. Phil says he loves to dance, and has made a million friends through his participation in square dancing.

In between his square dance activities Phil keeps active with the Masons, the Scottish Rite Society, and the Shriners. He has been a member of the YMCA for 52 years, and he golfs and plays racquet ball. In September of 1997 he won the gold medal for racquet ball in the Wisconsin Senior Olympics. He said he won in 1996 also, but it was by default; there was no one in his age category to compete with. Phil is 87 years old.

An Unusual Square Dance Program
by Ann Krueger

Wisconsin and Michigan square dancers have been holding an annual interstate hoedown on the docking areas of the Lake Michigan car ferry *S.S. Badger* since 1994. They board the ship for the trip across the lake on alternate years.

As the car ferry makes the scheduled four-hour run to the dock on the opposite shore, the dancers square up on the decks. They dance to the rhythm of the recorded square dance music and the melodious voices of the callers. When they reach the shore, a large crowd of square dancers from throughout the state are dancing dockside and waiting for them to start more squares.

The unusual dance program started when Michigan caller Dick Duckham brought more than 200 square dancers and callers to the Manitowoc dock, where the Wisconsin dancers were waiting.

The next year, Wisconsin callers Howie Fochs and Phil Doucette, with their wives Rosie and Joan, returned the visit. They took almost 250 Wisconsin dancers and callers, ranging in age from the late twenties to the early eighties, to the Ludington dock. There they were met by fellow square dancers from throughout Michigan.

In 1998, it will be the Michigan dancers' turn to board the *S.S.Badger*, in square dance attire, and dance their way across the lake to the chant of the callers.

Dancers from both states are enthusiastic about the annual hoedowns, and the eighty-year-old dancers hope their legs will hold out for a few more years of dockside dancing.

Our Hobby
by Norma Mader

One September evening the phone rang. It was a call from a friend asking a favor. He and his wife were square dancers and the new class needed one more couple. "Would you come to our get-acquainted dance to see if you would like it?" We said, "we'll come this once but we're not fond of that kind of dancing."

The next evening we danced, learned a few calls, met lots of fun people and had a great time. We never dreamed how our lives would change. We liked it.

There were 12 couples in our class and always many experienced dancers to help us. The class met Tuesday nights for eight months. Then at long last graduation. We were square dancers belonging to the Timber Toppers club in Oshkosh.

Eventually we decided to get into round dancing. After all, most of our friends did. This is actually ballroom dancing except we form a circle and the steps are "cued". We belong to the Valley Carousels Club. Next we decided to get into Plus, more advanced and difficult calls than our mainstream club offered. We belong to "Inter-Level Squares" club. We love all three.

We have made so many good friends throughout the years, friendships that have lasted more than 22 years. We have potluck dinners, golf outings, and always card games when we get together.

Our square dance instructors were Herb and Tilda Johnson. They were so patient as we learned, with Tilda always ready to step in to help. These people changed the lives of hundreds of people throughout the years. I remember the party for them when they retired. The room was crowded with square and round dancers. What a thrill that must have been to look out over that crowd and know how many lives they had made happier.

Then came the sad news that both Herb and Tilda were ill. It wasn't too many months later that Herb died. I wrote to Tilda after his death and told her how grateful we all were to have had such wonderful teachers and how square dancing had made our lives so much happier.

In January 1995, Tilda also died. We've lost two people we truly loved.

>─┼◆─◦─◦─┼─<

Mom and Me!
by Sue Ruf
Milwaukee, Wisconsin

Therese Ruf took square dance lessons in 1949 from Roy Christianson in West Bend. Square dancing was different then. There was one active couple who did the figure, usually couple number one, followed by two, three, and four. Sometimes all the couples were active. My mom tells me that we use some calls today that they used then, but the dancing was not as fast as today.

My mom wore a long dress with a skirt that was so full you could lift the side for a star promenade and not lift up the length of the whole skirt. Her dress was purchased at The Grand (a women's clothing store chain in Milwaukee at that time) for approximately $30. She wore regular shoes. She told me a story of how she was dancing at a benefit for the March of Dimes and the strap on her shoe broke. My mom just traded shoes with my grandma and danced some more. Mom still has her dress. I've worn it since then in a convention fashion show, and at special old-fashioned dances.

During my Mom's era, rounds were more like the Virginia Reel. She also competed in square dancing. St. Joseph Catholic Church in Oconto, Wisconsin, had a square dance contest at a church festival. She danced with her cousins, aunts, and uncles and came in second to a group from Green Bay that were all members of the same club.

Mom also square danced at her wedding. Her uncle did the calling and he got non-square dancers out dancing also.

Mom is the one who encouraged me to try square dancing. I had seen a demonstration at a cub scout pack meeting and thought it looked like fun. Several years later when the National Convention was in Milwaukee, in 1979, she urged me to go to it as a spectator.

I was hooked. Square Dancing looked like so much fun. I bugged the information booth until I found out about Swingin' Singles Squares and the rest is history. It was the beginning of a (so far) 19 year enjoyment of square dancing.

>─┼─◆>─○─<◆┼─<

They Square Dance To Belgian Calls
by Ann Krueger

Every square dance caller has a distinctive style of calling the squares. Ivan Draize, a caller from Luxemburg, Wisconsin, has a style that is unique. He calls in the Belgian language for exhibitions and square dance functions.

"As far as I know I am one of the first callers to translate our modern singing calls into a foreign language," he said. Ivan and his wife Margaret started to work on translation of the calls about 13 years ago when the local Belgian American Club asked them to furnish entertainment for one of the local meetings.

They wanted to present a program that was entertaining and interesting. Many of their regular square dancers were of Belgian descent and were able to speak well enough to hold a conversation. The Draizes realized that there would be no problem with the language after the translation was made. They were unprepared for the difference in the interpretation of some of the square dance vernacular.

Although the Draizes speak Belgian quite fluently they ran into problems when trying to translate the square dance calls. They received help from some of the older settlers of the area and new immigrants from Belgium, but still came up with a few missing words.

Translating square dance calls wasn't as simple as it would appear. After checking and rechecking Ivan and Margaret couldn't find the word "Swing" in the Belgian they spoke. They had to improvise by substituting the word "Dance". "Whenever I want to say 'Swing your Partner' I have to call out 'Dance your partner' or 'Donce vou Companie'", Ivan said. "The dancers have learned to follow that call with no trouble."

The words in some of the other calls had to be changed slightly to account for language differences but with a few lessons the dancers followed the calls easily.

"Many people don't realize that square dancing is as American as country music," Ivan said. "English is the language used when square dance sessions are held in foreign countries. If the people who dance can't speak English they have to learn the square dance jargon before they can enjoy this popular dance."

Margaret and Ivan Draize

In the summer of 1973 Margaret's cousin, who is a radio and T.V. program director in Liege, Belgium, came to this area. She was intrigued with American square dance calling, especially when it was danced to Belgian calls. She taped many of Ivan's calls while attending exhibitions and took them back to Liege to play on her radio and T.V. programs.

She informed the Draizes that the Belgian people enjoyed listening to the square dance calls. She also persuaded them to come to Belgium the following year with the Belgium American Club.

In Belgium Ivan and his dancers were programmed to dance on T.V. They realized that the people of that country were enthusiastic about the American square dances when they were called in the Belgium language.

The Draizes also found a sincere interest in that form of recreation when Margaret's cousin interviewed Ivan on her radio program.

Occasionally square dancers who have learned the translated

calls will persuade Ivan to surprise the dancers by adding a few of his Belgian calls. They enjoy watching the reaction of the dancers who have never heard the Belgian version.

"One time I called out 'Alla Mwa Gosh Al Gosh Komiere' which is translated from 'Allemande left with your left hand lady,'" Ivan said. "After the dance one lady asked me if that goose dance was a new one as she had never heard it before."

The Draizes are members of the Wolf River Area Callers' and Dancers' Association. At each meeting a number of callers are asked to workshop new or popular calls. They attended one of the meetings at Belgium, Wisconsin, where Ivan was asked to work-shop one of the new calls. "I was introduced as the Belgium from Luxemburg who came to call for the Luxembourgians from Belgium," Ivan said.

This article was first printed in 1976 in American Square Dance Magazine.

>─┤◆>─●─<◆┤─<

Russell's Hustle—A Tribute to Russell Burss
by Judy Hogan

When, in the mid-'80s, I was a young beginner caller eager to share what little I knew, I began to call at all the camps and resorts in the Rhinelander area, hoping someone would hire me. Upon call-ing Camp Northern Hills, a camp of the Milwaukee Girl Scouts, I became acquainted with Russ and D-D Burss who did not laugh at my brazen touting of my skills. They invited me to share some of their dance nights at the camp and added to my repertoire of dances, especially in the area of '50s-style line dances: Little Black Book, Ruby Baby, Dead skunk, etc.

Thanks to their encouragement I embarked on a wonderful ten-year career of teaching line dances to ladies groups in Minocqua, Rhinelander, and Three Lakes. I also used these dances to flesh out my "one-night stand" program, and gradually turned all my efforts to this particular style of calling and teaching. My collection of line dance choreographs eventually exceeded 80 dances, some of which I wrote. When Russ died I renamed a pret-ty little line dance for him; Russell's Hustle. It is a quick teach choreography designed for the dance leader to instantly judge the rhythmic skills of the dancers. So here it is "Thank you Russ and D-D!"

Russell's Hustle (Solo Dance)

Counts:
1, 2	Pat knees twice
3, 4	Clap hands twice
5—8	Wave hands left over right, then right over left, twice each *(hands are parallel to floor)*
9—16	Moving to the right, do 4 step-togethers, clapping on the "togethers"

Repeat the dance moving to the left.

>—◦—◦—◦—<

The Dance of My Life
by Agnes Thurner

"Stand still Agnes! Do you want me to poke you with this pin? The dress is almost finished so just be patient a little longer." Mama's words didn't come out quite the way she meant them to because of the stick pins in her mouth but I got the message. I tried very hard not to wiggle even though the fabric was itchy against my bare skin. My sister's dresses were already finished and we were going to wear them at the Grange Hall dance Saturday night. It was a grownup dance but the whole family was going. A few minutes later Mama took the dress off to finish sewing and I ran back outside to play with my brothers and sisters.

There were seven of us all told. My oldest sister, Leila was nine, and my brother Leonard was eight. They were my half-sister and brother from a time when Mama was married to someone else. I was six years old, my sister Bernice was five, brother Johnny, four, Frieda almost three, and Joey was one and a half. We were all very excited about going to the Grange Hall dance and wearing our new clothes. We had mostly hand-me-downs so new clothes were a real occasion even if we weren't going to a dance. There was very little in the way of formal entertainment where we lived, but we always seemed to have plenty to do.

There was a wind-up Victrola that we kids just about wore out and an old pump organ that used to stand in our living/dining (all purpose) room. Daddy moved it to the woodshed when Mama's nerves

Left to right — Leila, neighbor boy, Leonard, Agnes, Bernice. Mama is holding Johnny (1937).

wore out. Now we could go to the woodshed and pump and pound on the keys to our heart's content. 'Peter, Peter Pumpkin Eater' was our favorite song and we older kids knew it by heart. There were trees to climb, a tire swing, and sandy ditches to play in. In the win-

Bernice and Frieda.

tertime there was lots of snow. Daddy made several pair of skis, soaking them in hot water to form the curved tips. We often skied cross-country to school. I still have my skis in the garage. I can't bear to part with them.

We all had responsibilities such as feeding the chickens and pigs, gathering eggs, helping to weed the garden, and of course, washing and drying the dishes. For some reason when I look back, I remember everything being fun except doing the dishes.

We lived on a 40-acre farm in Upper Michigan. I always called it a farm even though all we had were two cows, a few pigs and chickens, a large vegetable garden, and an apple orchard. We raised only enough food for our own use. When we ran out of meat Daddy would butcher a pig or a cow. There was no refrigeration so Mama would cook the meat, render the fat and put everything up in glass jars to store in the cellar. She canned vegetables too, but some we were able to keep fresh in the root cellar Daddy had dug out near the maple grove. In the summer time, we would put milk and other perishables in a wooden box and lower it down into the well. In the winter things would keep cool in the pump house.

Every year Daddy smoked pork hocks, hams, and sausages, and sliced cabbage to make sauerkraut. In the spring he tapped the maple trees to make syrup. We always looked forward to hot pancakes and maple syrup. Sometimes in the summer we would all go to pick wild blueberries and Mama would simmer and serve those piping hot over our pancakes.

It was 1940, Daddy worked in the CCC camps and later for the WPA but he didn't make a lot of money. Neighbors would bring him odd jobs to do, like sharpening saws, fixing broken furniture, repairing cars. He even cut hair. He would set folks down on an old swivel stool that he had put together out of odds and ends and cover their shoulders with a big towel. He charged ten or fifteen cents for a haircut and often didn't even get that. If we hadn't had some of our own food, we would have been pretty hungry. Once things got so bad Daddy went to the courthouse in town to see if he could get some flour and rice from the "county aid people." He was told "this food is for Americans not foreigners." Daddy was born in

Bohemia but immigrated to this country in 1907. Although he hadn't taken time to get his citizenship papers he considered himself to be an American. It was difficult for him to "beg" for food in the first place. To be called a foreigner on top of it really "cut him to the quick."

Daddy was so angry "My kids aren't foreigners", he shouted. "Should they be punished because I wasn't born here?" He drove right over to the Mayor's house and told him what had happened. The Mayor was a friend of his and had often come to our house for moonshine and homemade wine during prohibition. Daddy kept the moonshine and wine hidden in the cellar. The trap door to the cellar was covered by a braided rug and a table stood on top of it. Daddy said it was hidden because "the revenuers used to come around looking for illegal liquor."

The next day a car drove into the yard loaded down with flour, cornmeal, rice, and oranges. The delivery man was the same man that had turned Daddy away at the courthouse. He told Daddy there was really no need to complain to the Mayor. Next time we needed food just let him know.

My Dad.

But I was telling you about the big dance. It seemed to take forever but at last the day arrived. The boys all wore corduroy pants and flannel shirts (except for Joey who was still in dresses), and we girls were dolled up in our new apricot-colored dresses with the big bows tied in back. Mama had put Leila's, Bernice's, and my hair up in rags the night before and we were so proud of our new curls. Frieda was lucky. She had naturally curly hair. Mama was dressed in a navy blue dress with a white lace collar. I had never seen her wear it before. She usually wore shapeless cotton house dresses. Her straight brown hair was cut in a shingle. Daddy wore overalls, a plaid shirt and suspenders just as he did every day, except these were clean.

And so we were off, all piled into our '29 Chevy four-door. After driving for what seemed like an hour and a lot of "are we there yets", we finally rolled into the driveway of the Grange Hall. There were a lot of cars already there and we parked next to them on the grass. We kids were amazed at the size of the hall. It was so big. Long tables formed a row on one end and they were filled with more food than I had ever seen all in one place. Punch bowls were filled with cold lemonade and ICE. I had never seen ICE before. I found out later that it had been cut in huge blocks from a nearby lake and kept in sawdust to keep it from melting.

On the other end of the room was a low platform where an accordion player and a fiddler were tuning up. I was surprised to see that the fiddler was Mr. Eagle, our neighbor from down the road. Years later, I learned that his name was really Ernst Huegle but I will always remember him as Mr. Eagle.

There were a lot of other kids our age in the dance hall but we were too shy to make friends easily. We hid behind our mother, hanging onto her dress, until she turned and said, "That's enough now, go over there and sit." She motioned to the chairs lined up along the walls. About that time the music started. Mr. Eagle had all the grown-ups line up and instructed them in the Virginia Reel. When that was finished, he told everyone to form squares of eight people and he called a square dance to the tune of "Pop Goes the Weasel." Mama and Daddy were having so much fun. It was one of the few times I remember hearing her laugh.

When the grown-ups sat down to rest, it was the kids turn. We all went out on the floor and began to horse around. We would run down the length of the hall and slide the last few feet on our bottoms. I don't have to tell you what our new finery looked like at the end of the evening. When the dancing started up again, Mama and Daddy were the first ones out on the floor.

Soon it was time to eat. There was fried chicken, homemade bread, potato salads, beans, and all the cake and pie we could eat. And eat we did. We had all learned early in life that we ate what was put on our plates whether we liked it or not. Thankfully all the food was as good as it looked.

When it was time to leave, we all bundled back into the car for the drive home. Joey had been sleeping for over an hour; wrapped in a blanket, straddling two chairs that had been pushed together. The rest of us kids were asleep almost before the car was out of the driveway. I woke up when we pulled into our yard but I pretended to be asleep so that Daddy would carry me in to my bed.

The memory of that day is particularly precious to me. None of us knew it then but our lives were about to change drastically. Less than six months later my 32-year-old mama went to the hospital to have another baby, the first of my siblings to be born outside of home. I never saw her again. I was told that she had died of "complications". We kids were sent to live temporarily with various relatives in Milwaukee, northern Wisconsin, and Upper Michigan. My Dad was 48 years old at that time and was overwhelmed by the thought of raising us all alone. He boarded up the house and set off to look for a steady job. One that would pay enough to support eight kids and a housekeeper (or a new wife that was willing to take on a ready-made family).

He applied for work at the A. O. Smith plant in Milwaukee but one of their hiring stipulations was that an employee had to be a United States citizen. He filed for and received his citizenship papers but worked for A. O. Smith for only a short time before following his heart to Kansas City, Missouri, where he had been corresponding with a lady he'd met through a "lonely hearts" column. While courting her he worked at the Pratt and Whitney Aircraft factory. They carried on a lengthy friendship but she finally admitted to my Dad that she had no desire to rear his children.

The years passed and my father's dreams of reuniting our family passed with them. My sister Bernice died in a traffic accident in Milwaukee; Frieda and Joey were adopted by my Aunt Emma, and the baby, Julius was adopted by my Uncle John and his wife. Leila and Leonard continued to live with my maternal grandparents, and John and I lived with various relatives and in foster homes until we reached the age of 18. When I was 12 my dad met and married his third wife and their marriage endured for over 35 years.

* * *

Gym class had just been dismissed when the bell rang signaling the beginning of the next class. I hurried to change my clothes, struggling behind the curtain of a small shower stall. The other girls were already leaving the locker room. They didn't seem to mind taking off their clothes in front of each other and were always finished dressing long before I was. I was too embarrassed to let the others girls see me undressed. For one thing, I was FAT, as my Aunt saw fit to remind me almost daily. Besides that, the buttons on my brassiere straps were missing and I had to fasten them together with big safety pins. I got teased enough as it was because of my long underwear and coarse stockings (all the other girls wore ankle socks). It seemed no matter how hard I tried I couldn't smooth out the wrinkles when I pulled my stockings on over the underwear. So there was just no way I would let those girls see my ugly body and ugly underclothes.

"Hurry up, Agnes." It was Lorna, one of my classmates. "You're going to miss dance class. We're square dancing today." "I'm coming, I'm coming," I said, tugging my dress down. We ran down the hall just as the class was lining up, girls on one side, boys on the other. As I took my place I saw the boys pushing and shoving each other in the line. My face turned beet red when I realized that none of them wanted to be standing across from me when the dance started. Sure enough, we were paired off by our position in the line, and Glen was my unlucky partner. I'd had a crush on Glen ever since school started, but when the teacher told us to join hands he glared at me, and stuck his hands in his pockets. I've never felt so humiliated. Tears filled my eyes and I ran from the room. I went to the girls room and cried until no more tears would come.

When I finally went back the class was almost over and Glen had a different partner. No one else was available so I ended up dancing with the teacher. At age 13, I thought it was the worst thing that would ever happen to me.

A few years later I went to live with a foster family. They belonged to a Seventh Day Adventist Church and I immersed myself (quite literally, since they believed in baptism by immersion) in this new religion.

I joined the choir and was frequently called on to sing a solo or a duet. I was asked to teach a junior religion class and invited to join the youth group. I wrote poetry, and it was actually published in the church newsletter. For the first time I heard myself referred to as attractive and talented.

No dancing was allowed in the Seventh Day Adventist Church, but one day I was invited to attend a "march". We had such a wonderful time. We marched by twos, fours, and sometimes eight in a line, all in time to lively (secular) music. A cuer directed us into various and intricate march formations. We even linked arms with the boys, and they didn't seem to mind having to hold my hand.

Gradually I came out of my shell, and came to believe that "just maybe" I was a worthwhile person after all. But it was many more years before I could look into a mirror and not see an ugly fat girl.

* * *

1965

Jim looked at the calendar. "This coming Friday, did you say. Sure we can make it."

"Make what", I said, as I came up from the basement where I'd been doing laundry. "Oh Hi, Linda, Steve. I didn't hear you come in."

"Steve and Linda have invited us to go square dancing." answered Jim. "It sounds like fun, doesn't it?"

"Square dancing! No Way! I hate square dancing." I said, more forcefully than I intended.

"How can you hate it—you've never done it." Jim said. I could hear the question in his voice.

"I have tried it. I did it in school and I hated it."

Steve and Linda laughed. "This is nothing like the square dancing you did in school", said Steve. "Look, why don't you just come along Friday. If you like it, fine, if not, you don't need to come back. You aren't doing anything that night anyway."

I reluctantly agreed and on Friday Jim and I went to Calhoun Hall to dance to the calling of Dale Wagner. We met Dale's lovely wife, Florence, and were introduced to a lot of smiling, happy, friendly couples. And yes, we did have fun. Steve was right—it was nothing like high school—but it was vaguely reminiscent of the fun I had marching at the Seventh Day Adventist Church. Jim and I went back every Friday night, usually stopping for breakfast with the gang after the dance.

The fun didn't stop after graduating. There were always visits to other clubs, bus trips, and the regular Friday workshops with Dale and Florence. In 1967 several couples formed a convoy to go to the La Crosse Convention. We stopped at a scenic wayside and shared a picnic lunch arriving in La Crosse about 3:00 p.m. After checking into our motel we changed into square dance clothes for our first convention experience. All the ladies were dressed alike in fuchsia outfits with white trim. The men wore matching vests and ties. We looked and felt terrific as we posed for a group photo. When the dance ended for the day we all gathered in one of the motel rooms for an after party, sharing our snacks, beverages, and (sometimes colorful) stories. Life was good!

Dale and Florence Wagner at a Christmas party at Calhoun Hall.

Since the only thing constant is change I shouldn't have been too surprised when my life changed again. I found myself raising my two teenagers alone. My time taken up with making a living for them and myself. The years sped by, the kids left, my elderly dad came to stay permanently, and I had a whole new set of problems.

Jim and Agnes Wegner —1967 La Crosse convention.

How to put some fun in my life and still make sure my dad was not left alone. He was almost 90 years old and very unstable on his feet. Then I ran into Eleanor Christianson at a Hartland craft fair and she handed me a flyer for square dance lessons at the Swingin' Single Square Dance Club. I could hardly wait for September.

Taking my dad with me, I started square dance lessons once again. Square dancing had changed during the years I had been away from it. The "allemande left" and "grand right and left" were still the same but there were many other calls that I didn't remember. What hadn't changed was the fun and the friendliness of the other dancers. After 36 weeks I had mastered Mainstream, then went on to learn Plus and round dancing. I joined the Swingin' Singles Club and not long after that was asked to do the Newsletter and Publicity. From there it was just a hop, skip, and jump, before I was involved in doing publicity for one of the conventions, and then to holding an office in the SDAW-SEA.

My Dad went with me to all the dances. He said he "liked to watch the leg show." He loved to talk and had made as many friends as I had in the square dance community. But one day he begged off going to a dance, saying the music hurt his ears. He went downhill quickly after that and in 1990, at age 97, he quietly passed away.

A few months later, a friend Sue Doers, asked if I would go along on a Mystery Trip with her club, the Square Benders. She said they had a single man that needed a partner. I canceled other plans to go on the trip, and so did he. We danced every dance that night, and have been dancing together ever since. He is my husband, my partner, my friend. And that is how square dancing became the Dance of My Life.

My Dad at age 95 plays the mandolin at a party held for square dance students.

Come Dance With Me!
by Olive "Skippy" Giese

Some people think it's corny
Others say square dancing's for hicks.
Our very best friends were dancing squares
Full of fun with a basket of tricks,

It takes eight to make a square
You can dance even though you're single.
Need exercise, would you like great friends?
Your heart and soul will tingle.

Yellow rocker's are great lovers
For they're hugging all the time
While they promenade or courtesy turn,
Put centers in, zoom from a line.

You can be part of a star family,
Sashay while you circle right
Or touch 1/4 then circulate,
Split couples holding tight.

Decide to pass the ocean,
Cast off, do a grand square.
Then wheel and deal or Ferris wheel,
Box the gnat, tag, spin, fan, share.

You can giggle, laugh, but should listen
To the caller's every call
Lest you break up the square, mess up the dance
Get flutter wheeled out of the hall.

Square Dance Stories
Compiled by Judy Barisonzi

"Then there was the time...." Heard any good stories about experiences in square dancing? Here's a few you might enjoy.

Bob Goebel of Port Washington, who has been calling for about 37 years, remembers dancing at Waupun for a Jail Bird Dance, and being wrapped up in toilet paper while calling a tip. This seems to be a common practice. At one Halloween dance of the Milton Village Squares, Carol Thorp remembers the caller being wrapped in toilet paper like a mummy, and calling from a coffin.

Dot Conrad, President of the Square Bender's Club, remembers

*Square Bender
club members
prepare Aggi
for her
"wedding".
Left to right,
Vi Brabender,
Aggi, Martha
Bolz, Betty
Rapp.*

holding a mock wedding for Aggi and Max Thurner in which Aggi
was pinned into a tissue paper wedding dress. Club member Fritz
Zemski held a shotgun on the groom until the "preacher", none
other than caller Alex Brabender, had performed the wedding ceremony.

Callers sometimes get carried away. Carol Thorp remembers a
caller who actually threw ping-pong balls during a ping-pong circulate.

Callers don't give up easily. Glenn Younger remembers driving
to a dance with his wife during a snowstorm. When their car ended
up in a ditch he just called his brother-in-law to pick them up, got

*Fritz and
Marie Zemski
watch as Max
and Aggi seal
their vows.*

to the dance on time, and went
back next morning for the car.
Mike Krautkramer recalls a
state convention in Oshkosh
in 1995 when dancers from
Green Bay removed his boots
while he was calling. He just
kept right on singing.

Callers can get strange presents. Nancy Steblik of
Kenosha remembers an April
Fool's Day when the 49ers
club members dressed up a
chicken in square dance
clothes and boots and gave it
to Delores "Boots" Laufenberg

to take back to her farm.

Camping and square dancing go together. Clare Anderson remembers interesting people they met when square dance camping—a man who crowed like a rooster to wake people in their campers, a couple who camped with a make-believe mongoose, and a man who brought a telescoping fork to grab his meals. John and Cal Stillson remember camping outside the Coliseum in Madison in 1986 and being awakened by dozens of colorful hot air balloons landing a few hundred feet from the campers.

Embarrassing things can happen too. Clare Anderson of Square Benders in Milwaukee, who has been dancing for 32 years, remembers a time when they were still taking lessons and her husband Chet knocked off a lady's hairpiece during a tip. Gert Schneider of Falls Promenaders, who has been dancing for 35 years, recalls the time a woman's petticoat got caught on a man's belt and it started to unravel, until finally the whole square was caught up in the threads. Olive "Skippy" Giese of Bayside remembers the elastic on her petticoat breaking and the petticoat starting to fall off during a tip. But men can have their problems as well. Reginald Buchanan of Dudes and Dolls remembers dancing one tip with his fly open.

Square dancers just never stop. Helen Rothman of Grafton recalls going to a caller's house one night after a dance and getting him out of bed to cue another round. Velda Quimby of Appleton remembers dancing in the parking lot at one convention in Madison with Red VanderLangt calling until the lights were turned off at 3 a.m. Gert Schneider remembers one time Art Weisensel was calling at an outside dance, and the police came and shut them down about 10 p.m. because someone complained about the noise. That was the end of outside dancing for them. Other groups have had similar experiences. At one state convention, a group was outside with Jerry Wenglewski calling until police came to break it up because of the noise, but the officers were clapping their hands in time to the music!

Square dancing is a way to make friends. Here's a strange coincidence. At the state convention, Vern and Dorothy Overbye of Country Promenaders met another couple named Overbye. Her first name was also Dorothy, and her husband's name was Tom, the same as their second son's name. They had two sons named Tom and Ray, and Vern's brother's name is Ray.

Sometimes you can make more than friends. Billie Weisensel started square dancing when her fiancé's mother sent the young couple to a square dance. She ended up marrying the caller instead. Now one daughter, in Virginia, is teaching a square dance class, their son is a caller, and another daughter, in Milwaukee, is married to a caller.

Favorite jokes? Glenn Younger has this to tell: "I can only please one person per day. Today is not your day, and tomorrow doesn't look good either!" Bill Schara reminds us that "square dancing is spelled with a three-letter word: F-U-N." Steve and Mary Gonske of Stevens Point say, "Any man that says he's the king of his castle will lie about other things too."

Square dance callers and cuers have a lot of good advice. At the end of the evening Dolores Laufenberg always tells dancers, "Watch the car in front of the car in back of you." And Ray Steinich recalls Pilachowski's three rules of round dancing: 1. Your feet don't work right unless you're smiling. 2. It is more important to have fun than to get it right. 3. If anything goes wrong it's the cuer's fault. Finally, here's some advice from Milton Ystad, square dance caller from Loyal: Treat everyone like you would like to be treated. Enjoy yourself, keep good humor, and never hurt anyone's feelings!

➤─┼─◆➤─○─◆┼─◄

It's Fun To Be Square
by Jean and Bob Brisk

Bob and Jean have been square dancers for over 13 years. They dance Mainsteam and Plus with the Falls Promenaders and also round dance and clog. They have been club publicity chairman and secretary, and have served on several committees. They heard about square dancing through a Menomonee Falls newspaper and have never been sorry they went to that first class. Following are some of their personal reminiscences.

Bob and I have had lots of good times over the years while members of the Falls Promenaders Square Dance Club. Besides meeting great friends, not only in our club but in all clubs around the state, we have even made friends nationally. We are glad we took up this activity when we did.

As l look back I remember some of the many fun activities we were involved in. Here are just a few: Usually on a night (no one knows which night) between Christmas and New Year's Day, someone will start this annual trek going caroling from house to house. We were new dancers and didn't know about this "Christmas Game" the club played.

One night I was washing clothes. I piled the dried clothes on chairs and on the davenport in the living room. I was wearing some old clothes and had my hair up in curlers. I was folding the clothes as I watched a show on TV when the telephone rang. It was a wrong number. Then about ten minutes later a lot of carolers came up our steps. I went to the door and there they were—Falls Promenaders. They came right in and said "this house is a potty stop." They wanted us to get our coats and come with them right away, just the way we were. There were lots of vans and cars. "Just hop in," they said.

We drove to the Uecker's house. Ray Uecker had played Santa Claus that day and he had a nice Santa suit which he donned. We caroled at lots of dancer's houses always adding them to our group. Ray would stand in the middle of some of the intersections waving our caravan on through. We ate cookies at one house, stollen at another, fruitcake and other goodies were offered at others.

Soon it was 10:30 p.m.—11:00 p.m. Then 12:00 p.m. It got later and later, but it made no difference. They made enough racket to get the dancers out of bed. It reminded me of Halloween when they rolled those empty thread spools against the windows.

I remember getting Dolly and Harold out of bed. She came downstairs with her nightie and robe on and turned on all the lights and served a beautiful big tray of cookies and wine. Then when we burst into Dotty and Dave's house, there they sat with big bowls of ice cream, but not enough for all of us. Gloria and Jim were entertaining guests but we went right in and were introduced to all.

We usually saved Buford and Chris Thingvold's house until last as she always had pies, cakes, and cookies, in the freezer. She is such a good cook. But this time it was 3 or 4 o'clock in the morning. Then some would stay for breakfast.

I will tell you one thing. When I found out it usually happened during the week between Christmas and New Year's, I picked up our house and made ready.

Another time the club members met in front of Lincoln School and boarded a big Badger bus. We were going on a Knothead trip. Everyone brought snacks and drinks. Of course no one knew where we were headed. Everyone had ideas, especially when we made the turn on Appleton Avenue driving toward Milwaukee. We got on Hwy 45 and Hwy 894. People were guessing Greendale, Racine, Kenosha. But then we made a right turn on Hwy 15 and started driving west towards Elkhorn, or Milton, or Madison. Lots of guesses now.

Terry Hanson brought along his accordion and started playing all the "golden oldies". Everyone was singing and passing their snacks and drinks. Such fun! Finally we came to a stop at Beloit. We all piled out of the bus and the Petunia Squares club was waiting for us. Their dancers all welcomed us with hugs. They had lots of decorated cakes all lined up and down two or three long tables. Big jars were set on the tables and everyone was to put slips of paper with their names in the jars. During the dance, names were called and you could go and pick out a cake. I bet nearly everyone in our club held a cake in their lap on the way home in the bus.

One night we had planned to get the caller out of bed. You could get a dangle to attach to your badge, which was a popular thing to do at that time. It was about 11:00 or 11:30 at night. We all drove one behind the other without our lights on and right past the Brabender's house in Mequon. We turned the corner and drove a little ways and parked. We walked back to their house. Some of us went around the back of the house and some to the sides of the house. At a given signal we knocked on the door and ran thread spools up and down the windows and made lots of noise. The front door opened and there was Gen Brabender, all dressed, hair combed and looking bright-eyed. She had been sitting on the davenport in the dark and watched our cars pass by, then saw us walking up the street. She called Alex to get up and dress. We didn't fool her but we sure had a good time. We all went down to the basement, Alex put on the records, and started calling. Gen brought out some goodies. We all wore our nighties, PJs, slippers, nightcaps and had curlers in our hair. Some brought Teddy bears and some wore those big bear slippers. A night to remember for sure.

One thing about square dancing, you meet the nicest people all over the country. One time Bob and I were visiting our daughter in Dallas, Texas. We looked in the telephone book and the National Square Dance Organization was listed. We made a call to the President and he said that there was a dance scheduled the next night at a school right near our daughter's house. We dressed and when we arrived everyone gathered around and introduced themselves. Then they saw to it that we were always included in a square during the dance. After the dance they asked us to come along and have a snack at a nearby restaurant.

Another time we arrived at a RV Park in Texas and after getting settled, Bob attached our square dance flag to our antenna. Soon, a caller who was parked across the street from us came over and asked where we were from and gave us a calendar of dances. Then he directed another couple to come pick us up in their truck and take us along to a big dance. This couple was from Seattle, Washington, and we have become very good friends. We have met them in Texas every time we go to the valley. We have been to their house three times. They have showed us how to fish in the Sound, and how to go crabbing. They have escorted us all around Seattle and many other places in the State of Washington.

A group of five couples from Falls Promenaders and a couple from Square Benders all gathered together like pioneers at the National Convention held in Portland, Oregon in 1994. We all drove out there in our RVs and trailers. We saw some of the sights around Portland together; we went to the famous rose gardens and the Japanese gardens. We partied together and entertained some other members of our club who had flown out to Oregon and were staying in motels. Most of us took extended vacations and spent two months traveling up and down the Washington, Oregon, and California coast. We have had lots of fun meeting new dancers at both national and state conventions and keep in touch with many of them.

At another National Convention that was held in Anaheim, California, Bob and I pulled into the county fairgrounds to park our RV. It was a big field with hundreds of different kinds of camping vehicles. California people were parked on either side of us. As soon as we got settled a couple came over and said "come join our party". We joined about five or six other couples and we all became good friends. We danced in squares together until it was time to travel over to Disney World to join square dancers from all over the United States. The grounds opened at 6:00 p.m. and stayed open all night just for us. One couple that had a big RV offered to drive everyone over there. We all piled into his motor home and off we went. We meet nice people like this everywhere we travel. It makes you proud to be an American. It is so easy to meet friendly people when you dance and camp.

Salvation
by Caroline Cook

There's a brief break in the line of people coming to the gate of the high school football field, and Neil says quietly, "Would you like to get something to eat after the football game?"

I count out change and hand out another program. "Nice idea, but where? High school teachers don't look good in bars, and my daughter won't appreciate our showing up together at the Steer. Better come up to the house for coffee."

"We could go to Eau Claire, but that makes it late when I have to milk cows, and you have to report to school in the morning."

"Settle for the house."

It's ten o'clock when I pour coffee. Daughter Barbara is home thirty minutes later. She goes to the piano stating, "I have to practice. I have a lesson tomorrow."

Neil shakes his head briefly. It's a problem dating a widow with a teenager. As we walk to the door, he says, "Ever thought about square dancing?"

"Nobody does anything like that in Osseo, Wisconsin!"

"They do in Fall Creek, Augusta, and Eleva," he replies naming three nearby communities.

"Could be fun, but I don't know how."

"Lessons at the Fall Creek school start Monday night."

"Where could I be more comfortable?"

"Monday night then?"

"I'll keep it in mind when I'm giving out assignments."

Neil has gotten good directions and parks close to the proper entrance. Full skirted women all carrying something converge on the door in front of us.

"Potluck after the dancing," Neil tells me.

"One more problem solved," I think, remembering that even in Eau Claire we frequently run into familiar faces.

Once inside, people quickly introduce themselves. "Will I ever remember the names?" I wonder. Of course I will. They're all wearing badges that say Twilight Twirlers with their names below.

The Zempels, whom I already know, tell us we'll learn faster if we split up. Dawn takes Neil to the far end of the gym, and John escorts me in the opposite direction. Harold Aanerud, the caller we've just met, explains our positions, then shows us a right and left grand—not hard since I've done it before. Next comes a right and left through. This gets trickier, but feels pretty good after half a dozen repetitions. I find I have to listen and think, no mind wandering back to school problems.

Finally the learners rest, enjoying the whirling patterns of the regular dancers neatly on beat with the music. A bountiful lunch counter reminds me I skipped supper because Barbara was at a friend's house. The conversation is as good as the food. It's obvious these people read and do all sorts of things as well as dance. Harold Aanerud tells us the lesson will be repeated on Wednesday at Augusta and on Saturday at Eleva. We are welcome to come. Talk about learning reinforcement!

Neil looks at me. I nod. I have not felt so comfortable any place since we started dating. No raised eyebrows, no wisecracks, no prying questions—just lots of friendly learning help.

By Saturday we feel a little ahead of those who are doing this for the first time. Three times a week is not always possible. We do try to hold firm on Mondays. Now we are learning scoot back. For some reason I can't remember to flip—a firm hand gently pulls on my shoulder and I'm back in position.

The weather turns cold. Roads are slippery, often drifted with snow, but dance night is something we are not going to miss. Christmas decorations glow. Neil appears at my house with a Christmas gift—matching square dance outfits. We wear them to the club holiday party and dance two tips without error. Then our square falls apart on a simple spin the top. Everyone laughs with us, but not at us. We square up again.

In March there is graduation complete with the four-candle cake which represents the square. I love the lines about friendship and think about how much this group has meant to us.

Five years later we have danced at civic celebrations, nursing homes, club meetings, and state conventions; and we keep learning. Many of the plus calls are no longer mysteries.

My older boys are established in homes of their own and Barbara is away at college. We return to the farm from our wedding trip, but a phone call tells me my father is gravely ill. I go to Montana and return only two days before school is to start. I am tired; the house is a mess; my lesson plans incomplete. I feel major depression setting in.

Doing supper dishes, I look at walls that have splotchy, ghostlike shadows where patching plaster has been smoothed in. Neil has put on a coat of primer, but has not had time for more. Curtainless windows look out on a mowed yard that needs edge trimming and flower beds that are empty.

"This place is no credit to you, lady," I say out loud as I jam kettles on an overcrowded shelf. The cupboard contents clatter to the floor. A rolling pin spins in one direction, a frying pan in another. I empty the shelf, scrub it well, discard some items and see the beginning of organization.

"That's better. The bathroom is the smallest room in the house. It needs attention so do it now!" Talking out loud seems to be good discipline, and I go into action. Filling a kettle with hot soapy water and taking a cake pan to hold the content of the medicine cabinet, I head down the hall. Many of the bottles are sticky and old. I fill a waste basket with discards and wash off the rest. Then I scrub down the shelves and turn to the linen closet. Yellow edges on unused towels and sheets attract my attention. I whip these items into the washing machine and carry the rest to the bedroom. Above the sound of the washing machine, I hear a car in the driveway. A glance out the window tells me our neighbors, the Deinhammers and Larsons have picked tonight to visit. I dump the scrub water, grab the cake pan filled with bottles and park it in the bedroom. Seizing a fresh blouse from the closet, I reach the living room just as I fasten the last button.

Aggie knocks and opens the door. "Anybody home? I've got fresh chocolate bars so I hope so. I know you haven't had time to bake since the Montana trip."

"Come in, come in. It will be great to visit." I mean this with all my heart but I do wonder if there's enough coffee left to make a full pot.

Before I have a chance to check, Neil comes in the back door dripping wet milk. "Hi, neighbors. Be with you in a minute as soon as I get some dry clothes. Those damned calves upset two buckets on me before I got 'em fed."

A crash tells me Neil has collided with the bathroom stuff in the bedroom, but I pretend not to notice as I empty the coffee can and set the coffee perking. Back in the living room, I start to ask about fall square dancing plans. My voice is blotted out by a hideous clanging which seems to echo over the whole farm. This is followed by dozens of horns honking. "There must be a horrible accident," I cry, racing for the door and turning on the yard lights. I fail to notice my guests are laughing.

Gazing fearfully up the road, I see cars driving bumper to bumper. They circle into the yard and begin to unload. The noise increases. People bang spoons and hammers on old pieces of metal. Cowbells ring. Whistles shrill through the air. "Shivaree! Shiveree!" come the shouts.

I shake my head and yell at Neil, "The neighbors will think we've gone mad."

He laughs. "Forget it. The neighbors are all here!"

I surrender my kitchen to square dance friends who plug in huge coffeepots and load my refrigerator with great bowls of salad and mountains of sandwiches. A table holds elaborate cakes, bars and gift-wrapped packages. Someone tosses a cord through the living room window. A card table is set up outside. Harold Aanerud's familiar voice calls out, "Square your sets."

I am tired no longer. The music throbs in the cool night air, fragrant with third crop hay. The cows join in the chorus and Steve Deinhammer says, "That's what I call real country music."

Sometimes we slip a little on the grass, but these are experienced dancers who have performed on floats at many parades. It does not bother them. Neil and I move from square to square. The hand clasps are warm and familiar. The smiles and congratulations are clearly genuine. Never have I felt so surrounded and included by a group of friends.

This all happened nearly 20 years ago. Some of these good people including Harold Aanerud have gone on to another life, but the wonderful fellowship is still there each time we dance. The three clubs, A-Gay-O of Augusta; Howdy Pardners of Eleva; and Twilight Twirlers of Fall Creek, have now merged to form the Triple Scooters who meet at Fall Creek on the first and third Mondays of each month and dance to the lively calling of Bud Cote.

>−·◆⟩−·Ο−⟨◆·−·≺

Haiku's
by Olive "Skippy" Giese

Joy is dancing square:
four girl fluffs, four clothespin's turn,
circle, swing in pairs.

Giddy energy:
Gals and guys allemande left
zoom, cloverleaf, sing.

Square dancing is like
champagne: bubbling energy:
art: a picture framed.

Fleeting movements squared —
box the gnats, sashays, star thru's,
It's called square dancing.

A Couple of Squares
by Margaret L. Been

My husband Joe, and I entered the world of square dancing at a county fair. As we wistfully viewed the exhibition, a pair of dancers grabbed our hands and greeted us with unabashed smiles. This couple urged us onto the stage to try a few entry level moves, and we were hooked. We agreed to sign up for square dance lessons.

Our classes started on an upswing. We memorized square dancing protocol (always wear deodorant, always smile, always say "thank you") and we learned to distinguish our right foot from our left. We reviewed the basics—things like "Do-Si-Do" and "Allemande Left" that most of us mastered in first grade gym class. And we thought THIS IS EASY!

Ha! I get dizzy just thinking about the weeks that followed that first lesson. The word "easy" disappeared from our vocabulary. Joe and I discovered that there are not six Mainstream calls, but approximately sixty-six. To say nothing about those seemingly unreachable levels beyond mainstream with remote sounding names such as Plus, Advanced, and Challenge. (After several years of dancing, Joe and I are still convinced that "Challenge" entails four couples parachuting simultaneously from four planes, meeting in a perfect square, and executing unimaginably complex steps prestissimo without an error—wind velocity notwithstanding.)

Somehow we charged through our first season of lessons, despite time out for flu—after which we

Margaret and Joe Been — "A Couple of Squares".

felt like we were in THE LAND OF THE LOST. Miraculously, we graduated. Graciously, we were urged to attend the regular club dances. In addition, we were encouraged to "get out and DANCE" at other clubs.

Square dancers, as a group, may be the friendliest people in the world. In the process of getting out and dancing at other clubs, we traveled around southeastern and central Wisconsin—and as far afield as Aurora, Colorado, trying to hit a different location each week. I say "hit" because that is what new dancers frequently do when they visit around; they pop in, receive the warmest of welcomes, and then proceed to stumble, bumble, break up squares, and prove conclusively that square dancers really are the friendliest people in the world. People who wear deodorant, keep right on smiling, and never cease to encourage beginners.

As we attended various club dances a second and third time, we began to be "known". Sometimes it seemed that seasoned dancers "squared up" rapidly when we entered the scene. I don't blame them a bit; I wouldn't have wanted to dance with us either!

Despite recurrent bouts of humiliation and chagrin, and inspired by the words of Sir Winston Churchill ("Never give in, never give in, never, never, never, never ..."), Joe and I have persisted at square dancing. We try to dance at least one night a week, and sometimes more. (One week we danced three nights out of five; during the days between those nights, we limped around in a state of near terminal exhaustion.)

Our times of chaos and confusion on the dance floor are definitely on the wane, but occasionally we still scramble the calls. Sometimes we frankly forget; other times we simply forget to remember. There are disastrous moments when I mistake "Slip the Clutch" for "Shoot that Star". And there are occasions when I blank out altogether. My mental screen says, "Too many files; list truncated". I know the necessary information is buried somewhere in the hard drive, but I just can't bring it up to my directory!

Now, after five years, there are incidents where Joe and I actually believe that someone else messed up—maybe some beginner. But we don't mind. We just wear our deodorant and smile!

Joe and Margaret learned to dance at Limber Timbers in Elkhorn. Although they no longer belong to a club they are still actively dancing. They even have a personal badge; they call themselves the "Sheepy Hollow Squares, as they live on three acres of land and have a couple of silly sheep."

>―◦―◦―◦―◦―<

What is Square Dancing?
by Dolores Tock

That was the question I asked myself about 20 years ago. After a day of teaching I came home, made myself a cup of coffee and picked up the evening paper. Somehow my eyes rested on a small ad that read "Square Dance Lessons". I knew a waltz and a polka, but what was a square dance? I decided to find out. I would go just that first night.

The most important thing I learned is that square dancing is fun—so much fun, in fact, that I went back each week. The fun has never stopped.

There were other things I learned. Square dancing is simply listening to and following the directions of a caller as you walk to the beat of the music. So I can honestly say that square dancing is good exercise.

Perhaps the most significant thing I've learned is that square dancing is people. It is the acceptance of all ages and all sizes. It is the welcoming hugs and handshakes, the thank you's just for being there. It is strangers who join hands and have fun together in the square. It is the concern and care, the consideration of each other, that have become so admirable to me.

A song that we frequently sing together says, "remember that a stranger is just a friend to be." The reality of those words strikes me every time I hear it, as my husband, Roy, was a stranger who acted as my "angel" during lessons and soon became my dearest friend.

Just this past weekend we were up north and stopped in at the square dance club in Waupaca. All of these people were strangers to us when we walked in, but one would be hard put to find a more friendly, welcoming group as we danced, visited, and snacked with them.

Yes, I have, and still do, enjoy the polka or a waltz. But I believe that it is the people I square dance with that enables me to say at the end of an evening, "That sure was fun!"

⊱┈⊰⊹⊱──⊰┈⊱⊱┈⊰

Northwoods Square Dance Stories
by Judy Hogan

(1) Ann Ross often said that in the "old days" the ironing of the dress was a major part of getting ready for the dance. That was because the dresses were all cotton and decorated with miles of rickrack, silver and gold braid, and other trims. Ann and her husband Don, loyal members of Rhinelander area clubs from the '50s through the early '90s, danced all over the state and in many other places including Hawaii and Norway. They were given a special lifetime membership in the Hodag Twirlers, the only couple to ever be so honored.

(2) Wes and Eileen White who began square dancing in the early '50s had to stop when they moved out of town and no longer had her mom available to baby-sit. They returned to the world of dance, first with ballroom and polka, and then to square dancing in the late '80s. They still do a bit of polka dancing, but had to give up square dancing due mostly to Wes' development of hearing problems.

(3) Bob and Marj Fease kept square dancing alive in the northwoods in the late '50s with dances at their resort, Shady Rest Lodge, renaming the club the Shady Squares. About this time they also began hold the first square dance weekends held in Wisconsin. The first event had Bob Dawson, Milwaukee caller and Harry Lukens, a round dance cuer from St. Louis. Their son John, recalls dancing at the lodge as a teenager and dreaded having his weekend plans interrupted when he'd be called down to the rec' hall to fill in a square and "dance with the 'old' people".

(4) Barb Busche Craig who danced with the Casswood Promenaders as a teen dancer remembers dancing on Channel 7 T.V.

(5) Carole Jacobsen recalls a mid-'60s dance exhibition done for mentally retarded people. One Downs syndrome young woman was so enthralled by Carole's red dress that she followed her all evening. The people were so appreciative that the event was very memorable. Carole began dancing in Michigan and as a 13-year-old with a good singing voice, she was called out of her regular school classes to call squares for the gym classes.

(6) Late in December of 1968 the Jacobsens and the Langloises returning from a square dance noted a bright orange sky and upon investigating found all of downtown Rhinelander in flames. They hurried home, instructed baby-sitters to stay longer and returned to witness this historic event.

(7) Vern Baudhuin remembers many good dance times exchanging dances with dancers from Antigo in the '60s. He recalls a time when dancers from Rhinelander traveled to Milwaukee for a car ferry trip on Lake Michigan with all night dancing (six callers) on the boat. They met Art Gorski who was there with a group from Chicago and invited him to Rhinelander. He called once in the winter for about $15 or $20 and again when he was in the area on vacation in the summer. He and his wife Fran eventually moved to Rhinelander because he loved to fish the muskie and call square dances.

(8) I remember dancing to Leroy Hitzke while working at Fease's Resort. He frequently did singing calls with his back to the crowd. He also loved "hot hash" and he'd say, "I'll just do an inch more," and then go on for ten more minutes, hardly taking a breath.

(9) Favorite party and graduation stunts:

Dancing on Jello: Actually what we did was have the dancers remove their shoes and put on blindfolds. We then placed wet pieces of sponge on the floor and told them they were dancing on Jello.

The pair of Bloomers: Two artificial flowers were placed in a gift box and tied with a ribbon. Dancers were to pass the box around while dancing and when the music stopped the dancer who was holding "the bloomers" was told to "open the box and put them on."

The Spool Trick: One dancer placed a spool of sewing thread in his pocket and tied the end on another dancer without the dancer knowing it. As the dance progressed the spool unwound and everyone became tied up in the thread.

The Square Dance Exam: Tom Hogan invented a short "final test" for his students. There were some rather cleverly worded questions, but most important were the initial directions: "Do not answer any questions until you read the whole test." The last statement on the test was "Do not answer the questions," "Write your name at the top and hand in your test."

(10) In the mid-'90s when the departure of "snow bird" dancers for wintering in Texas, Arizona, or Florida was causing a financial

emergency, club president Wendell Schenck helped institute a new form of dance membership which undoubtedly saved the club. He suggested that belonging to a square dance club be similar to having a golf course membership. All dancers were strongly encouraged to pay for a full year of dances in the fall. The price was slightly reduced from what individual dance prices would be if paid one dance at a time. The message was clear, "If you want your club to still be here when you return, we need your financial commitment now." It worked! Membership dollars in the treasury got the club through the lean winter dance months. Our club survived thanks to the generosity of dancers who paid for dances they were not here to enjoy. Other dancers discovered that since their evening out was already paid, they were more likely to attend, even when the chilly northern weather tempted them to remain home in their cozy living rooms.

>─┤─◄►─•─O─•─◄►┤─◄

Welcome to Our World
by Doug Kindschuh and Judy Barisonzi

As we *pass thru* the world to go to a healthy, fun-filled evening of square dancing, we've had to *pass to the center* and then *pass to the outside,* enabling us to *pass the sea,* en route to *pass the ocean,* which leads us to a final *grand pass through* to our square dance hall.

On the way, though, we have to *load the boat* or *unload the boat* so we *don't sink the boat.* Then we *transfer the wave* and *paddle thru* our *paddle wheel.*

On dry land, we may have to *wheel in and out, wheel back, wheel across,* and even *wheel and deal* to get to the dance. Sometimes we'll have to *deal around* or go *around the flutter* to *spin the top* or *spin the windmill* if times are tough.

Then we have to deal with the insects and animals. We may have to *spin the flea, swat the flea, box the gnat, scatter the pack,* or *chase the rabbit.* If there are spiders we may have to *spin a web, fan the web,* or *top the web.*

Finally we're at the door, and it's time to *turn the key* in the *key line chain,* start a *chain reaction,* and *chain across.* Now *lock it* near the *hinge,* and step on in.

Now at the dance, we'll make a *transaction* to *transfer the column* before the *lines trade.* Then we'll *line up* and *unwrap the hourglass.*

If it gets too warm and we get *red hot,* we'll go outside to *bat the breeze* while we look up at the sky and *roll the star, flare the star,* or even *shoot the star.*

If we're not happy with our corner girl, we'll let the *couples trade,* and if we're still not satisfied we can *trade about* or *swap around* some more, or *trade and roll*. We'll be careful not to *roll around* and *roll away* until we *pass out*.

If we're still not ice cold it might be time to *lead out to the right, flip around* and *follow your neighbor* over to the *swing* and *slide*. Careful, don't *slip* while you're looking for the *cloverleaf. Zoom!* Once we get to the *yellow rock,* we'll *zigzag* right out to the *Ferris wheel,* where we'll find the *cycle and wheel.* We'll *walk and dodge,* make a *horseshoe turn, turn back* at the *crosswalk,* and then *scoot back* to the hall.

We'll be just in time to *cut the diamond* and *weave the ring*, and when the caller calls

"Muddle in the middle and fast back,"

we'll all be ready to *swing and mix* with our friends in this world of fun we call square dancing.

All the words in italics are square dance terms taken from the 1982 edition of The Square Dancing Encyclopedia *by Bill Burleson.*

A Grateful Square
by Olive "Skippy" Giese

I'm grateful for square dancing women
secure enough with their partners
who smile and share their handsome men
with bumbling women slow starters.

I'm grateful for men dancers
sensitive to women demure
who struggle with a new folk art
alone in a couples' culture.

I'm grateful for cuers and callers
who teach a wholesome pastime,
for the friendly helpful people
who lift spirits, help others shine.

I'm grateful for all these crusaders
who keep square and round dancing alive.
They're a group of world-over parleyers
making sure this dance idiom survives.

CHAPTER 10

Wheel and Deal
Square Dance Enterprises

Allemande left and a right to your girl
It's a wagon wheel, so make it whirl.
The hub flies out and the rim flies in,
It's a right and a left and you're gone again.
Now a right-hand whirl and another wheel,
The faster you go the better you feel.
Now the gents step out and the ladies sweep in,
It's a right and left and you're gone again.

Getting The News Out

You may be wondering how news about dances, and goings-on in the square dance world, finds its way all over the state.

In 1951, Howie Bernard, a Milwaukee area caller, began distributing *Fiddle and Squares*. Under the masthead were the words "Wisconsin's Own Square Dance Magazine." It was supported by advertising and subscriptions. For $1.50 dancers would receive ten issues per year (one each month except in July and August). The first issues were mimeographed on legal size paper, folded in half and stapled, and contained news about clubs, callers, and dances, as well as a calendar of where to dance. Within two years it was being printed in offset form and had an overall more professional look. Although it still featured Wisconsin happenings, it also featured an Illinois page and one for national news. By 1953 the subscription price of the 20-page magazines had gone up to $2.00.

When *Fiddle and Squares* ceased publication, Bob Dawson started a new magazine called *Here 'Tis*. This history of *Here 'Tis* was published in the Winter 1980-81 issue in recognition of the magazine's 25th anniversary.

Fiddle and Squares *magazine cover.*

In the winter of 1956-'57, *Here 'Tis*, a quarterly square dance magazine, came into being with Bob Dawson and Carl Larson as editors. The first issue had the following statement of purpose. "We, like many folks throughout our state, have talked about a method whereby the many dances held could become known to all. Wisconsin has some of the country's finest callers and many excellent halls. Through the cooperation of the Square Dance Association of Wisconsin (SDAW) and Milwaukee, Wolf River, Racine, and Madison Areas, and other caller's associations, we hope to be able to bring direct to you, the square dancer, a complete list of all Wisconsin square and round dance activities."

The state was divided into four areas and listings were made by counties within the areas. Each area was requested to have one or more correspondents to gather the listings and news items and send them in. Art and Mary

Weisensel from the South West Area were the first correspondents. Favorite calls of Mel Schoeckert and Art Weisensel (3/4 chain and Let 'er Go) were featured.

The response was tremendous. Our Spring issue saw the addition of a caller's roster, Club of the Month, a listing of round dances, miscellaneous articles by callers and leaders and an Idea Exchange, a section devoted to fun stunts. The annual subscription cost was $1.00. Lyle and Margaret Leatherman became North East Area correspondents. Ruth and Harry Johnson reported for the South East Area. Rosemarie and Elmer Elias wrote an article beckoning dancers to join the round dance movement.

By the time the third issue went to press there was a complete staff. Bob Dawson became editor and Carl Larson took over the North West Area correspondent job. Irv Igorski became Production Assistant. He and his wife Mary were still on the staff in 1981. Irv had many interesting stories to tell about the early days and some of the things that made it so interesting. Such as, the many trips around the bed-collating. Or the night the kids jumped on the bed and the time it took to make order out of the chaos. This was the year Milwaukee's "Fun Factory" Club Calhoun, was given a face-lift with caller Dale Wagner, and the dancers, uppermost in the plans. The first subscription dances were held in Kenosha, Racine, Whitewater, Madison, and Oshkosh.

Summer 1958 saw the first cooking page called "Recipe Roundup" and the Round of the Month, another feature in the Spring of 1959. This was also the summer of the first state convention in Appleton. Ed Dunn was General Chairman.

With the start of the third year the magazine was taken over by the MACC and Mel and Loretta Schoeckert were the new editors with Hug and Norma Hugdahl as assistants. By now the sewing, cooking, and round dance columns were regular features.

In 1961, Bill and Betty Kersey became editors with Jack and Lu Olsan as assistants. Kersey's recreation room became the home of the magazine for the next couple of years. It seems that fancy flourishes not taught at lessons were a problem even then, along with club members who wanted "stacked squares" and more calls.

Tony and Lu Berget became editors in 1963 with most of the same staff remaining. The Illinois news column was picking up steam. There were a lot of Illinois subscribers then. Gene Dreyfuss had a Saturday morning radio show featuring square dance callers and club news. The 5th State convention advertised a Challenge Level Dance with "no walk-thrus or sympathy."

1970 brought another change in editors with Gene and Vi Dreyfuss taking over the reigns. Their staff included people who had worked with the publication for many years. Names such as Elias, Ferderer, Hugdahl, Leatherman, and Ziemann. The subscription rate had gone up to $1.50 cents per year. The attractive covers were produced by Erv and Isabelle Jahn.

Elmer and Rosemarie Elias became editors in 1972 after

having served continuously in various staff capacities. One of their first official acts was to change the name of the publication to *Wisconsin Squares and Rounds*, so it would be more descriptive of the magazine content. The spring 1979 issue carried the following paragraph.

> "WE SURRENDER—After three or more years of trying to have square dancers use the name *Wisconsin Squares and Rounds* we still receive over half of our mail addressed to *Here 'Tis*. We are now waving the white flag of surrender and have once again become *Here 'Tis*.

Elmer and Rosemarie remained editors until 1979 when Bill and Colleen Wilton agreed to take over the publication.

Things have changed over the years, in the square dance movement, in the *Here 'Tis* staff and in the way the magazine is put together. No more bloody fingers from tying bundles of books; we now have a binder. No more walking around the bed to collate; we sit and the table goes around.

This little history can't begin to list all of the people (callers and dancers) who have donated many, many hours of their time to insure that Wisconsin square and round dancers are informed about where to go, what is new in dances, sewing, cooking, and sharing club activities.

As with most 25th anniversaries, there is always the anticipation of celebrating the 50th. If the past is any indication *Here 'Tis* will still be going strong when that time arrives.

* * *

A Letter to the Editor from Elmer Elias, published in the summer 1996 issue of *Here 'Tis*, shed a little further light on the publication's history. Elmer wrote "I thought you might be interested in the history of the magazine. It was started in '55 or '56 by Bob Dawson, a Milwaukee area caller. Many dancers had talked about a newsletter so when this one started Bob said "Here 'Tis" and that became the name of the magazine. I missed working on the first issue but started on the second issue and was active in all subsequent issues until after Wilton's took over. In fact, I helped on the magazine when Bill and Colleen lived in Waukesha and drove about 150 miles round trip to help them after they moved to the Montello area.

"When Bob Dawson moved to Florida, he sold the magazine to the Milwaukee Area Callers for $1.00, with the understanding that its publishing would continue. The MACC was not interested in becoming the *Here 'Tis* publisher so ten callers each contributed 10 cents to become the owners. As their interest waned their share of the magazine was purchased by the *Here 'Tis*, or they relinquished their claim to partial ownership.

"When the Wilton's expressed an interest in owning the magazine after Bill's retirement I was the only one left with an interest in *Here 'Tis*, and ownership was transferred to them."

* * *

Bill and his wife Colleen continued as editors of *Here 'Tis* until summer of 1996, when they turned over the reins to Dennis and Karlene Leatherman. Bernie and Carolyn Coulthurst took over from the Leathermans in 1998.

Wisconsin's official magazine for square and round dancers celebrated its 42nd anniversary in 1998 and has grown to 90 pages over the years. At $5.00 per subscription it has to be one of the best bargains in the square dance world.

Bill and Colleen Wilton got into square dancing in 1973, after taking lessons from Bert Rietz. They were members of Circle D for a short time, then joined the Dousman Derby Dancers where they were president for one year. They served as South East Area delegates for the club until they moved to Westfield in 1983, and joined the Westfield Jolly Squares.

The Wiltons were Chairmen of Social and Special Events for the National Convention held in Milwaukee in 1979 and in 1983 chaired the state convention in Whitewater. They were general chairman-elect when Wisconsin made a bid for the 1995 National in Houston. Wisconsin lost that bid to Salt Lake City, Utah. Bill and Colleen regularly attended the state SDAW meetings and when the "Where to Dance in Wisconsin" brochure was separated from the publicity chair duties they volunteered and have had the responsibility since the mid-1980s.

In 1989 Bill became a round dance cuer. Someone suggested at a meeting that it would be nice if the club had someone to teach rounds. Colleen said "We can teach you—we will teach you as much as we know." Colleen began teaching the group but when Bill told her she had no rhythm Colleen told him to do it himself. He's been cuing ever since. They have been members of ROUNDALAB and WRDLC for six or seven years.

Bill and Colleen Wilton

* * *

Bernie and Carolyn Coulthurst were "talked" into attending their first square dance in September of 1971 by friends, Gene and Berla Edwards. The dance was a beginner's "Round-Up" held by the Plover Circle Eights Square Dance Club. It took only one lesson to convince them that this was an activity they could both enjoy. They lined up a baby-sitter and attended lessons faithfully once a week. Their caller-teacher was Bryce Anunson. After graduation the Coulthursts became very active members of the Plover Circle Eights. Three years ago they took up round dancing.

Bernie and Carolyn served as vice president (1973) and president (1974) of the Plover Circle Eights. They were General Chairmen of the 1978 Wisconsin State Square and Round Dance Convention and Assistant Directors of Floor Hospitality for the 1979 National Convention in Milwaukee. Those early years set the pace for the Coulthursts and they have remained active in various aspects of the square dance activity. They served as president of the SDAW Central Area for over ten years and in 1989 were general chairmen for the bid to have another National Convention in Wisconsin. They were Chairmen of the Board of LEGACY International from 1995 to 1997.

Carolyn and Bernie Coulthurst

Writing and editing seems to come naturally for Bernie and Carolyn. They are editors of LEGACY's *Club Leadership Journal* (an international newsletter) and they write and edit the *Chit-Chat*, the SDAW Central Area newsletter.

In addition to their new responsibilities as editors of *Here 'Tis*, the Coulthursts manage computer services for the Wisconsin state conventions. In spite of their busy schedule they manage to dance as often as three nights a week.

>–·◆·–O–·◆·–·◄

Square Dance Fashions
by May Donna Gilmore
Fashion Show Chairman 1991

Our square dance dresses of today, like our dance, can trace their history back to the elegant ballrooms of France and the grand manors of England. In those countries the minuet, polka, waltz, and quadrille were danced. As people emigrated to America, they brought their customs, dress, and dance with them. Gowns were made of damask, taffeta, silk, or fine muslin. The fullness in the skirt was obtained by wearing a hoop skirt underneath. Coiffures were often high and possibly powdered. It was an era of stately music, stately dances, and stately dress.

We move forward a hundred years and the move to open the West is on. Days are long and hard with both men and woman settling the land, working in the fields and tending the livestock. There is not much time for gaiety, so every occasion is used for socializing. Barn-raisings, weddings, and holidays were prime examples when gatherings were held. Often people came from miles around to see their neighbors, catch up on the news, and dance the night away. These dances were held in kitchens, barns, out-of-doors, even in the saloons. Women's dresses were long; starched petticoats and floor-length pantaloons were worn underneath. The costuming allowed free and exuberant movements in the squares, circles, and couple dances.

We move forward to the 20th century, the 1920s in particular, and we find Henry Ford endorsing and sponsoring early American square dancing in Lovett Hall. Lovett Hall was complete with teakwood floors, crystal chandeliers, and formal straight chairs on either side of the ballroom. A live orchestra and a dancing master were on hand to teach and prompt the evening's dances, which consisted of waltzes, two-steps, early squares, and contras. Formal attire was mandatory with the ladies in long gowns and white gloves.

In the late 1930s Dr. Pappy Shaw and his young Cheyenne Mountain Dancers toured North America presenting cowboy dance exhibitions, dressed in colorful calico with simple blouses and long, full-flowing skirts.

Following World War II there was a resurgence in square dancing. In choosing their costumes ladies remembered the long dresses of the earlier years. At first these dresses were straight, and worn without a petticoat. It wasn't long before the length came up to just above the ankles and starched petticoats and pantalettes were added. Cotton was the fabric used which meant hours and hours of ironing, not only for the dresses but the petticoat as well.

By the early 1950s squaw dresses were "discovered." Some of the newer cottons could be washed, crushed together while wet, and pulled through something tubular like a stocking or tied at intervals. When dry, a three or four-tiered skirt would present a pleated look, much like the skirts worn by Indian women. Miles and miles of rick-rack were used as trim which made these dresses weigh eight or nine pounds. Square dance hemlines had gone up to ankle- or calf-length, and pantalettes to below-the-knee bloomers. By the late '50s some of the embossed cottons would be washed carefully and be presentable without ironing.

In the 1960s came the nylons; nylon net, Dacron, polyester, and novelty blends that did not need to be ironed. The drip-dry era was in full swing. So were the petticoats. Layers of nylon net were used for the petticoats which held the dresses out beautifully. The hemlines were rising and now we had fanci-pants with row after row of lace trickling down the leg.

Along with the '70s came the border prints. These prints can be used not only with the print providing the decoration around the bottom of the skirt, but working the design into the bodice and sleeves. Skirt lengths got shorter, petticoats also got fuller and with the hemline creeping up the thigh, the look began to be more like that of a tutu-skirted ballerina.

The 1980s gave us a return to a fancier dress. Most of the patterns feature rows of ruffles, lace, and ribbons with very full skirts and petticoats. The colors were bright and eye catching. Many women now wear color coordinated dresses, petticoats, and pettipants. The length of the dress and the pettipant is left to your good taste. They can range from knee-length to the "sissy britches" style.

Now as we enter the '90s, square dance clothes are no longer the authentic covered-wagon type. Men wear well-fitting western shirts, western pants or jeans, and boots or comfortable shoes. Women may be as individual as they like in their dress, letting their imaginations run free. Sleeves, necklines, skirts, trims, colors, combinations—there is no limit. Some of the choices that we have today include denim western dresses, prairie skirts, belts, accessories to change, and mix and match outfits. Dance shoes are available in many styles, heel heights, and colors. The choice is always yours. Good taste in underpinnings, in skirt lengths and necklines should always be considered. What looks well on the wearer and to the beholder are the criteria.

Down through the years and time to come we will see costume changes in the square dance movement, but the fun and satisfaction of dancing to music with friends will remain constant.

⪼∹◆⟩•O•⟨◆∹⪻

Where Do They Buy Those Fancy Outfits?
by Agnes Thurner

Western wear has been the standard square dance attire for men for many decades. Since this type of clothing was favored by ranchers and farmers, it was readily available by catalog and in retail stores. In the early 1900s, however, most ladies had to make their own costumes, or have them made to order by skilled seamstresses. The invention of the sewing machine made it easier for women to sew their own clothes and most department stores stocked fabrics and patterns.

During the increased square dance activity of the '40s and '50s

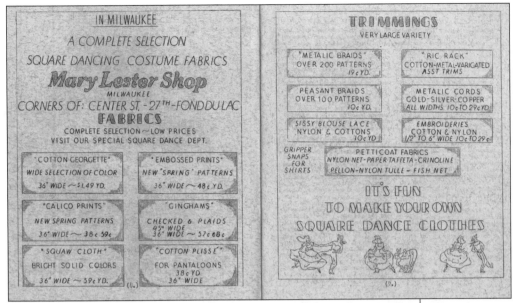

*Mary Lester
Ad — 1958.*

many stores began to carry ready-made square dance apparel for ladies as well as men. Square dance dresses and skirts could be purchased at Milwaukee dress shops such as The Grand and Rosenbergs. Sears and Penney's joined the competition and made square dance items available by catalog and in their retail stores. More women were joining the work force, so they had less time to spend making their own clothing. They appreciated the convenience of buying retail.

Entrepreneurs saw the business potential and soon square dance specialty shops began to appear on the scene, providing everything you could ask for in square dance attire. Skirts, blouses, dresses, crinolines, pettipants, shoes, belts, as well as men's clothing to coordinate with the lady's outfits. Convention committees began to choose specific colors for the annual event, and square dance shopkeepers would be the first to know, so they could order fashions in the color for the year.

Square dance callers liked the new fad of color-coordinated outfits for men and ladies. It made it easier for them to match up the right lady with the right gent when calling a square dance.

Wisconsin had its share of square dance related businesses. One of the earliest in the Milwaukee area was MIDWEST RADIO located on West North Avenue. Art Knoblach, a square dancer, started the business in the late 1940s. It was "the" place for callers to go for records, sound systems and microphones. In 1970, Art sold the record portion of the shop to Ralph and Faye Wheaton.

Ralph and Faye, who were also square dancers, opened MID-WEST RECORD AND ENGRAVING at 5428 West Hampton Avenue. Their ads announced that they had "everything for the caller and dancer." They stocked square and round dance records, square and round dance clothing, and provided a badge-making service. Square dance badges "made to order—any shape or size." In the late 1980s they phased out their square dance apparel line and eventually the name changed to Midwest Engraving. The Wheatons sold their business to Ken Parbs in 1997.

THE SQUARE DANCE SHOP in Milwaukee opened for business in 1958 and was in operation for almost 30 years. It was owned by Darryl and Emily Youngs, and located in their home at 125 North 70th Street. It was a favorite place to shop for square dance clothing and accessories. They carried many one-of-a-kind square dance dresses. The shop was closed after Emily's death in the late 1980s.

Leo and Pat Carroll opened DO-SI-DO ON TIME in 1984. The shop, located at 6026 West Greenfield in West Allis, combined a clock repair service with the square dance business. The Carrolls began square dancing with the Swinging Stars Square Dance Club in 1981 and opened DO-SI-DO ON TIME after the tool and die company Leroy worked for moved out-of-state. They closed the shop in mid-1991.

In summer of 1991 Elissa Pischke and Donna Luber teamed up to open E & D'S GRAND SQUARE in West Allis. Elissa and her husband Bob, were square dancers for about four years when he talked her into calling. About two years later she began cuing as well and continued for 15 years. Ray and Donna Luber were members of Elissa's 1988 square dance class and the two couples developed a good rapport.

Leo and Pat Carroll

Elissa's dream was to open a square dance shop. DO-SI-DO ON TIME had just closed when space became available in a small strip mall on 84th Street, south of Greenfield. Elissa and Donna decided

The Square Dance Shop Ad.

Midwest Record and Engraving Ad.

the time was right. The first two years were a struggle. There were fewer dancers in the area and not enough sales to support the high rent at the mall. They moved the shop to the corner of 81st and National where they continued to struggle. Although they were able to meet expenses, they were never able to pay themselves. The shop closed in 1996 after five years of operation. In 1998 Elissa Pischke announced her retirement from calling and cuing.

Lyle and Faye Long purchased the PALOMINO SQUARE DANCE SERVICE in 1989. It was chiefly a mail-order business operated from their home in Waukesha. Their inventory included over 30,000 records for squares, rounds, and clogging. They operated the business for almost four years, selling it in 1991 when the

Record jackets.

stress of their busy schedule began to take its toll.

Lyle and Faye were high school sweethearts and were married in 1957. They had never danced a step before taking beginners square dance lessons in 1980. The next fall they drove 140 miles round trip to take beginners round dance lessons. Graduation came in the spring of 1982 and they cued their first dance on the following New Year's Eve. Beginners lessons were needed in their area and the next fall the Longs taught their first class. The following year they took and gave intermediate lessons. Two clubs, the Merry Go Rounders, one for Phase II and one at Phase III and IV, were born.

Lyle cued regularly for six square dance clubs and guest cued for others. A schedule with only one free night a week led to semi-retirement.

Lyle and Faye served as presidents of the Wisconsin Round Dance Leaders' Council, in which they were active since 1983. They were members of ROUNDALAB, and served as chairpersons of Wisconsin's annual Accent on Rounds.

During the summer, they enjoyed extended motorcycle trips across the country to attend cuers' colleges, seminars, and square dance weekends. They also spent two weekends a year on staff at Fease's Shady Rest Lodge in Rhinelander, Wisconsin.

Lyle believed that in order to have an active round dance club, one needed to be active at square dances and help to promote square dancing. He believed square dancing was the lifeblood of round dancing, and round dancing was equally important to square dancing. The Longs gave up cuing in 1995, for health reasons.

PAULY'S SALES, Wausau, was owned by Pauline Holup and her caller husband Bob. The shop specialized in badges of all kinds—fun badges, Knothead badges, Aurora Borealis Rhinestone Badges, and an engraving service.

Some other Wisconsin square dance shops: PETTI-PANTS UNLIMITED, Windsor, moved out of state; H & H PETTICOAT JUNCTION in Kenosha, DIXIE STYLE SQUARE DANCE SHOP in Granton, and W & F SQUARE DANCE SHOP in Sheboygan are closed.

Bernice and Jim Bolek operated THE COAT TREE in Oshkosh, for many years. The shop specialty, coats designed to fit over voluminous square dance skirts, were usually made to measure. When Bernice passed away on April 12, 1997, Jim took over running the shop. He still brings his goods to the state convention every year.

CHAR'S SQUARE DANCE SHOP in Janesville, opened in March 1995 and is still operating in the state. Charlotte Wegart bought out the Dixie Style Square Dance Shop in Granton and the square dance apparel from Betty's Square Dance Shop in Illinois, to start her business. Char runs the shop, and her husband John, and son Jim, help out when they can. Floyd and Jean Schultz, current treasurers of the SDAW, also enjoy helping with the business and often travel with the Wegart's when they take their merchandise to clubs and conventions. Like most square dance business owners the Wegart's are ready and willing to "take their show on the road." They have a trailer that is used to travel to conventions and special square dance events, at the request of sponsoring clubs or organizations. The store handles new and resale goods, special order items, and alterations.

With the decline in the number of square dancers in Wisconsin there has been a move toward relaxing the square dance dress code. Casual dress is considered acceptable in most restaurants and even at church. Some advocates of casual attire believe allowing women to dance in blue jeans, slacks, or shorts, will attract more new dancers to our classes. Others believe strongly that we should uphold the current standard of dress that is a hallmark of the square dance activity. Proper attire for women is a full circle square dance dress or skirt and peasant-type blouse. The longer prairie skirts are also appropriate. Men should wear jeans or western cut trousers, and long-sleeved western style shirts. Proper square dance attire is required at state and national conventions.

>–⊹–⊙–⟨⊹⊢⟨

In Days Gone By
by Dolores Rabe, Oconomowoc 1985

Oh, the world it is a-changing,
Faster than you or I,
And we wish for things as they used to be
And we long for days gone by.

In days gone by things were simple
And seemed so right and good.
The world wasn't then so upside down
And we did the things we should.

Doesn't everyone want a way of escape
Out of their troubles and cares?
Wouldn't we like to go Over the Rainbow,
Or climb a magic stairs?

We don't need to go to a Fantasy Isle,
Or the Love Boat, or place far away,
We just need to go to Square Dance Land
And dance our troubles away.

In Square Dance Land, in Square Dance Land,
We can smile and we can swing;
We can dress in buttons and bows
Even though it's not the thing.

Once again we can be ladies and gents;
(In the world they can't tell them apart.)
We can have all the old sentiments
And we don't mind sharing our heart.

In Square Dance Land time is standing still
While the hours happily fly.
We can steal away to Square Dance Land
And live as in days gone by.

CHAPTER 11

Cross-Trail Thru
Promoting the Fun

Heads go forward and back that way,
While two and four do a half sashay.
One and three you cross-trail thru,
Go up the outside and go around two,
Catch right on, that's what you do
Go forward eight and back with you,
Go forward again and pass on thru,
Arch in the middle, the ends turn in,
Criss-cross thru and don't just stand,
Pass your partner, left allemande
Partner right, go right and left grand.

Havey-Sauer Tours
Information provided by Don Sauer

Havey-Sauer Tours came about almost by accident. Wayne and Evelyn Havey are members of Kettle Squares who dance in Plymouth on the 2nd and 4th Saturday of the month; Don and Alice Sauer belong to Country Promenaders who dance in Saukville on the 1st, 3rd, and 5th Saturdays. Members of the two clubs regularly attended the other's dances and sometimes planned special activities together.

Someone suggested that a bus trip might be a fun thing to do so Wayne and Evelyn made arrangements for the group to take a four-day bus trip to Opryland. The trip was so well accepted by the square dancers that the Havey's were persuaded to undertake a bus trip to the National Convention. This trip was also successful and they were encouraged to do it again the next year. About that time, the Havey's asked Don and Alice to join them in setting up the next tour to the National Convention.

The two couples have thus far planned 15 tours to National Conventions, and four trips to Canadian Conventions. They have gone on a Caribbean Cruise and a 16-day trip to Germany, Austria, and Switzerland.

Havey-Sauer Tour poster.

Celebrate Statehood Day
with a Havey-Sauer Tour
May 29-30, 1998

Square dancers are invited to join in a weekend celebration in Wisconsin's capitol city of Madison. The State Sesquicentennial Committee has planned some exciting festivities for the occasion. This tour includes many of the weekend highlights:

An old-time barn dance on the streets of Madison... An open Square Dance *(indoors-sponsored by the Southwest Area SDAW)...* **A tour of the Capitol Building** *(opt.)...* **A Civil War Reenactment... A Statehood Day Parade...**

Depart Friday morning from several southeast area pick-up points, arriving in Madison in time for the roll call of counties. After checking into the room reserved for you at the Park Hotel you may want to lunch at one or more Taste of Wisconsin Food Stands, or browse the many art and craft booths on the square. Everything is within walking distance. Before returning home on Saturday you will have dinner *(included)* at Quivey's Grove, a restored Italianate Fieldstone mansion just south of Madison. Total cost of the tour is $120.00. Price includes all transportation, hotel lodging on the square, full breakfast, and one dinner.

Watch for our flyers, or contact Don (414-284-4330), or Aggi (414-241-4152) for more information. Make checks payable to Havey-Sauer Tours. Send to: Don Sauer, 601 N. Holden St., Port Washington, WI 53074-1512, or Aggi Thurner, 1711 W. Fiesta Lane, Mequon, WI 53092-5731

The Caribbean Cruise was a little disappointing because there wasn't as much time for square dancing as they expected. The cruise lines pretty much planned the activities. They did have a square dance one evening. The cruise lines always have an amateur talent night and during this cruise there were only two talents in addition to square dancing. Those two were pretty bad and when the square dancers came on they stole the show.

For the European trip they decided to avoid the usual tourist places and stayed in small pensions and gasthaus'. They danced with German square dancers in Darmstadt and Munich. The Germans were such good dancers—and they partied between each tip. "Of course we partied with them," said Don. "It was a great experience and we came away with many good memories."

On May 29, 1998, the Haveys and Sauers took a group of 38 square dancers from the Port Washington, Milwaukee area to celebrate Statehood Day in Madison. Square dancing on the Capitol Square was one of the highlights of the two-day trip.

The Havey's now spend their winters in Florida and with Wayne's health deteriorating, they no longer participate much in the actual planning. Alice always does a lot of research before a trip so she can recount the history and points of interest along the way and Don now does most of the legwork arranging for sleeping accommodations and meals. Both the Haveys and the Sauers are outgoing people and their personalities make them natural tour guides. They get a lot of repeat people on their trips because the tours are well planned and organized. The 1998 trip to the National Convention is sold out and they have a waiting list.

When asked how long they would continue planning the tours, Don said "We don't know. We just take it year by year."

⪼⫯⟡⫯⪻

What Kind of People Are Square Dancers?
by Judy Barisonzi

We're frequently asked, "What kind of people take up square dancing?" There are as many ways to answer this question as there are square dancers. Some of us are outgoing; some of us are shy—some of us have families; some of us are single. We're farmers, teachers, physicists, insurance salesmen—any profession you could name.

But after eight years of square dancing, I've concluded that there is one quality many square dancers have in common. We're creative. We tend to be people who enjoy not only dancing, but also many other forms of creative activity. We like to express our artistic sense in many ways, not only on the dance floor.

Sometimes I'm amazed at the different things square dancers create in their spare moments, in between dancing sometimes five or six nights a week and maybe having a job too.

For instance, let me tell you about Art and Ethel Pade who recently retired from dancing with the Lakeside Twirlers in Fond du Lac. Art is a retired farmer but I don't know when he ever found time to farm. He keeps busy helping serve meals at his apartment complex and tending the garden—he's especially proud of his beautiful moonflowers. But the rest of the time he paints, draws, and makes things. Stained glass is Art's specialty; he makes suncatchers in all different shapes but my favorite is his square dance couple suncatcher. He makes stained glass lampshades but he will make lampshades out of anything, even glass beads from Lite-Brite sets. He designs his own greeting cards, writes the verses and

Oil by Art Pade.

Art Pade displays his stained glass art.

sends them to friends and family. The walls of his apartment are so covered with his lovely oil paintings that he worries about where he can possibly put another one. And what does Ethel do while Art is busy doing, well, art? She crochets slippers and wall hangings and rugs, and she's working on writing the autobiography of their life and travels based on the journal she's kept for 26 years. There's a busy retired couple! But they're not unique among square dancers.

If you ever travel up north, you'll have the opportunity to observe the handiwork of another square dance couple, Lucille Kallio-Schenzel and her husband Vern Schenzel. Dance with the Hodag Twirlers in Rhinelander and you'll admire the beautiful club banner crafted by Lucille. The figures are made of thousands of sequins, each one individually attached. Or maybe someone will be do-si-doing in Lucille's homemade Hodag costume. Perhaps on your visit, you'll have time to go to a holiday parade in the north-woods area, and there you'll be sure to see Vern's famous float—a monumental purple martin house that is a model of the U.S. Capitol. It took Vern seven years to complete this project. He loves to display the 14-foot-long birdhouse and has pulled it on a trailer behind his truck as far as Appleton. But if you want something smaller, he can make you a birdhouse shaped like a Soo Line caboose for your local swallows.

This is just a sample of the creative talents of Wisconsin's square dancers. In my years of dancing, I've exclaimed over many hand-embroidered square dance dresses with intricate designs. I've admired men's handcrafted belt buckles and tie clasps. I've eaten delicious cakes and cookies and enjoyed beautiful flower arrangements decorating refreshment tables. I've visited square dancers' gardens, listened to them tell me about their paintings and hand-made quilts and have been given presents of delicate objects carved from wood and nutshells. It's clear to me that Wisconsin square dancers are active, creative people who enjoy life to the fullest. They're great people to be with.

Thirty-Eight Years Ago
by Don Niva, Madison, Wisconsin

Thirty-eight years ago I learned to square dance. I started learning to call shortly after lessons were over. The amazing part of this occurrence was that I had to be practically dragged to my first lesson! My cousin and her husband pleaded, threatened, and cajoled me to "try it at least once." My wife was rarin' to go and added a few choice bits of advice.

I went with a great deal of reluctance, fearing the worst. I found to my amazement that the music was terrific and you didn't have to know how to waltz, two-step or line dance. Just shuffle your feet to the music and know left from right. (After two years in the army, what could be simpler?) Even though, at times, the moves didn't work out, it was still fun and laughter.

We were fortunate in having a caller/instructor who was patient, kind, and had a sense of humor when confronted by a student suffering with extreme enthusiasm and directional stupidity. Let me explain that in those days, circa 1956-'57, ten lessons covered the list of commonly used basics (Square Thru was considered quite advanced).

My wife and I, along with some other beginner couples, took some additional lessons considered more "advanced", in the callers basement. In the course of these lessons, I was invited to take a shot at calling. Thinking back, probably the others present thought that anything that got "Mr. Whoops I'm going the wrong way" off the floor was worth the effort. To everyone's surprise, especially my own, I did the singing call "Hurry, Hurry Home" on a Windsor record, almost on key,

Joan and Don Niva

in rhythm, and ended when the record did, (thanks to singing lessons in the church choir and guitar lessons).

I was hooked! I couldn't resist going to any square dance within reasonable driving distance. I bought equipment and records. I haunted my favorite callers' dances (all the local callers). I'd walk into the hall and the caller would say, "Are you here again?"

Finally, I got the opportunity to attend a caller's class sponsored and put on by the local callers' association. I found out what a person had to learn and how much practice was necessary to be able to call a passable square dance.

I'd like to give special mention to the late great Ed Gilmore for his callers' classes and also Mr. Jerry Helt for the extra super help he gave me in his callers' workshop. It's fortunate that I started out when young and optimistic. I feel sorry for the new guy just getting started. After 38 years, I'm still learning something new.

A special mention for my wife, general manager, keeper of calling dates, connoisseur of fine music, and the one who tells me where to go and when. Joan, "that music is not your style" Niva is the greatest!

Previously published in American Square Dance, *August 1995*

>─┤◆>─◆─O─◆<─┤─<

Badges, Rings, and Thieves
by Agnes Thurner

Banner Stealing, Knothead Trips, Fun Badges, Club of the Month, and the Friendship Ring are a few of the ways clubs encourage their dancers to visit other square dance groups. New dancers are especially encouraged to dance to other callers. It strengthens their dance skills and makes them smoother and more versatile dancers. Various badges can be earned by participating in these visitation programs, and square dance clubs benefit by the extra attendance at their dances.

Banner stealing was designed to promote cooperation between area clubs. A banner is made of any pliable material, in any shape or color, not to exceed four feet. Each participating club starts out with no more than ten banners and each banner must have the official seal (provided by the area) on the facing side.

Originally, a visiting club had to register at a dance with at least one square of dancers (eight people) to take a banner from the host club. (This requirement was later changed to six people when club memberships declined). If the host club already has a club banner belonging to the visitors, the club must retrieve it before they can take the host club's banner. They need six dancers to retrieve their own banner and another six to steal one from the host. Records must be kept by the host club of who has what banners and the visiting club records the names of the dancers who did the stealing. Dancers are awarded a Master Thief badge when they record a certain number of steals, and dangles are added to the badge for additional steals.

Clubs are given a three month time limit in which to retrieve their banners. If a banner hasn't been retrieved by that time, a written notice is given to the Secretary of the area and the reported club is given one more month to retrieve the banner. If a proper report is made and the banner still not retrieved, the club holding the banner may attend the negligent club's dance with six members, return the banner and their dancers get free admission.

Many clubs choose not to participate in the Banner program. If the club has a small membership, or dances only at Plus level, the Banner program can prove detrimental rather than beneficial. For that reason, the South East Area—(SDAW–SEA) looked for other options to compensate those clubs.

A Club of the Month program was started in about 1965, which was meant to honor a different club each month as well as to help their attendance. The club had to request Club of the Month status and designate one of their dances as a Club of the Month dance. Member clubs were urged to send their members to attend the Club of the Month dance. Banner stealing was not allowed on that date but some clubs gave their members banner stealing points for attending.

Vic Doers designed the Club of the Month traveling banner which included names of all the area clubs and space to indicate each club's attendance. The program continued until about 1975. It was restarted again in 1989 with Vic Doers once again designing the banner. There was marked lack of participation by clubs requesting Club of the Month designation and by dancers attending. Clubs honored reported either no change or poor dance attendance and the program was eventually dropped. Similar programs have been reported in other areas with more success.

A Friendship Ring program was conceived by the SEA in 1995 to enhance visitation among all clubs in the area, including non-banner stealing clubs. To qualify, a participant must dance at least once at each member club, attend at least one SEA sponsored dance and one SDAW Jamboree. To begin, dancers are given a card listing the member clubs, SEA dances, and Jamborees. A club or area officer must date and sign the card for each dance attended. When the card is half filled the dancer may purchase a Friendship Ring dangle; at three-fourths filled, a simulated ruby can be added to the center; and, when it is completely filled, the dancer may exchange it for one with a diamond zirconia in the center. The completed dangle is paid for by the SEA and is usually presented at an area dance or function. To date, 11 dancers in the South East Area have achieved completed status and ten more are at the three-fourths mark.

Knothead badges are earned when a dancer travels at least 100 miles one way to attend a dance. Knothead badges are made in the shape of the state. Clubs often plan Knothead bus trips for their members to attend special dances in other parts of the state. If the trip is not a full 100 miles away the driver will often double back or take detours to gain enough mileage to qualify.

On a Mystery trip, the destination is kept secret and must be at least 50 miles away. The passengers have fun trying to guess where the bus is taking them. The driver travels circuitous routes designed to confuse the dancers as to the location of the dance. A different badge can be earned for Mystery trips.

There are almost as many fun badges as there are dances. The Boot Snatcher is earned when dancers remove a caller's boots while he is calling and the Mummy badge for wrapping the caller in toilet paper while he's calling a tip. Wear an Idiot badge and everyone will know that you woke up a caller after midnight to call

Fun Badges and Kissin Kuzzin's Membership Card.

one or more tips. This has been done in caller's homes and at times in motel rooms during conventions. The Cuckoo badge is the caller's revenge for the Idiot party. He contacts four or more couples after midnight, has them meet, and makes them dance a couple of tips.

The Torture badge is for enduring a dance tip by an amateur or beginning caller, and the Purple Heart is given for dancing with three callers in a square.

You can get a Duck badge for dancing in a swimming pool, lake, river, etc. The deeper the water, the harder it is to move around and the more fun you will have. The "basic" call for this one is "Splash your right-hand lady." Get a Grasshopper badge for dancing in the grass and a Barefoot badge for—"what else"—dancing barefoot. For the Jailbird badge, you must dance in jail behind closed doors. It's usually no trouble at all to get locked up but it takes a friendly jailer to "unlock the door". Earn your "Church Mouse" pin for dancing in a church, get a Tombstone badge for dancing in a cemetery, a Crackpot pin when you dance in a bathroom, or a Cloudhopper for dancing at a high altitude. Forget your club badge and have to pay a fine to the club?—you've earned a Dog House badge. You can even earn one called "I Danced with the Devil" if you dance with someone wearing a Devil's costume at a Halloween party. Get the Barn Stomper when you dance in a barn, and the Bedbug when you dance in a motel or bedroom (on the bed).

Some badges can only be attained through initiation, such as the Turtle or Donkey badge (ask a pin wearer about these). For the Kissin' Kuzzin' you must be initiated by a certified KK (or your caller or club president might initiate all members at a special dance or party night). The Kangaroo is another secret club that only people with pins know about.

There are Monkey badges, Raft Rocker's, Royal Order of Pickle Eaters, Seagoing Squares, Out-House Squares, Traffic Stoppers, Trestle Trotters, Slip and Shirt Snatchers, Stable Stompers (watch your step), Topless pins (dance with three bald-headed men) and many, many more.

Clubs often hold badge nights where dancers are given an opportunity to earn particular badges, such as the Lemon, where participants dance with slices of lemon in their mouths. It's a chance to earn a badge and have some fun with the caller.

There are various ways to display a pin collection. Some people make a "Badge Vest"; some pin them onto shoulder sashes, like the Scouts, and others may mount them on exhibit boards. To give dancers a chance to show off their, sometimes immense, pin collections, clubs periodically sponsor badge dances. There may even be a badge for the person with the most badges.

The Promotion Committee

In the late 1980s, the South East Area came up with the idea of a promotion committee composed of callers and dancers to help area clubs promote their lesson programs. The MACC and the SEA each donated $500 to give the committee some seed money to work with. Dwayne Olson was the chairman and he recruited dancers and callers to serve on the committee. The intent was, not to do things for the clubs but, to give them the tools they needed to do it themselves. The group held brainstorming sessions to generate promotion ideas. Some things sponsored by the group, as a result of these meetings, included seminars for club officers and interested callers and dancers. Information on proper public relations, how to write press releases, how to create flyers, etc., was distributed. The committee also prepared business-size handout cards with captions such as "Looking for a great time—Try Square Dancing" or "Wanted—Fun-loving People Interested in Learning How to Square Dance." Space was provided at the bottom of each card for clubs to add a name and contact phone number. The cards were distributed free to area clubs to hand out at exhibitions and open dances.

In 1996, The Lightning Trio (Jimmie Burss, Randy Tans, and Mike Krautkramer) arranged for a square dance booth, several demonstrations, and an open dance at the Wisconsin State Fair. They held fund-raising dances to raise the money for the booth and petitioned dancers and callers statewide to help them out with demonstrations, to man the booth and, of course, to attend the open dance. Handout materials were designed with contact numbers for clubs throughout Wisconsin. Radio commercials were prepared to air the week prior to the Fair. The Trio hoped this would become an annual state sponsored event. Although there wasn't a big difference in lesson attendance that fall, square dancing did gain needed visibility.

In 1997, Dwayne Olson resigned from the Promotion Committee and Greg and Joan Polly became chairmen. About the same time The Lightning Trio asked the SEA to take over the State Fair Booth. It was suggested that it would be a good annual project for the Promotion Committee. Working with the Trio, the committee arranged fund-raising dances, took up collections and urged Wisconsin clubs to make donations or hold their own special fund-raisers earmarked specifically for the State Fair.

The Pollys also had square dance T-Shirts and sweatshirts designed and sold the shirts throughout the state and by mail order. The income from the shirts helped to boost the general Promotion Committee treasury. Enough income was generated to pay for radio advertising in Racine, Hartford, West Bend, La Crosse, and on WTMJ, whose signal reaches most of Wisconsin. There was enough in the general treasury to rent billboards for the Milwaukee area. Three boards were rented for a two-month period beginning in August, with locations changing the second month. The billboards proved to be a good investment, several of them were left up for over six months and one in the downtown area was still in place in June of 1998.

The committee is continuing the State Fair Promotion in 1998 and is currently recruiting dancers and callers to help at the fair and soliciting funds for the advertising campaign. They have added static cling and bumper stickers to their product line and hope to raise enough money to do more radio advertising in other parts of the state. Billboard advertising using a different slogan from last year is being considered.

The success of the promotion venture is difficult to measure at this point, but the committee feels strongly that repetition of the square dance message and repeated visibility are the key to attracting new people to our lesson programs. However, Promotion Committee activities are intended to supplement, not replace, what square dance clubs normally do to promote their lessons. If the club does exhibitions, appears in parades, adver-

Joan and Greg Polly

tises in local papers, etc., they should continue to do so. The one-on-one approach is still one of the best ways to get students. If each club member were to bring one new person to lessons, the club would prosper and the entire square dance industry would benefit.

Greg and Joan Polly started square dance lessons during 1960-'61 and joined the Acey Deucy Club after graduating. Jim and Pat Collins were the club callers. They danced through 1964 and then left the activity for awhile. They came back to square dancing in the 1980s, taking lessons with Jim Noonan, and graduating in 1981. In 1983 they became SEA delegates for R Squares and served as SEA President for two years. They were president of R Squares three different times, for two-year terms, and just completed a two-year term as treasurer for the Suburban 8's Square Dance Club.

Greg and Joan were Special Events Chairmen for the 1986 and 1991 Wisconsin Square and Round Dance Convention, and in '93 were Ass't. General Chairmen-Facilities for the annual event. The Pollys served as Vice President of the SDAW for two years and on the SDAW Board where they helped on the budget committee. They became LEGACY members in '89 at the LEGACY convention held in Reno, Nevada.

Flail Tail
by Don Niva

(A new poetic dance movement)

You gotta do the Flail Tail,
You gotta do it right.
You shuffle to the left,
Put your hand up to the right.

You turn a quarter right
And touch with the left,
You move around one quarter,
Get the feelin' get heft.

The lady walks under,
The man turns around.
When the movement's done proper,
You'll be close to southern bound.

Wiggle just a little
And get up on your toe,
The end is coming up
And you settle down low.

The man slides under
His own right arm,
The lady shuffles left
So there isn't any harm.

By then you see your corner
And you're flying off the floor.
Put your partner on the right
And swagger out the door!

CHAPTER 12

Crossfire
Squaring Off

Heads to the right and circle to a line
Centers trade you're doing fine.
The ends fold in then turn right back,
Go straight ahead on the same old track.
Stop right there!—you can't do thet,
Everybody home and square your set.

Introduction to Square Dancing
The One-Night Stand
by Don Niva

Every so often, I am hired to call a one-night stand. I have always regarded this as a golden opportunity to recruit new members for a beginners class. As a result of this feeling, I find this dance causes two opposite and conflicting emotions, sometimes three.

First of all, stress! What if the dance (the basics) doesn't click with this group? Secondly, a glow of satisfaction when the material works. Third, either sadness or elation, depending on how well the people responded.

Another part of my problem is what I regard as the amazing tendency for people to rehire me time and time again to call these one-nighters. This makes me worry about repeating a successful dance. Finally, after a fabulously successful dance, I decided to analyze my successful ones as well as my failures and pass it along for what it's worth.

Participation: one of the most important parts of a successful dance. It helps to discuss this aspect of the dance with the sponsor or group that is putting on the dance. Be sure they know how important it is to have everyone participate from the beginning of the dance.

I remember and will NEVER, and I mean NEVER, forget two one-nighters that were completely unmitigated disasters. The first one was in a public high school in a large city. I could not get a large circle formed to start the dance because disruptive students kept wandering through the forming circles, and refused to join in or leave. When the school principal asked me if I could "control those people," I smiled sadly, said "No," and I packed up and left.

The next group was at a technical school. The people refused to get up and participate. Joking, cajoling, and darned near pleading, had no effect. They were not going to participate. I ended up giving them a lecture on the history of square dancing, playing records to show the music used, and closed with some square dance verses used in old time squares. To my chagrin the students applauded. Talk about expectations.

I remember these two dances because I regard them as spectacular failures. Then there were all the good ones. People formed a large circle as requested, responded enthusiastically to the music, chuckled and smiled at my self-depreciating remarks, danced and clapped noisily at the end of each dance.

These groups were indescribably uplifting. Any time a caller can watch inexperienced dancers laugh and smile while finding they can square dance is an incredibly rewarding experience.

I find that simplicity is the hardest thing for a caller to keep in mind and use. Repetition of simple basics in various formats, with a variety of lively music makes for a successful evening. Keep teaching to a bare minimum.

Following is a list of basics I used for a 1-2 hour, one-night stand. (An asterisk next to the basic indicates I teach it while the people are standing, others are taught while dancing the movement.)

1. Circle left and right.
2. Promenade single file, by twos, fours, and eight.
3. *Squared set, home position, number, sides, heads.
4. Circle four, right, left.
5. Right/left hand stars.
6. Allemande left.
7. *Swing, elbow or dance position.
8. Do-Si-Do.
9. *Grand right and left.
10. *Roll away half sashay.

In addition I use two or three simple line dances, including the "Chicken" if there are children present. (It's surprising how many adults join in.) I also use two very simple circle mixers, "Jiffy Mixer" and "Bingo Waltz." I try to close with the Virginia Reel.

The most gratifying experience happens when I finish the program and the people ask for "Just one more." I am always overjoyed to comply.

Previously published in American Square Dance, *August 1998*

The Community Dance Program
A Personal Perspective,
by Dennis Leatherman

At the time I retired from the U.S. Air Force in 1989, I had not called a square dance of any kind in over five years. After I returned to the Fox Valley in Wisconsin, Mom (Margaret Leatherman) convinced me to start up again; so I taught a class, married one of my students (Karlene), got involved with the Wisconsin Square and Round Dance Conventions, started calling and teaching weekly for the Waupaca Squares, and life was good.

In 1991, Karlene and I opened a new type of square dance program at Dot & John's Bar in Menasha. We called it simply, the Thursday Night Hoedowns, a weekly one-night fun dance for whomever might show up. We advertised in the area "Buyers Guides" and soon had square dancers from Waupaca, Wrightstown, Fremont, and Appleton, as well as non-dancers from everywhere and we all had a wonderful time. We danced whatever fit that evening's crowd, sometimes squares, sometimes reels, sometimes mixers, sometimes line dances, most of the time a little bit of everything.

We'd been at it for a couple of months, bragging wherever we went, when a fellow caller mentioned that it sounded as if we were doing the CALLERLAB Community Dance Program. I didn't have a clue as to what he was talking about since I had not yet fully returned to CALLERLAB's fold nor kept up with their literature. A little research soon proved that caller absolutely correct and opened my eyes to the wonderful world of the CDP.

In 1989, after years of discussion, planning, editing, trial and error, and worrying, CALLERLAB's Community Dance Program had been born. In the preface to the 44-page CALLERLAB Handbook entitled the "Community Dance Program," Ken Kernan, then Chairman of the CALLERLAB CDP Committee described the program as "an easy access, limited basics program that demands little commitment on the part of the dancers but, at the same time, provides an almost unlimited scope of variety, friendship, and fun". This was almost exactly what we had discovered; however, we also addressed the partnerless condition of so many of today's adults.

We wholeheartedly embraced the CDP and became well-known throughout the state and across the nation as successful implementers. We have been asked to share our experiences in the *Club Leadership Journal,* in *Here 'Tis,* at a LEGACY Convention, at a CALLERLAB Convention, during several WSDLCC Worksprees, several ECCO Mini-LEGACY Seminars, and at many Wisconsin State Square and Round Dance Conventions.

The thrust of that original program was to use six two-hour lessons to teach the following 24 easy square dance basics:

1. Circle Left and Right.
2. Forward and Back.
3. Do-Si-Do.
4. Swing.
5. Couple Promenade.
6. Single File Promenade.
7. Allemande Left Right.
8. Arm Turns, Left Right.
9. Right and Left Grand.
10. Weave the Ring.
11. Star Right/Left.
12. Star Promenade.
13. Pass Thru.

14. Split the Couple/Ring.

15. Rollaway with a Half Sashay.

16. U Turn Back.

17. Separate.

18. Courtesy Turn.

19. Ladies Chain, Two/Four.

20. Lead Right.

21. Right and Left Thru.

22. Circle to a Line.

23. Bend the Line.

24. Grand Square.

Those basics were then to be used in any, or all, of the following types of Pattern Dances: Squares, Quadrilles, Contras, Reels, Circle Mixers, Couple Dances, Sicilian Circles, Trios, Mescolanzas, and Solo Dances.

This program is nothing new. It is square dancing as it was about 50 years ago, when I started learning to dance. During the late '40s, my mom and dad, Margaret and Lyle Leatherman, were hired to teach square dancing in the Neenah Summer Recreation Program. Once a week, we'd set up Dad's equipment in that old green pavilion in Riverside Park and we'd start a dance. Most of the boys and girls, like me, came every week but some came only when they felt like it or their folks forced them. I don't rightly remember too many adults being there and I can remember Mom and Grandma grumbling about having to baby-sit other people's kids.

Dad never let the turnout phase him; he'd just get us all into circles, put on some lively music, and off we'd go dancing to his prompting. It never felt like he was directing us or ordering us, or scolding us; it was more like he was having a good time singing and we could follow his advice and have a good time dancing.

We learned how to do the Danish Schottische and we knocked the cobwebs off of the ceiling when he taught us the Teton Mountain Stomp. We learned to do the "Cotton Eyed Joe" and the "Jessie Polka," then used that same Jessie step as we learned the "Jessie Polka" Square. We did the Virginia Reel and lots of its variations. Sometimes, if we had the right number of people we even managed to get into squares. We learned how to dance some Sicilian Circle dances. We went "Marching to Pretoria" and glided along to the "Isle of Capri". Dad had us going "Around That Couple," to "Take a Little Peek," and we could make circles and stars. We learned how to swing our "Red River Gal", "Pull That Other Couple Down", "Dip and Dive", "Duck For The Oyster", and "Dig For The Clam". We could "rip and snort" and dance a "grapevine twist".

We learned a lot of the same square dances that he was teaching in his adult programs (and sometimes we learned them first). Dances like "Hot Time in the Old Town Tonight", "Swanee River," and one of my personal favorites "Hurry, Hurry, Hurry". We laughed with "Solomon Levi" and "Margie". We loved "Oh, Johnny" and "Just Because". When children came who hadn't been there for a while (or never) everyone helped everybody else and we all laughed at ourselves when we made mistakes.

Sometimes Mom would take me along to dance with her at one of their adult dances and I could dance everything they could, because what we kids were being taught was what the adults were being taught. We kids got ten weeks of lessons in the summer and the old folks got ten weeks of lessons in the fall. I guess I must have danced in that program until about fifth grade when we moved to Oshkosh and my two little brothers needed a baby-sitter.

While I attended school in Oshkosh, my teacher approached Dad to do some square dancing for the kids in my class. Dad just couldn't take off of work to do so but loaned me some of his equipment and gave me a few records (still in use today) so I could teach them. I know we danced the "Jessie Polka" and we did "Hurry, Hurry, Hurry". I didn't know it then but I had become a CDP caller just like my dad.

Throughout all of the intervening years, I never lost Dad's sense of "keeping everybody dancing". When I discovered the CDP, I felt like I'd come home. I later discovered that Dad was one of the CDP committee members who helped shape the program. No wonder it was so easy for me to make the minor adjustments needed to turn our Thursday Night Hoedowns into a full-fledged CDP program. To this day, I still use almost everyone of Dad's dances and a lot of his old records.

In June of 1992, Karlene and I bought a home in Oshkosh and one year later, under the auspices of the Oshkosh Recreation Program, launched "Classic Square and Country Dancing," offering six weeks of square dance lessons, every six weeks. The program caught on, flourished, and grew. That September, I was asked to start a similar program in New London, 30 miles away. That same December I was asked to take over a Line Dance program at the Oshkosh Senior Center and the Classic Country Dancers were born. By 1994, we had moved the entire Oshkosh program into the air-conditioned comfort of the Oshkosh Senior Center where we now dance four days a week.

Classic Country Dancing today is a Community Dance Program that works. Every Thursday evening at the Oshkosh Senior Center, we have a fun-filled dance with squares, Contras, reels, quadrilles, mixers, Sicilian circles, and trios. One modification that we have made, and that the CALLERLAB CDP Committee will most likely make this spring, is to back away from the concept of a "set" of lessons. We make every dance open to anyone, and everyone is invited.

CHAPTER 13

Passed Thru
In Memoriam

Many dear ones have gone on ahead
To that square dance hall in the sky,
To pave the way for that glorious day
When we'll meet in the sweet bye and bye.

Our friends have "passed thru" to the other side;
Some day when we meet once again,
We'll join our hands in the promised lands
And "square our sets" in heav'n.

—*Agnes Thurner, 1998*

In Memoriam

Although it is impossible to mention all the well-respected and beloved callers, cuers, and dancers that have passed away, we have listed just a few of those who left us during the last decade. Others will always be remembered in our hearts.

>─┼◄►─○─◄►┼─<

Clarence and Enid Dorschner
by Stanley DeBoer

The tragic, swift, loss of Clarence and Enid Dorschner on September 16, 1997, ended the long careers of two caller/dancers. They were taken from us through a tragic automobile accident that took both their lives. We are all saddened, not just by the memories of what they brought to square dancing, but also because they were such kind, thoughtful, friends.

Clarence grew up in a musical family taught by his father. As a young adult, he was drawn to square dancing. Later he ventured into calling and part of his life changed. His circle of friends expanded. Always, Enid was at his side, his faithful and helpful taw.

It was at the Clarence Dorschner Birthday Picnic at Winneconne Park in 1953, that the Timber Toppers Square Dance Club was born, a "closed club" of 32 couples. Herb Johnson became the club caller. But, Clarence was always the club's dependable back-up and teacher.

For many years, Clarence also called and taught for the K C Squares in Appleton. They later became the Apple Ciders Square Dance Club. He did the same for the Sovereign-Aders at Winneconne. In addition, he was popular as a caller for hundreds of one-night stands throughout the region.

Clarence was active in the Wolf River Area Callers' Association, The Wisconsin Square Dance Callers and Leaders, the Pioneer Chapter of the National Square Dance Campers' Association, (which he helped create) and a charter member of the Timber Toppers Square Dance Club.

Clarence and Enid were square dance teachers and callers for more than 30 years. Failing health forced them to give up their active role. However, when urged, Clarence still called a good tip at the Pioneer Campers winter picnic last January. He said, "That felt good!"

So, Square 'em up, Clarence and Enid; you are remembered and you will be missed!

>─┼◄►─○─◄►┼─<

Eddie Urban
Submitted by Mary Urban

Eddie Urban, a well-known square dance caller in the Central area, passed away February 1, 1998, at the age of 66 years, after a brief illness caused by a stroke. Eddie started calling in 1965 for the Plover Circle Eights, Rapid 8s, Marathon Squares, and Edgar Squares. In 1972, he retired from calling and dancing until 1986 when he and his wife, Mary, decided they needed to stop being such couch potatoes and start dancing again. His intention was not to start calling but Bob Holup, a well-known Wausau caller, handed him the mike one night and the rest is history.

Mary and Ed Urban

He joined Warren Gruetzmacher in calling for the Lincoln Squares in Merrill. He later started a group called the "Hap 'P' Hazards" which was not an organized club—just a bunch of dancers out to have a good time on a Saturday night when no other club was dancing. The Tomahawk area wanted to start a square dance group and contacted Ed. Tomahawk graduated their first class in 1991, and for a few years, in order to build up the club, Eddie taught two classes a year. He was still calling for the club at the time of his death.

Not only was he active in the local square dance scene but he and Mary were assistant Fashion Show chairmen for the 1989 State Square and Round Dance Convention in Stevens Point and General Chairmen for the 1994 State Square and Round Dance Convention, also held in Stevens Point. At the time of his death, he and Mary were Vice Chairmen of the Wisconsin Square and Round Dance Convention Corporation.

Bob and JoAnne Engum, who graduated from one of Eddie's first classes, wrote the following tribute to their square dance teacher.

In the Fall of the year as the leaves lost their green,
A square of beginners came onto the scene
We came in all sizes, short and with height,
And it took us awhile to learn left from right.
One step at a time, we started out slow,
Red wing, steal, promenade home you go.
With all the explaining, walk-thru's and goofs;
Yellow rocks, Mike's help, raising of roofs,
We've come to the end; Eddie still has his voice.
Our lessons are over, not really by choice.
He thinks we can make it, he's letting us go.
We'll all miss the lessons, we liked Friday's so.
Thanks again, Eddie, for all you have done.
Not only did we square dance, but also had fun.
So when Fall rolls around, with a new ten or twenty,
Just give us a thought, the "Swingin' Class of '70".

Clayton A. Pigeon

CLAYTON A. PIGEON of Green Bay died unexpectedly on March 23, 1995, at the age of 56. He was a member of the Wolf River Callers' Association. He loved calling square dances but especially loved to teach. He was club caller for West Turners, Twin City Squares, Roundups and Peninsula Promenaders square dance clubs. Clayton and his wife, Joan, were General Chairmen for the 1990 convention in Oshkosh and members of the convention Board of Directors. He and Joan were serving as Chairman of the Board at the time of his death.

DAVID A. KUMM, age 41, of Wisconsin Rapids passed away on April 9,1995 at his home. He was a square dance caller and round dance leader in the Central Wisconsin area. He called for the Happy Steppers and Galaxy Rounds. David represented his area for many years as a delegate to the Square Dance Association of Wisconsin and the Wisconsin Square Dance Leaders' and Callers' Council. He was a member of the Central Area Callers' Association, Wisconsin Round Dance Leaders' Council, and ROUNDALAB.

WILBERT "BILL" WILD died November 27, 1994, in Monroe. Bill and his wife were very active in the Wisconsin square dance world for many years. They designed and copyrighted the Wisconsin Square Dance Flag and were chairmen of the Flag Foundation.

ROBERT W. KOERNER died suddenly on October 19, 1994. He was a member of Romeos and Calicos Square Dance Club in Appleton. He and his wife, Verla, were serving as Camping Chairmen for the 36th Wisconsin Square Dance Convention in Oshkosh at the time of his death.

HERBERT "HERB" JOHNSON died at home on November 23, 1994. He had been a caller for over 36 years. He called for Square Swingers and Timber Toppers and was instrumental in organizing the Valley Carousel Round Dance Club. He and his wife "Tilda" helped to establish the National Square Dance Campers' Association, the Wolf River Area Callers' Association and the *Hoedown News*.

MATILDA "TILDA" JOHNSON left this world on January 2, 1995, after a courageous battle with cancer. She and Herb had been married for almost 60 years and were well-known in the Wisconsin square dance community.

LEWIS "LEW" SNYDER, of the South East Area, passed away January 4, 1995, after a bout with cancer. Lew called square dances for over 20 years. He was a member of the MACC, and CALLERLAB.

DIANE WALKER, President of Greendale Village Squares, was killed October 22, 1995, in an auto accident. She was active in the square dance activity for over 20 years. She became a member of Swingin' Single Squares after the death of her husband, Chet.

ED PLACZKOWSKI, a member of the EMBA Square Dance Club passed away on November 26, 1997, at the age of 83. Ed and his wife, Hedy, were very active members of EMBA and held many club offices including president. Ed and Hedy attended their first square and round dance convention in 1962. Two years later, they were general chairmen for the 6th Wisconsin Square and Round Dance Convention.

ALICE SPOOR, wife of cuer Milt Spoor, died in January, 1998. Alice was a well-loved member of the South East Area square dance community and will be greatly missed.

ELROY NELSON, age 80, of Appleton died February 9, 1996, at his home. He will be remembered for his love of Square and Round Dancing. He and his wife, Gertrude, were square dance leaders in the Appleton area and worked on several state conventions.

BERNICE G. BOLEK of Oshkosh passed away April 12, 1997. She was a teacher in Wisconsin prior to beginning a career as a social worker for the Winnebago Mental Health Institute. Bernice and her husband, Jim, were members of Timber Toppers Square Dance Club in Oshkosh. Jim and Bernice were seen each year at the State Square and round Dance Conventions—mostly in the retail area, as they were owners of The Coat Tree.

The name **MEL SCHOECKERT** is synonymous with the Square Dance Association of Wisconsin and the Wisconsin Square Dance Leaders' Council. A former caller in the Milwaukee area, Mel passed away June 11, 1992, at the age of 85. He was actively involved in the formation of the SDAW and was elected its first Vice President. Mel and his wife, Loretta, are former editors of *Here 'Tis*.

RALPH TAYLOR passed away August 14, 1992, at the of 78 years. Ralph and his wife, Ann, were charter members of the EMBA Square Dance Club for 46 years. They were general chairmen of the 9th Wisconsin Square Dance Convention and worked tirelessly promoting the square dance activity.

JACK ROEHR died unexpectedly on September 25, 1992, in Arizona. Jack and his wife, Mary, were longtime members of the Square Benders Square Dance Club. They worked on many state conventions and the 1979 National Convention in Milwaukee. They served their club as delegates to the SEA for many years. They were members of LEGACY and worked on many ECCO seminars.

Margaret Leatherman 1917-1993

The 34th Wisconsin Square and Round Dance Convention was dedicated to the memory of Margaret Leatherman. Margaret was a founding member of the Square Dance Association of Wisconsin, the Wisconsin Square Dance Leaders' Council and the National Square Dance Campers' Association. She was the Executive Secretary to the Wisconsin Square and Round Dance Convention Corporation for more than 25 years.

Closer to home, she was a founding member of the Wolf River Area Callers' Association. She founded *Hoedown News*, the Wolf River Area Square Dance Newsletter.

Square dancing will miss her tireless efforts, her steady hand, and her seasoned devotion. Square dancers will miss her down-home friendliness, her welcoming smile and her "joking" around.

Through her legacy to square dancing, Margaret will continue to touch the lives of square dancers throughout the Wolf River Area, the state, and the nation.

Reprinted from the 34th Wisconsin Square and Round Dance Convention booklet — 1993

> ⊱ ⟡ ⊙ ⟡ ⊰

Remembering Russ
by D-D Burss

When Russ was alive he always said "When I die, I want the words 'I'd rather be calling' on my tombstone." He said it many, many times, jokingly, but the kids and I felt it was something he really did want. It was a hard decision but after much discussion with the family we came to an agreement. Now, at Woodlawn Cemetery in Milwaukee, his stone has a "mike" engraved with the words "I'd rather be calling," Russ Burss. So far we haven't regretted doing what we believe to be his final wish.

CHAPTER 14

Promenade Home
What Were We Doing in 1998?

Good night Sal, Good night, Sue,
Good night Elmer, Good night Lou,
Hurry up girls, don't be slow,
Come kiss the caller before you go.
Now promenade one and promenade all,
Lead right out of this old dance hall.
You know where and I don't care,
Take her out and give her air.

The Square Dance Association of Wisconsin

The quarterly SDAW Jamboree was held Sunday, May 3, 1998, at the Community Center in DeForest, Wisconsin. This was the first Jamboree with the new format. All meetings were held in the morning with the square and round dance workshop and mainstream dance in the afternoon. Previously the square and round dance workshop was in the morning and the SDAW joint meeting was in the afternoon, followed by the mainstream dance.

The morning education session for dancers was conducted by Dennis Leatherman who discussed his very successful Community Dance Program. The session ended with an on-the-floor demonstration and questions from the audience.

Historian's John and Gloria Rindfleisch, announced they were giving up the historian's position in November.

Convention publicity chairmen Al and Vera Schreiner, passed out flyers for the 1998 convention and encouraged all dancers to register.

Aggi Thurner reported the progress made by the Anniversary Committees: Delegates were given pre-publication order blanks for the anthology for distribution in their areas. If ordered before July 15 buyers will save $5.95 off the retail price. June Myklebust is working on the Memory quilt; she has sewn the pieces together but still needs to add a border. The South West Area is hosting a sesquicentennial dance during Statehood Days in Madison. There will be an old-fashioned barn dance on the Capitol Square in the afternoon of May 29. Two busloads of dancers from the Wolf River and South East Area will attend.

The Wisconsin State Fair Promotion Committee reported on this year's booth and the square dances and demonstrations that will take place at the fair August 6-16 in West Allis. They are encouraging square and round dancers and callers statewide to come out and help with this annual effort.

The next SDAW meeting will be held in Racine on Sunday, July 19, 1998, at the Wisconsin Square and Round Dance Convention.

><+>-O-<+><

1998 SDAW Officers

President—Vern Weisensel, Lodi, Wisconsin

Vice President—Lloyd and Joyce Gatzke, West Bend, Wisconsin

Secretary—Roger Buettner, Appleton, Wisconsin

Treasurer—Floyd and Jean Schultz, Lake Mills, Wisconsin

Historian—John and Gloria Rindfleisch, Clinton, Wisconsin

Area Associations

Wolf River Area:
President, Ellery and Karen Gulbrand, Green Bay

Member Clubs:
    County Cousins
    Millstream Wranglers
    Fox Valley Squares
    Green Bay Squares
    Lakeside Twirlers
    Ripon Twirlers
    Romeos and Calicos
    Timber Toppers
    Twin City Squares
    Jacks 'N Jills
    Kettle Squares
    Whirl-A-Ways
    Waupaca Squares
    West Turners

South East Area:
President, Mel and Merrylou Green, Thiensville

Member Clubs:
    Allemande
    American Heritage Dancers (Exhibition Group)
    Circle 8s
    Country Promenaders
    Dudes and Dolls
    EMBA
    Falls Promenaders
    Greendale Village Squares
    Hartland Hoedowners
    Kettle Moraine Squares
    Lamplighters
    MACC (Milwaukee Area Callers' Council)
    49ers
    Ridge Runners
    Spring City Squares
    Square Benders
    Suburban 8's
    Swing-in-Families
    Swingin' Singles
    Swinging Stars
    T-P Taws & Paws

South West Area:

President, Floyd and Jean Schultz, Lake Mills

Member Clubs:

- Badger Rovers
- Circus City Squares
- Crosstrails
- Diamond Squares
- Good Time Squares
- Limber Timbers
- Markesan Wheels
- Milton Village Squares
- Petunia City Squares
- Prison City Squares
- Rhythm and Rounds
- Swingin' Beavers
- Watermelon Squares
- Westfield Jolly Squares
- Westport Squares
- SDAW-SWA Callers' Association

West Central Area:

President, Tim and Charlotte Manning, La Crosse

West Central Area Clubs

- Tim's A-Team
- NorJen Dancers
- Prairie Partners
- Country Squares
- Squarenaders
- Happy Twirlers

The following West Central clubs had not rejoined the SDAW as of May 1998.

- Friendly Twirlers
- Merry Mixers
- Pairs and Squares
- Rice Lake Twirlers
- Square Wheelers - Durand
- Sweetheart Swingers
- Triple Scooters

Central Area:
President, Joe and Phyllis Kretschmer, Merrill

Member Clubs:
    Saints and Swingers
    Merry 8's
    Loyal Circle 8's
    Marshfield Hoedowners
    Hodag Twirlers
    Country Corners
    Gateway Squares
    Levis and Lace
    Lincoln Squares
    Wheel and Deal

Callers' Associations

Wolf River Area Callers' Association

    Charlie Bitter, Oshkosh
    Roger Buettner, Appleton
    Larry Cockrum, Oshkosh
    Phil Doucette, Neenah
    Howie Fochs, Hilbert
    John Glasgow, Fond du Lac
    Warren Gruetzmacher, Merrill
    Marvin Hechel, Neshkoro
    Pat Kelm, Deerbrook
    Dennis Leatherman, Oshkosh
    Betty Schumacher, Appleton
    John Stillson, Appleton
    Lloyd Vertz, Algoma

Milwaukee Area Callers' Council (MACC)

    Tim Beneke, Menomonee Falls
    Jimmie Burss, Milwaukee
    Scott Campbell, Germantown
    Elmer Elias, Mendota
    Will Ferderer, Waterloo
    John Fruit, Waukesha
    Wayne Gessner, Janesville

Joyce Gibour, Wauwatosa
Bob Goebel, Port Washington
Wayne Irwin, Delafield
Kevin Jochims, Waubeka
Buzz Kaczmarek, New Berlin
Bob Koser, Hales Corners
Mike Krautkramer, Racine
Chuck Muecke, Oconomowoc
Jim Noonan, New Berlin
Dwayne Olson, Wauwatosa
Doris Palmen, Bristol
Ted Palmen, Bristol
Elissa Pischke, Racine
Howie Reoch, West Allis
Jerry Ridley, Milwaukee
Rob Sanderson, Greenfield
Harry Schopp, Germantown
Len Siegmann, Rubicon
Ruth Siegmann, Rubicon
Pat Tans, Racine
Randy Tans, Racine
Jeff Whipple, Cudahy
Gordy Ziemann, Cedarburg
Mary Ann Ziemann, Cedarburg

Eric Tangman chats with author between tips at a Greendale Village Square Dance.

Eric Tangman, a popular caller in the South East Area, is not a member of the MACC. He teaches lessons for Swingin' Singles Squares and Square Benders and is club caller for Square Benders. Eric is a member of CALLERLAB.

South West Area Callers' Association

Bob Asp, Rockton
Darrah Chavey, Beloit
Dwayne Dhuse, Rockford
Nyle Germundson, Whitewater
John Herschman, Fort Atkinson
Bob Lindemann, Beloit
Tom Nickel, Madison
Kathy Nickel, Madison
Don Niva, Madison
Bob Paull, Rockford
Dale Ryan, Sauk City
Bill Schara, Madison
Ray Steinich, Pardeeville
Vern Weisensel, Lodi

West Central Callers' Association

Bud Cote, Chippewa Falls
John Dittner, Marshfield
Tim Manning, La Crosse
Jerry Portis, La Crescent
Joel Vanderzee, La Crosse

Central Area Callers' Association

Darlene Bennett, Wisconsin Rapids
Amanda Gruetzmacher, Merrill
Warren Gruetzmacher, Merrill
Gale Hartlerode, Mosinee
Richard Hartlerode, Mosinee
Judy Hogan, Rhinelander
Tom Hogan, Rhinelander
Pat Kelm, Deerbrook
Al Montgomery, Gleason
Harry Stubbe, Schofield
Glenn A. Younger, Mosinee
Violet Kumm, Mosinee

1998 Club News

Wausau Merry 8's purchased a group liability insurance policy to cover clubs in northern Wisconsin.

Kettle Moraine Squares hosted its annual "Amateur Night" in January.

La Crosse Happy Twirlers graduated 12 new square dancers in April.

Racine County Dudes and Dolls celebrated St. Patrick's Day with the "Wearing of the Green".

Square Benders will dance in July to accommodate the new dancers who need to keep dancing through the summer to maintain their skills.

Swingin' Single Squares are celebrating their 23rd anniversary on June 10. Doug and Don Sprosty will call and cue.

Falls Promenaders celebrated the 40th Anniversary of their club.

Suburban 8's held a "Have-a-Heart Dance" in February. Over 100 pounds of non-perishable foods were collected for St. Boniface Parish in Germantown.

Plymouth Kettle Squares assisted with a program for the Nu Dawn Club for developmentally disabled adults. Dancing was led by Jerry Ridley.

Dwayne Olson calls for American Heritage Dancers exhibition at Boerner Botanical Gardens. Milwaukee Clogging Company also performed.

Milton Village Squares is hosting a "dangle" dance July 25. Don Niva is caller for the dance which will be held at the Janesville Senior Center.

The Lightning Trio is calling for Suburban 8's dance at the Todd American Legion Post on October 16. Mary Edge is cuing rounds.

American Heritage Dancers performed three exhibitions at the Boerner Botanical Gardens on June 14 and 20.

The SEA Promotion Committee hosted a dance at the Grobschmidt Senior Center on Flag Day, June 14, 1998. The dance was to raise funds for the annual Wisconsin State Fair promotion. Calling was The Lightning Trio, who donated their time.

>─┼─◄►─·─O─·─◄►┼─◄

Vern and Billie Weisensel
SDAW President

Vern and Billie Weisensel started their calling career in 1961 for the Crosstrails youth club which later became a family club. Vern and Billie married in 1966 and have three daughters and one son, Vern II. Vern Sr. retired in 1993 and is the club caller for six different clubs: Badger Rover Square Dance Campers, Circus City Squares in Baraboo, Crosstrails in Madison (the original youth club), Swingin' Seniors (at the Madison Senior Center), Westfield Jolly Squares and Markesan Wheels. He calls an average of four dances per week including one-night stands.

Billie and Vernon Weisensel

Vern likes to promote lessons and workshops whenever he finds enough beginners to form a square. Billie harmonizes with Vern on many of the singing calls. They are members of the Badger Rovers Chapter of the National Square Dance Campers' Association and attend as many camp outs as possible, including the International Square Dance Camporee. They guest call for most of the clubs in the area and have called for the Wisconsin Square and Round Dance Convention for the past four years, and the Iowa Square Dance Convention for the past five years. They are members of CALLERLAB, the Wisconsin Callers' and Leaders' Council, and the SDAW-South West Area Callers' Association.

>─┼─◄►─·─O─·─◄►┼─◄

Tim and Charlotte Manning
West Central Area President

Tim and Charlotte Manning met on a dance floor in 1950 during a circle two-step. They seem to be destined to dance through life and are very happy doing so. They did some traditional square dancing before they were married but didn't learn the western style until the fall of 1967. They were talked into joining a group at Eagle Cave near Muscoda and that's where Norm and Jenny Indvick taught them their first round dances. When the Muscoda club disbanded they traveled 110 miles round trip almost every week to take round dance lessons.

Charlotte and Tim Manning

In 1969, Tim and Charlotte helped organize the RC Twirlers square dance club in Richland Center, now disbanded. They served as president the first year with Dale Ryan as caller. In 1973, they began to teach and cue rounds to a small group in Richland Center, in the hope of starting round dancing in the area. One thing led to another and in 1975 Tim took up calling, teaching his first class that fall in the Manning recreation room.

Tim has called for many clubs since then. The Coulee Region Promenaders of La Crosse and Hill and Gully Twirlers of Wilton are disbanded. He still calls for the Sweetheart Swingers of Tomah, Prairie Partners in Lansing, Iowa, the Spring Swingers in McGregor, Iowa, and an advanced club, Tim's A Team. The Manning's are also cuers for the NorJen Round Dance Club originally started by Norm and Jen Indvick.

Tim and Charlotte were Vice Chairmen of Education for the national convention held in Milwaukee in 1979. In 1980, they were round dance chairmen for the state convention and president of the West Central Caller's Association. They have been in charge of programming for the state convention every five years since then, each time it was held in the Madison area. In addition they chaired advanced dancing for the '93 convention and were assistant convention chairmen in '87. In 1992, they were General Chairmen for the convention held in La Crosse. The Mannings are members of the Wisconsin Round Dance Leaders' Council and have participated in the annual Accent on Rounds weekends.

Dale "The Auctioneer" Ryan
Sauk City, Wisconsin
Caller—South West Area

Dale Ryan announced plans to retire from calling at the end of 1999 and will not be accepting bookings for dates later than December 1999. His last calling engagement will be with the club where he called his first out-of-town dance in Westfield.

Dale graduated from high school in Prairie du Sac in 1956 and in the spring of 1957 he attended Auctioneer School. What caller could ask for a better background. In the fall of 1957 he followed up with his education and attended a beginners class in square dancing with Milt Thorp as the instructor. During a break one night he picked up the mike and started to chant an auction cry. Milt was impressed and gave him a singing call to learn. Dale made his debut as a caller on graduation night and has been calling for 40 years. Would you believe Dale's favorite singing call is "The Auctioneer?"

Dale Ryan

The following year Dale purchased used calling equipment and started teaching a beginners class. Dale has called for many clubs in Wisconsin and one-night stands are a part of his itinerary. He is a member of the South West Area Callers' Association and the American Callers' Association.

Dale believes the future of square dancing is with the limited basic or fun level clubs. "We need to accommodate those dancers who have a limited amount of time to spend dancing. They need a place to go for fun and dancing without having to participate in workshops to keep up, or take extended lessons to further themselves," he said.

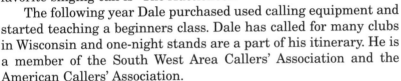

Thanks For The Memories
Jim Noonan, New Berlin
Caller, South East Area

How do you put 28 years into a couple of paragraphs? For about ten years, Bette persistently tried to convince me to try Square Dancing. When I learned that a fellow member from the Rifle Club I belonged to was a square dancer, we finally decided to give it a try. Our first night of square dancing was spent in the basement of R-Squares caller, Ernie Randall. We did enjoy the dancing but, because Ernie's class night conflicted with my Rifle Club night, we decided to look for a different night to take classes. In September 1969, Ernie suggested we go to caller Elmer Elias, of the EMBA Club who offered lessons on Sunday nights at The Knotty Pine on 17th and Mitchell in Milwaukee. We found The Knotty Pine very convenient since it was only one block away from our home.

After learning to dance that season, and helping out as "angels" for the new dancers, I found myself becoming more interested in calling. One night, at a class in February 1971, I was telling fellow dancers of my interest in calling, and Elmer overheard. Tapping me on the shoulder, Elmer told me that there was a box full of records on the stage, to pick one, take it home, practice it, and then to come to the Club Dance on Friday to call it. My first singing call was Summer Sounds.

Jim and Bette Noonan

In 1971, I taught my first class at the Christian Center on 23rd and Greenfield. We had four squares, mostly teens or preteens. Our son, Tom, who was 13, and our daughter, Barbie, age 6, were in that first class. Out of our four children, three square danced. Our son, Jim III, surprised us by taking square dance lessons while in the navy, stationed in Florida. He met us at the 1977 National Square Dance Convention in Atlantic City, where he met his wife, Pat. Our daughter, Susie, never square danced, but did get into Country Western Dancing with her family recently.

Jim III and Pat's children, Jim IV and Rebecca, are also dancers. Jim IV went to his first State Convention, when he was six weeks old, to enjoy hearing Grandpa and Grandma singing a duet while Mom and Dad danced. Rebecca attended her first Convention two months before she was born. Both Jim IV and Rebecca danced with Jimmie Burss' Swinging Family Exhibition Group.

Three generations of Noonans — Back left to right — Pat, Jim I, Jim II, Bette. Front — Rebecca and Jim III.

We have been deeply involved in square dancing and calling, attending six National Conventions, from Kansas City in 1975 to Memphis in 1980. I called at 22 Wisconsin State Conventions, and Bette attended 1996 and 1997 as a spectator. In June 1977, we were Assistant General Chairmen for Caller activities for the Wisconsin State Convention, and in 1979, we were Vice-Chairmen of Hospitality for the Wisconsin National Convention. I have been calling for 27 years, and have been a member of CALLERLAB, the International Association of Square Dance Caller's, since 1976. I have held numerous positions in the Milwaukee Area Callers' Council, and was club caller for R Squares, Jeans & Queens, Swinging Singles, and Allemanders. Today, I teach classes every fall for our Dance-N-Squares, and share Mainstream Workshops with other callers through the summer. I also enjoy doing one-nighters with local community groups. I recently called for a sesquicentennial event at the YMCA in Brown Deer, when the Wagon Train reenactment camped there for the night.

Bette and I have been involved in Square Dancing for 28 years—all of them good. It is one of the best things that ever happened to us. We have met thousands of people, and have made as many friends— many who have become part of our extended family. God Bless Square Dancing.

>─+◀▸•─O─◀▸+─◀

The Lightning Trio
South East Area

Jimmie Burss and Randy Tans sang a duet in the Youth Hall at a state convention a few years ago, and the dancers thoroughly enjoyed it. The next year Mike Krautkramer joined them and afterwards everyone encouraged them to form a group. It wasn't long before "The Lightning Trio" became a reality. Swinging Stars engaged the "Trio" for their first calling date in 1994. Since then, the "Trio" has called for several clubs and state conventions. They

have volunteered their time for the past three years to raise money for the State Fair Promotion and have called dances at the fair.

The biggest problem is coordinating dates when all members of the talented threesome are available. They each have a full-time job, in addition to other calling commitments. Jimmie and Deanna Burss are busy raising their first child, Joe, born in February, and are General Chairman for the 1998 Wisconsin State Convention in Racine.

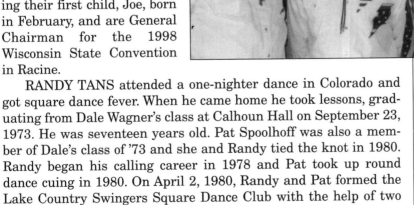

Lightning Trio— Left to right— Randy Tans, Jimmie Burss, Mike Krautkramer.

RANDY TANS attended a one-nighter dance in Colorado and got square dance fever. When he came home he took lessons, graduating from Dale Wagner's class at Calhoun Hall on September 23, 1973. He was seventeen years old. Pat Spoolhoff was also a member of Dale's class of '73 and she and Randy tied the knot in 1980. Randy began his calling career in 1978 and Pat took up round dance cuing in 1980. On April 2, 1980, Randy and Pat formed the Lake Country Swingers Square Dance Club with the help of two other couples, Herb and June Tannis, and Ned and Carol Bradley.

The Tans' danced with several clubs over the years: the Silver Buckles, Wagon Wheels, and Suburban 8's. They are members of CALLERLAB, MACC, and WSDLCC.

MIKE AND JULIE KRAUTKRAMER met in college where they were both theatre majors. They were married in 1982. Julie's mom and dad were members of Dudes and Dolls Square Dance Club. Art Radoll the Dudes and Dolls club caller was a guest at the wedding. In 1985 Mike and Julie graduated from Art Radoll's lesson program. Art had heard Mike sing a few songs with the band at his wedding reception and encouraged Mike to try his hand at calling. He gave him a record and suggested he practice a singing call. However Mike didn't really get started as a caller until New Year's Eve 1988. That was when he called his first official dance for Dudes and Dolls. He worked with Bill Webster and the Square Wheelers during 1989 and '90 and when Bill passed away in 1993, Mike and Julie took over his chairmanship of the Sound and Music programming for the state convention. The Krautkramers are chairing the Sound and Music programming again for the 1998 convention in Racine. They are also helping with the Fashion show; Julie is designing the stage set and Mike has a solo in the finale.

>─┤─◄▷─◇─◁▷─┤─◄

Crosstrails Square Dance Club
by Vern and Billie Weisensel

In the fall of 1960, several teenagers and young adults attended lessons at the Verona Square Dance Club. In January 1961 these young people decided to start a club primarily for teens. This was the birth of "Crosstrails Square Dance Club." We started dancing in the basement of the First Baptist Church on Madison's west side. From there we migrated to the Seminary Springs School in the Sun Prairie District, and from there moved to the Burke Town Hall on East Washington Avenue on the north side of Madison.

We moved to the YMCA on West Washington Avenue in 1964. When the YMCA was renovated we moved back to the Burke Town Hall. Shortly thereafter, arrangements were made with Kermit Bliss at the Madison Community Center on Doty Street, and we were able to use the "Loft" for our dances. When the Community Center moved to Fairchild Street, we moved along with it. Subsequently, the Center changed its name to the Downtown Arts and Activities Center.

During this period of time we started to have more University students joining our group. Eventually some of the older members formed a separate single adult club.

During the summer months we danced under the stars at the Weisensel residence, first on Syene Road south of Madison and later at Sam Road near Lodi. In the fall of 1995, we relocated to the

Neighborhood House on Mills Street for the winter. In the fall of 1996 we were at the Stoner Prairie School on Devora Road in Fitchburg (off Lacy Road between Fish Hatchery Road and Seminole Highway).

Several callers and one cuer got their start through membership in Crosstrails. One of them, Tom Nickel, brought his family to take lessons with Crosstrails. He began calling in 1992 and includes some line dancing in his lesson program. His wife, Kathy, was not entirely new to the activity. She began square dancing in the Pardeeville/Beaver Dam area at age eight. She has been cuing for the last two years. The Nickels are club caller/cuer for the Watermelon Squares and the Swingin' Beavers.

Tom Nickel, left, with Vern Weisensel call a duet at a club dance.

Cuer Darrah Chavey of Beloit also took lessons with Crosstrails. It was there he met Vern's niece, Peggy, who later became his wife. If he hadn't started with Crosstrails he wouldn't have known what round dancing was, and he wouldn't have met the girl he eventually married.

Many of our dancers met in lessons and began romances that led to matrimony. Most of them are still together and some are still dancing.

As of right now, the club is temporarily at a standstill with no new students but we plan to start lessons again in October 1998. Crosstrails held an open house in January and will hold another in September. We do have a few interested people. Hopefully things will change with our son starting to call. Young people like to see someone younger at the "mike". Vern II started calling three years ago and for the last two years has been registered with the South West Area Callers' Association as a beginner caller.

Cream City Squares
by Don Dilges

Cream City Squares began in October of 1991, when Joe Frazier, from Foggy City Squares in San Francisco, California, introduced the Milwaukee lesbian, gay, bisexual, and transgender (LGBT) community to modern square dancing.

Cream City Squares was chosen as the club name. It was taken from Milwaukee's old nickname, Cream City, because of the color of the local clay bricks used in so many of the city's historic buildings.

Cream City Squares joined the International Association of

Gay Square Dance Clubs (IAGSDC) in 1992. Members have enjoyed the annual IAGSDC square dance conventions and fly-ins around the country, and have danced at all but one of the Wisconsin Square and Round Dance Conventions since 1993.

The club has taught a Basic/Mainstream class every year, with class size varying from two to ten people a year. Cream City Squares is a Mainstream Club, but held Plus classes in 1994, 1996, & 1997.

One of Cream City's dancers, Don Dilges, attended the Gay Callers' Association (GCA) Caller School in Chicago in conjunction with the 1995 IAGSDC convention, and became a licensed caller. He shares calling duties with Joe Frazier. Both are members of CALLERLAB.

In 1997, the club was introduced to Advanced dancing but presently has only three Advance level dancers. They only dance at that level when visiting other clubs, or if enough Advanced dancers visit a club dance, and an Advanced caller is available. The club officers feel that the club is too small to divide the group into too many levels of dance.

Cream City Squares members consider their group a Mainstream Club. They dance two Mainstream tips and every third tip is a Plus dance.

They like to dance by definition (DBD) to keep the Mainstream interesting. Most of the club members dance in all positions and the club stresses that practice rather than moving the dances up to another dance level. The weekly club dances are held on Sundays from 3:00 p.m. to 5:30 p.m. unless the club is running a class.

The club dances wherever space is available at low, or no cost, because the group is not large enough to attract more than one or two squares at most dances. They originally danced at B's Bar (which no longer exists), then in members homes, and now at Just Us Bar located at 807 South 5th Street, in Milwaukee.

Cream City Squares officers had hoped to be away from the bar scene by this time, but haven't found a suitable alternative space. The majority of members and prospective members prefer an alcohol- and smoke-free environment. Classes for fall of 1998 depend on where they can be held, and our instructor/callers' work schedules.

>―┤◄►・O・◄►┤―<

Joyce and The Yellow Rocker's
by Joyce Gibour, Wauwatosa, WI

Several years ago, at a state convention, I purchased two singing calls and proceeded to listen to the caller's side, which I now know is a no-no. I learned both of them by heart. I had been thinking for some time about surprising Eric Tangman by learning a singing call. I was singing along with the callers anyway. I was born, it seems, with a natural ear for music. I've always loved to sing and have been involved in music since I was very young.

Eric was calling for a Single's weekend at Camp Byron, and after our Saturday afternoon session, I asked him if I could do a singing call that evening. He said, "You learned a singing call?"

"Yes, I learned two of them," I proudly answered.

Eric proceeded to tell me that this was great but if I was to call a "tip" I must also call some "hash." He kept me after for almost the entire break before dinner, attempting to teach me how to call a hash tip.

Joyce Gibour calls...

That evening I made my debut before the Swingin' Singles. They were all my friends so I felt pretty comfortable—except for the hash. Everyone was surprised that I was able to do this and delighted that I chose to do it for them. That happened over Memorial Day weekend in 1987. In August of that year, Eric told me that he was considering starting a caller's class and asked if I would be interested in joining. There were four of us and I was the only female.

Classes were held once a week for fifteen months. When the class ended, there was no place for us to go to call so Eric suggested we have a dance where the four of us could develop some confidence and experience. The New Callers' Jamboree started in the fall of 1989 in the Rathskeller at the Red Carpet Bowlero in Milwaukee, with the four new callers from Eric's class: Joe Bott, Joyce Gibour, Mike Jessup and Bill Webster. Other new callers and cuers were invited to join us to try out their skills in "friendly" territory. We changed the name of the Jamboree to "New Callers' Dance" when we learned that "Jamboree" was reserved for the SDAW quarterly Jamboree and meeting. Later the name was changed to the Yellow Rockers.

...as (left to right) Bill Webster, Mike Jessop and Joe Bott critique at a caller's class.

In the beginning, we charged no set fee but welcomed donations to offset hall rental. Whatever balance still owing was split four ways. The dance was held on the third Saturday of each month so we didn't compete with any other club dances. Most of the dancers who came out to help us practice continued to support us the whole first year, for which we were very appreciative.

As we entered the second year, Bill Webster left the group to become club caller for R Squares and we changed our dance night to the third Wednesday. The expenses were lower and we hoped to see some new faces among the familiar ones.

In Fall 1990, I started my first beginners class. You can't be a full-fledged caller until you've taught a class. In 1992, I invited the new dancers from my third class to the Yellow Rockers' Christmas Holiday dance. They had so much fun that they wanted to come

Now it's Jerry Ridley's turn.

back. Since they hadn't finished lessons yet, we decided to change to a dance/workshop format in which we used only calls that the class had learned up to that date. Other beginner classes were invited and several dancers that had dropped out of other clubs also came to relearn their skills.

Then two more callers left the group because of conflicting work schedules. I wanted to keep the dance going so I invited other new callers to join. Rick Scharlau accepted and later Wayne Irwin signed on. We lost a lot of our following when we changed our dance night to Thursdays. The dances continued for awhile but classes had dwindled and turn-out at the dances was poor. Then Rick Scharlau left. I finally had to put the club on hold until a new location and another willing caller became available.

The Yellow Rockers was on hold for almost two years. Jerry Ridley joined me when the dance resumed in June 1998 at the Northwest Senior Center. We call Basic and/or Mainstream dances which gives new graduates in the area a place to dance. Of course, experienced dancers are invited too. This fall, Jerry and I are planning to start a Yellow Rockers Plus on a different night, in addition to the Basic/Mainstream dance.

>─┤─◆〉─○─〈◆─┤─<

WAYNE IRWIN, began square dancing during fall of 1986 with caller Jack Gaver. Wayne and his wife, Eileen, graduated from lessons in May of 1987 and in 1992, he began calling and cuing. The Irwins are president of the Hartland Hoedowners Square Dance Club and Wayne is the club cuer and lesson instructor for the group. He is a member of CALLERLAB, MACC, and WSDLCC.

JERRY RIDLEY took square dance lessons with Eric Tangmans' Swingin' Singles class in 1990, and started calling three years ago after getting his license and joining CALLERLAB. He teaches for the Washington Park and the Kenosha Senior Citizens. He also calls with the Rolling Thunder, a group of beginning callers. Several new callers from one of Eric's classes started the group in order to have a place to call. The dances are held monthly on the 4th Saturday. Ridley is a member of the American Heritage Square Dancers. He recently joined Joyce Gibour to resume the Yellow Rockers dances.

JEFF WHIPPLE is another new caller in South East Wisconsin. He has been dancing for nine years and took up calling just four years ago. He and his wife, Sue, took lessons at the 49ers when Johnny Toth was the club caller/instructor. The Whipples are members of EMBA where Jeff is club instructor for lessons. They also belong to the Pine Tree Square Dance Campers' Chapter 002. Jeff is a member of CALLERLAB, MACC, and the WSDLCC. He does mainly guest calling.

>–+–+>–+–O–+–<+–+–<

Wisconsin Square and Round Dance Convention

The 39th Wisconsin Square and Round Dance Convention was held in Racine, Wisconsin, on July 17,18, 19, 1998. Jimmie and Deanna Burss are General Chairmen. Dwayne Olson, Assistant Chair-Programming and Lloyd and Joyce Gatzke, Assistant Chair-Facilities.

Planning was begun and convention colors chosen three years before the actual date. The committee was unable to locate available space for August, the usual convention month, so the new J. I. Case High School was reserved for the event. A promotional skit at the Saturday Special Events programming, during the 38th State Convention in La Crosse, reminded dancers that "We've Changed the Date in '98—So Don't Be Late," and encouraged dancers to register in advance.

Jimmie and Deanna Burss

Since 1998 was the sesquicentennial of Wisconsin, Dwayne Olson sent a letter to the state anniversary committee requesting that the convention be designated a sesquicentennial event. The request was approved. The fashion show, co-chaired by Agnes and Max Thurner and Lucy and Wayne Mattson of Milwaukee, and the Special Events, chaired by Wayne and Judy Gauthier of Green Bay,

Cy White and Joyce Gatzke watch as Aggi Thurner and Lloyd Gatzke dance to some "Voices from the Past" —Showcase of Ideas—1995.

233

used the sesquicentennial theme in planning their programs. A special presentation of a Memory Quilt, will be made to Leslie Bellais, Curator of Costumes and Textiles for the State Historical Society.

A song entitled "Wisconsin" in honor of the sesquicentennial year was written by Agnes Thurner and dedicated to the state. Mike Krautkramer will sing the song during the Fashion Show finale.

THOMAS (FLASH) GORDON has been a familiar figure at Wisconsin conventions since 1979 when he volunteered to provide emergency medical service for the National Convention held in Milwaukee. Flash, who is an EMT (Emergency Medical Technician) was persuaded to offer his medical skills by Bill Wilton, father of the young lady he was dating at the time. He had just graduated from lessons that May. After that Flash volunteered sporadically for the conventions until 1990. That was the year Flash and his wife, Mary Ann, participated in the fashion show "Fashion Wizardry in the Land of Ahhs". Flash was playing the role of the Tin Man in the skit.

There were two shows that year, and sure enough he got an emergency call just before the second show. He answered the call wearing his costume with silver makeup still in place.

Flash is participating in the 1998 Fashion Show in Racine in July and is hoping he won't need to answer an emergency call wearing his Hodag costume.

>−!◂▸•O•◂▸!−≺

The 50th Anniversary of the SDAW— The Sesquicentennial of Wisconsin
by Agnes Thurner

At the November 1996 meeting of the SDAW, I suggested that with the 50th anniversary of the organization and the Wisconsin Sesquicentennial both coming up in 1998, it would be a good idea to begin making plans for some kind of recognition. Dennis Leatherman was president of the SDAW and, being the savvy leader that he is, asked if I would be willing to chair a committee to come up with some ideas. Everyone that knows me is aware that I have difficulty with the 'N' word, so of course, I said yes.

At the next meeting, in February of 1997, I proposed several options for consideration.

1. A Memory Quilt. We would ask all Wisconsin square dance clubs and organizations to submit a quilt patch based on their club badge or banner.

2. A Square Dance Anthology to incorporate the history of the association with biographies and anecdotes of Wisconsin square dancers, callers, and leaders.

3. Encourage all clubs and area associations to hold special dances and sesquicentennial activities during the anniversary year.

After some discussion of the ways, whys, and wherefores, all the suggestions were accepted. I agreed to work on the anthology if June Myklebust would take charge of the Memory Quilt. (At a follow-up meeting of the association, it was voted to donate the Memory Quilt to the State Historical Society.) Several other people had volunteered to serve on the committee and we proceeded to publicize our plans. We distributed flyers and advertised in *Here 'Tis* for clubs to send their quilt squares to June and their square dance memories to me.

It is now the beginning of June in 1998. Clubs and associations throughout the state have held special dances and activities for the sesquicentennial and the SDAW anniversary; the Wisconsin State Convention has been designated a Sesquicentennial event. The Memory Quilt is finished except for some final touches, and the anthology … well if you're reading this then you know it was completed. The intent of the committee was to do something that would trigger warm memories of square dancing and leave a lasting heritage for future generations of "Square Dancing in Wisconsin." I believe we have successfully accomplished our goals.

Anthology committee members, **WAYNE AND LUCY MATTSON,** met while Wayne was taking lessons with Swingin' Singles Squares and Lucy was "angeling". They have been married for seven years. They are members of Square Benders and American Heritage Dancers. Wayne and Lucy serve as delegates to the area association and alternate delegates to the SDAW. They have worked on the SEA promotion committee for three years and are currently co-chairing the 1998 convention fashion show. The Mattsons make their home in Milwaukee.

JUDY BARISONZI of Fond du Lac, also a member of the anthology committee, has been square dancing for eight years. She learned mainstream and plus dancing from John Glasgow and has been a member of Lakeside Twirlers in Fond du Lac since she graduated from lessons. Judy has been club secretary, treasurer, vice president, and president on various occasions. For the last three years she has danced Plus with the Neenah Advanced Dancers, caller Glen Krakower. Judy is interested in the history of square and folk dancing as well as local cultural history in general.

MARILYN and **RAY STEINICH,** who live in Pardeeville, Wisconsin, are members of Diamond Squares and Diamond Rounds. Ray is a round dance cuer and instructor and teaches round dancing at the DeForest Community Center every Sunday. The Steinichs are active in their area association and in the SDAW. Marilyn was one of the first to volunteer for the Anthology Committee.

JUNE MYKLEBUST and Bob Dahnert belong to Diamond Squares in the South West Area of Wisconsin and June is a founding member of the club. The couple met when Bob was in lessons and June was angeling.

June has been square dancing for 24 years and has round danced for 20 years. Bob has square and round danced for 10 years. June served on many square dance convention committees with her husband Elvyn (deceased). They were Special Events Chairmen for the 1978 Convention, Services Secretary for the National Convention in Milwaukee in 1979, and Registration Chairmen for the Madison Convention, 1981 and 1986. She and Bob have served as co-chairmen for the 1991 and 1996 conventions and were chairmen for the Retail Sales area in 1993.

>─┤─◆>─O─<◆─┤─<

Memory Quilt Contributors
Club name, area and designer

49ers (SEA)—Dorothy Primuth
Allemande (SEA)—Diane Ruzicki
Allemanders (SEA) 1951-1994—Jim Noonan
American Heritage Dancers (SEA) est. 1964—Charlotte Udovich
Badger Rovers NSDCA-031 (WRA)—Floyd and Jean Schultz
Belles & Beaux (WCA) 1970—1984—Marlys Galoff
Boots and Slip-ers (SWA) 1959-1992—Fae Milquet
Boots and Slippers (SEA) 1964-1996—Fela Chapa
Circle 'n Star (SEA) 1959-May 1989—Donald Bahr
Circle 8 (SEA)—Jean Wishau
Circus City Squares (SWA)—Laurie Wilson
Clar-Adel Dancers (WRA) 1959-1986—Pat Kelm
Country Squares ('64-'84) Pistol's & Petticoats ('72-'77)
      Metric Squares ('74-'81) (WCA) (Jack Daily, Caller)—Dorothy Daily
Country Promenaders (SEA) est. 1979—Merrylou Green
Country Villa Squares (WCA)—Joanne and Rosy Cote
Country Cousins (WRA)—Rosie Fochs
Country Corners (CA)—Airabell Beyer
Crosstrails (SWA) Est. 1961—Billie Weisensel
Diamond Squares (SWA) est. 1979— June Myklebust
Dip\N\Dives (Hollandtown) 1960-1965—Verla Koerner & Donna Cartwright
Dudes and Dolls (SWA)—est. 1958—Rose Tom & Jacquie Kovach
EMBA Square Dance Club (SEA) est. 1946—Marilyn Hall
Falls Promenaders (SEA) est. 1958—Gert Schneider
Fas-N-Eighters (WRA)—Bernice Zimmerman
Fox Valley Squares (WCA)—Rosie Fochs
Friendly Twirlers (WCA)—Arlene Gustafson
Good Time Squares (SWA)—Deloris Hubbard
Grand Squares (SWA) 1974—1997— Margaret Skolaski
Green Bay Squares (WRA) est. 1948—Flo Bungert
Greendale Village Squares (SEA)—Phyllis Pionkoski
Happy Twirlers (WCA) est. 1961—Sue Comeau
Hartland Hoedowners (SEA)—Elaine Irwin & Janet Hinkley
Hodag Twirlers (CA) est. 1968—Janice Johnson
Jacks 'N Jills (WRA) disbanded—Pat Kelm
Jeans & Queens (SEA) 1964-1977—Jim Noonan
Kettle Squares (WRA)—Christine Short

Kettle Moraine Squares (SEA) est. 1981—Joyce Gatzke
Lake Country Swingers (SEA)—Sue Ruf
Lakeland Promenaders (CA) 1973-1996—Mary Ann Anderson
Lakeside Twirlers (WRA)—Mildred Osborn
Lamplighters (SEA)—Yvonne Schiesl
Limber Timbers (SWA)—Marion Morse
Lincoln Squares (CA)—Airabell Beyer
Lodi Valley Squares (SWA)—Billie Weisensel—Club has ceased dancing—
     balance of treasury donated to Lodi Valley School System
Markesan Wheels—(SWA)—Marilyn Babel
Marshall Stars (SWA) Disbanded—Jean Dunham
Merry Mixers (WCA)—Mary Hagens and Eileen Martinson
Merry 8's (Wausau) (CA) est. 1961—Joyce Corder
Millstream Wranglers (WRA)—Judy Hechel
Milton Village Squares (SWA)—Donna Hobbs & Sue Balog
Milwaukee Area Callers' Council (SEA) est 1951—Jim Noonan
NorJen Dancers—(WCA) est. 1971—Sue Comeau
Northern Star (WCA) 1952-1992—Florence Rand and Mary Ann Kies,
OK Swingers (WRA) 1988-1997—Pat Kelm
Overseas Dancer Association—Gladys Bishop
     (Wisconsin Reunions held in 1988 & 1998)
Paddock Lake Squares (SEA) 1972-1992—Gladys Bishop
Pairs and Squares (WCA)—Evelyn Petass
Petunia City Squares (SWA)—Judy Heidenreich
Pistols 'N Petticoats (West Central 1966-1986—Laurel Hutchens)
Prairie Partners (WCA) est. 1981—Vi Wilklow
Prison City Squares (SWA)—Ona Johnson and Dorothy Parduha
Promenaders (Coulee Region) (WCA) 1993-1996—Sue Comeau
Pyramid Squares (SWA) 1956-1968—Floyd and Jean Schultz
Rhinelander Square Dance Clubs—(CA) 1954-1968—Judy Hogan,
     (Hodag Square Dance Club, Casswood Dancers Childrens Club,
     Shady Squares, Belles & Beaux)
Rice Lake Twirlers (WCA) est. 1968—Nancy Stein
Ridge Runners (SEA)—Dorothy Primuth
Ripon Twirlers (WRA)—Orion Fashun
Romeos and Calicos (WRA)—Barb Sharpe
Saints and Swingers (CA)—JoAnn Koehler
SDAW-SWA—June Myklebust
SDAW-SEA—Lucy Mattson
SDAW-Central (CWSDA)—Airabell Beyer
SDAW-WRA (Wolf River)—Karen Gulbrand
Shirts & Skirts (WRA) 1976-1988—Pat Kelm
Spring City Squares (SEA)—Claire Dundon
Square Wheelers (Durand) (WCA)—Rosemary Achenbach
Square Benders (SEA) est. 1965—Ruth Witt
Square Generations (WRA) 1991-1996—Pat Kelm
Squarenaders (WCA)—Elaine Long
Suburban 8's (SEA) est. 1960—Janet Pelky
Swingin' Single Squares (SEA) est.1974—Charlotte Udovich,
Swingin' Beavers (SWA)—Marion Gade
T-P Taws & Paws (SEA)—Dorothy Anderson, Ceanna Hartmann,
     Loni Singer, Cele Marascalco
Teen Twisters (WRA) 1971-1980—Dawn Zimmerman
     Bruce Busch started club, he and Dan Flynn were club callers
Timber Toppers (WRA) est, 1953—Barbara Reabe
Triple Scooters (WCA)—Inez Pettis
Verona Squares (SWA) 1956-1984—Cathy Garfoot & Arlene Larson
Watermelon Squares (SWA) est. 1975—Jean Alfredson & Joyce Hare
Waupaca Squares (WRA) est 1949—Joanna Rheingans

West Bend Square Steppers (SEA) 1951-1983—Joyce Gatzke
West Turners Square Dance Club (WRA)—Karen Gulbrand
Westfield Jolly Squares (SWA) est. 1953—Esther Brancel,
Westport Squares (SWA)—Marilyn Buechner
Wheel and Deal (CA)—Mary Gonske
Whirl-A-Ways (WRA)—Jean Palmer
Yellow Rockers (SEA) Est. 1989—Joyce Gibour

Trail's End

In May of 1998, the Square Dance Association of Wisconsin reported that 93 clubs and 76 callers had paid the annual association dues for the year. At the end of 1948, there were 33 member clubs in the association. There was no caller roster but the names of 40 callers were mentioned in the first SDAW handbook. In other words, we currently have 60 more clubs and 36 more callers than we had in 1948. When looked at from that perspective, it doesn't sound so bad. What's missing from that picture is how many dancers we have now, compared with 1948.

In 1990, LEGACY did an international census of square dancers. They came up with an estimated 374,494 dancers in the U.S. and 30,729 in Canada. Of that figure 6,648 were from Wisconsin. Soon after those figures came out, the Wisconsin LEGACY trustees did their own survey in Wisconsin and came up with about the same number. However, we have no count of the number of square dancers in Wisconsin in the early years of the association so we have nothing to compare it to. Another factor to consider is the average age of the dancers which is presently estimated at 55.

LEGACY is currently discussing the possibility of conducting another census, possibly in the year 2000. The numbers are expected to be down about ten percent from 1990.

Wow! If those figures are accurate, it means there are over 6,000 people in the state still actively enjoying America's Folk Dance. With that many people, this book could go on forever. There is so much more I could add—so many callers, cuers, dancers, and leaders that haven't been mentioned. Every day, I think of someone or something else that really should be included.

D-D Burss once told me how the square dance "tip" got its name. In the 1800s and early 1900s, fiddlers traveled from place to place calling dances. When the caller got tired and was ready to quit, the guests would collect money from the dancers in the square. They would give the "tip" money to the caller in exchange for another dance. These came to be known as "Tip" dances. The dancers would keep collecting money and the caller would keep calling until eventually, like all good things, the dance had to come to an end.

And so does this book.

Glossary

ACA—American Callers' Association, the second largest association of square dance callers in the United States. See also CALLERLAB.

Advanced—Skill level in Modern Western Square Dancing requiring prior knowledge of Basic, Mainstream, and Plus movements.

Afterparty—A gathering of square dancers after a dance. This can be something simple like going out to a restaurant, a quiet get-together at someone's hotel room, campsite, or house, to something more elaborate, like planned skits or initiations for fun dangles.

Angel—Dancers at a class that are already at (or beyond) the current dance program, there to help those who are actually in the class. Very often, angels are club members helping at their club's classes, helping new dancers learn the basics of square dancing.

APD—All Position Dancing. Dancing either the belle's or beau's position from standard formations of square dance calls. At many dances, calls are only called from certain standard positions. For example, the caller keeps the man on the lady's left most or all of the time—so if you are a man, you will always turn to your right during Square Thru—which means you don't have to think as hard about where to go next. Other calls also have standard positions, and so most people only learn how to do half (or less) of the call.

Banner—Usually a square or rectangular piece of cloth, with the club's logo. One method square dance clubs use to encourage dancers to come to their dances is to award visiting clubs (with a minimum number of attending dancers) banners with the sponsoring club's logo upon it. The tradition follows that the club giving the banner must then return the visit back to the club who captured the banner, in order to "recapture" their own banner back.

Banner Steal—A planned visitation to another club, with enough attending club members present to "steal" the visited club's official banner. Many areas use a single banner for their club, while other areas have many banners. See Chapter 11.

Basic—Introductory skill level in Modern Western Square Dancing. It contains about 48 movements.

Beau—The dancer in the left-hand position, relative to his (or her) partner. See also belle.

Belle—The dancer in the right-hand position, relative to his (or her) partner. See also beau.

Breakdown—When the square is no longer able to continue dancing because too few dancers know where they're supposed to be. This is considered to be a "broken" square, and is commonly referred to as "breaking down". If the current song is a singing call, the couples should all return to their original home positions and wait for the rest of the floor to return as well; if it's a patter call, they should form two facing lines and wait for a call that brings all the lines "up to the middle and back", their signal to join in and resume dancing.

Caller—The leader (male or female) who directs dancers through a square dance tip, calling either a patter or singing call. This can be at a class or dance.

CALLERLAB—An international organization, this is the larger of the two primary square dance caller organizations that has formalized what we call modern square dancing, responsible for the consistent definition of square dance calls and programs throughout the world. See Chapter 8.

CAW—Clogging Association of Wisconsin

Challenge—Skill level in Modern Western Square Dancing. Requires prior knowledge of Basic, Mainstream, Plus, and Advanced movements.

CLAW—Clogging Leaders' Association of Wisconsin.

Clogging—See Chapter 6.

Community Dance Program (CDP)—Fun level in Modern Western Square Dancing requiring only a portion of the Basic program. No prior experience is needed to attend a CDP dance. See Chapter 12.

Clyde Tanglefoot—A large doll which is passed from square dance club to square dance club. Each club pins their own badge on it and passes it on to another club.

Contra—Dances done in long facing lines and prompted, or cued on the last beats of one phrase so the dancers may start on count one of the next. Dance movements date back to the sixteenth century and are similar to square dance choreography used today.

Corner—From the gents' position it is the person dancing to the immediate left; from the ladies' position it is the person dancing to the immediate right.

Cuing—Another name for the concept of directional calling, where the caller will add directions after a call to help dancers who might be confused (or not familiar) with the call. In round dancing, the directions the cuer gives to direct the round dancers through the current song. Only cues are used when round dancing (vs. calls and singing during square dance singing calls).

Cuer—Similar to a caller, a cuer is responsible for directing round dancers during a round dance.

CWCA—Central Wisconsin Callers' Association.

Dangle—A small plastic or metal object which attaches to a badge, using only a single metal ring as the attachment. This object can symbolize a variety of things, including such items as visitations, callers, special events. See also Fun badge.

DBD—Dancing by Definition. Dancing such that the individual calls can be broken into their component parts so that a call can be danced from any position on the floor, including a call from a different starting point (non-standard position) than was originally taught.

EAASDC—European Association of American Square Dance Clubs.

ECCO—Education, Communication and Club Organization—Wisconsin branch of LEGACY. See Chapter 8.

Fiddle and Squares—A square dance magazine published in the early 1950s.

Fun Badge—A badge or dangle, usually earned by performing an unusual stunt or trick pertaining to square dancing such as attending a specific dance, (i.e. barn dance), or going on a bus trip with a group of dancers. There are literally hundreds of these dangles, representing everything from dancing a tip in the bathroom to dancing a tip in an airplane hangar.

Hash—Caller spontaneously calls a variety of calls moving dancers around the square and returning them to home position each time. Caller usually uses different sequences of calls until he/she decides to stop—length of time normally varies from 5-7 minutes. Usually followed by a singing call. See also "Patter".

Here 'Tis—A Wisconsin square dance magazine.

Home—The original positions within the square in which the men were located at the start of the song. The ladies, technically speaking, do not have their own home, but return with their current partner to his home. In a patter call, this would be her original home; in a singing call, her home would move between each of the four sides of the square, returning, at the end of the song, to her original home position. Simply put, her home is the home of her current partner.

IAGSDC—International Association of Gay Square Dance Clubs.

Line Dance—Partnerless dancing done to a wide variety of music. Specific choreography, usually short, is repeated over and over for the duration of the music.

LEGACY—LEaders GAthered for Commitment and Yak—A leadership and communication resource center. See Chapter 8.

Dr. Lloyd "Pappy" Shaw—The father of modern western square dancing. His greatest influence was felt in the 1940s through 1960s.

Lloyd Shaw Foundation—A non-profit organization established to preserve and disseminate our American square dance heritage. See Chapter 8.

MACC—Milwaukee Area Callers' Council.

Mainstream—Skill level in Modern Western Square Dancing requiring knowledge of Basic and containing about 20 additional new movements.

Mixer—Dance form designed to move dancers through specific choreography ending with a new partner each time the dance is repeated; couples dance in a big circle formation changing partners 6 to 10 times per record.

NEC—National Executive Committee (National Square Dance Convention).

NSDCA—National Square Dance Campers' Association.

NASRDS—National Association of Square and Round Dance Suppliers.

One-Nighter—A dance event designed to entertain and instruct people who have seldom or never square danced. Usually includes mixers, line, and other solo dances, reels, and some folk dances in addition to square dances.

OSDA—Overseas Dancer Association.

Partner—From the gent's position, usually the person to the immediate right; from the ladies position, usually the person on the immediate left.

Patter Call—Originally meant short rhyming phrases used to fill in between directional calls. Example: "Circle to the right; hurry-up boys, don't take all night." In present usage patter calls are often regarded as synonymous with "hash".

Plus—Skill level in Modern Western Square Dancing requiring knowledge of Basic and Mainstream, providing about 25 additional movements.

Reel—Contra dance with facing lines; gents in one line, ladies in the other.

ROUNDALAB—International Association of Round Dance Teachers, Inc.

Round dance—Couples dancing in a large circle formation prompted by a cuer. The dance movements are choreographed ballroom steps with each movement having a precise definition and name. In club dancing tips or squares are usually alternated with one or two round dances.

Square—A set of four couples, in a four-sided formation, each couple facing one of the four walls of the room. Each square is comprised of two head couples and two side couples. Set is sometimes used to denote a "tip".

SDAW—Square Dance Association of Wisconsin. An association made up of callers, cuers, instructors, and dancers in or near Wisconsin. See Chapter 2.

Singing Call—Usually done to a familiar Pop or Country tune; the caller will intermix square dance directions with the original song lyrics. The ladies move from one gent to another (usually counter-clockwise) around the square, ending up with their original partners.

SSDUSA—Single Square Dancers, USA.

SWACC—South West Area Callers' Council.

Taw—A reference to either partner (male or female) of a couple or just the female half of a couple. A common usage is to the "caller's taw" as well as in "Seesaw your pretty little taw."

Tip—The time you spend dancing in one square without a break. (This is usually a combination of a patter call and a singing call.) In the '50s and '60s it was usually two singing calls and a hash call, often lasting 20 minutes. Sometimes referred to as a "set".

Trail-In Dance—A dance held prior to a festival or convention, at the city or area, but not necessarily related to the festival or convention. Commonly sponsored by a local club or organization.

URDC—Universal Round Dance Council.

USDA—United Square Dancers of America.

Visitation—A club-organized event where the club "visits" another club, usually in the local area (though sometimes it may be a non-local club, usually with some sort of group transportation, such as a bus). In many clubs, a banner is given to the visiting club(s). Many clubs track each member's participation in the visitations throughout the year, and award members with swingers or dangles to indicate the current level or plateau obtained by that member.

Workshop—A formal class, designed for reviewing square dance calls that have already been taught to dancers at the workshop's program. The class instructor may review known calls in their standard positions, or teach these calls in new formations or orientations that the dancers may never have learned before. For example, you could have a Plus/DBD workshop, expanding the dancer's use of existing calls at the Plus program that the dancer is already familiar with, but previously known only from the standard positions.

Another type of workshop is called a Brush-Up Workshop. This would be oriented toward square dancers who have been unable to dance on a regular basis. Rather than go to a dance where they would, most likely, break down squares, they, instead, go to a refresher/brush-up workshop, allowing them to receive a quick review of all the calls and receive the confidence they need to go out on the dance floor—knowing their skills are up to par with the rest of the dancers on the floor.

WCCA—West Central Callers' Association.

SDAW-WRA—Wolf River Area Square Dance Association of Wisconsin. *(also referred to as WRADA—Wolf River Area Dancers' Association.)*

WRACA—Wolf River Area Callers' Association.

WRDLC—Wisconsin Round Dance Leaders' Council.

WSDLCC—Wisconsin Square Dance Leaders' and Callers' Council.

WSSDA—Wisconsin Single Square Dancer Association.

Yellow Rock— 1) A hug. 2) When used during a square dance it is a call that signals dancers to give a designated person in the square a hug.

Index

A

A-Gay-O 170
A. O. Smith plant 156, 157
Aanerud, Harold 168, 170
ACA 85
Accent on Rounds 188, 224
Acey Deucy Club 201
Achenbach, Rosemary 237
ADA—American Dairy Association . . . 63
Adopt-a-Highway program 112
Adrich Junior High 31
Alfredson, Jean 237
Alice in Dairyland 62
Allemande 217, 236
    Club 113
Allemanders 226, 236
Allen
    Bradley Company 41
    Charles (Grandpa) 27
Allis-Chalmers 40
America's Bicentennial 85
America's Folk Dance 238
American Callers' Association 225
The American Dance Circle 5, 132
American
    Heritage Dancers 69, 70, 71, 217,
        222, 223, 232, 235, 236
    Square Dance . . 28, 123, 152, 196, 205
Anderson
    Andy 83
    Chet 103
    Clare 103, 163
    Dorothy 237
    Mary Ann 237
Anhalt, Art and Helen 106
Annual Reunion of Overseas Dancers . .
    128
Anunson, Bryce 182
Apple Ciders Square Dance Club . . . 210
Arkansas
    Square Dance Federation Festivals . 87
    State Square Dance Federation 86
ASCAP 122
Asilomar Conference Grounds 121
Asp, Bob 221
Auctioneer School 225
"The Auctioneer" 225
Auer Avenue 39

B

Babel, Marilyn 237
Bachelor and Bachelorette clubs 101
Badger
    Middle School in West Bend 112
    Rover Square Dance Campers
        NSDCA-031 . . . . 218, 223, 236
    School 26
Bahr, Donald 236
Baker, Norbie—Hall 87
Baldwin
    Charlie 123
    Dorothy 40
Balog, Sue 237
Bammel, Harold 55
Bar-None Square Dance Club 23, 26
Barisonzi, Judy 161, 175, 193, 235
Barr
    Bill 6, 38, 84

Barr, cont'd.
    Dolly 116
Barth, Donna 96
Bashaw, Dale 91
Bastens Hall 27
Baudhuin, Vern 174
Baumann, Paul 113
Bay Beach Pavilion 27
Bear Lake, Manawa, Wisconsin 127
Beauchamps, R. W. 9
Been
    Joe 172
    Margaret L. 171, 172
Belgian American Club 150, 151
Bellais, Leslie 234
Belles and Beaus 92, 94
Belles and Beaux Square Dance Club . .
    . . . . 39, 49, 50, 236, 237
Beloit Square Dance Club 23, 31
Beneke, Tim 219
Bennett, Darlene 221
Berg, Lorraine and Frank 142
Berget, Tony and Lu 179
Berna, Gordy 146
Bernard
    Howie 7, 9, 37, 84, 178
    Hildegard 84
Bero
    Jim 126, 144
    Mitzie 126
    Vern 144
Berquam, Warren 74, 144
Betty's Square Dance Shop 188
Beyer, Airabell 236, 237
Bickford
    Lorraine 56
    Robert 55, 56
Big John's Hall 103
Bishop
    Gladys Elda 113, 129, 130, 237
    Martin 129, 130, 131
Biskobing, Bob and Gerri 103
Bitter, Charlie 219
Black
    Americans 77
    Hawk Cross Trailers, Chapter 0 14, 127
    Light Dancers 29
    Wheel in Cedarburg 103
Blankenheim, Ben 9, 45
Blessed Sacrament parish 45
Bliss, Kermit 228
BMI 122
Boerner Botanical Gardens 222, 223
Bolek
    Bernice G. 188, 213
    Jim 188
Bolz, Jerry and Martha 104
Boots 'n Bows 129, 130
Boots
    and Slip-ers 236
    and Slippers Square Dance Club . . 65,
        94, 130, 236
Bott, Joe 68, 231
Brabender
    Alex 83, 86, 87, 103, 104, 162
    Gen 103, 104, 166
Bradley, Ned and Carol 227

Brancel, Esther 238
Braun, Roland 18, 19
Brisk, Jean and Bob 164
Brock, Del and Jan 106
Brookfield East High School 68
Brown
    Brownie and Regena 117
    Deer Park Square Dancers 24
    Street School 140
Buchanan, Reginald 163
Buck, Ann Ratajczyk 40, 136, 137
Buechner, Marilyn 238
Buettner, Roger 216, 219
Bungert
    Flo 236
    Lloyd 27
Buoys and Belles 113
Burdick, Stan 123
Burgraff, Henry 134
Burke Town Hall 228
Burlington Square Dancers 47
Burss
    Deanna 110, 233
    D-D 73, 214, 238
    Jimmie 72, 110, 147, 200, 219,
        226, 227, 233
    Russell 73, 152, 214
Busch, Bruce 237
Busy Bee's 75

C

Calhoun Hall 40, 73, 143, 147,
    158, 227
Calico
    & Kerchief Square Dancers 23,
        24, 26
    Square Dance Club 47
    Country Cloggers 78
Callaway
    Don 129, 131
    Nancy 131
CALLERLAB 46, 54, 85, 86, 89, 121,
    122, 123, 206, 212, 220,
    223, 226, 228, 230, 233
Callers' College 106
Camp
    Byron 231
    Northern Hills 152
Campbell, Scott 219
Capitol
    at Washington D.C. 107
    Pladium 38, 47
    Squares 36
Carlson, Carol and Margaret 117
Carroll, Leo and Pat 186
Cartwright, Donna 236
Casper, Dr. Max 36
Casswood Dancers Childrens Club . . 237
Casswood Promenaders 173
CCC 154
CDP 208
Cecil, Jim 18
Cedarburg Firehouse 95
Central Area (SDAW-CA) 21, 219
    Callers' Association 212, 221
Certified Clogging Instructor (CCI) . . . 79
Chaffee, John 69
Channel 7 T.V. 173

Chapa, Fela 236
Chapman, Doris. 104
Chapter
    001. 127
    002, Pine Tree 127
Char's Square Dance Shop 188
Chartier, Tricia 68
Chavey, Darrah 221, 229
Checkmates. 75
Chestnut
    Don 62, 65
    Vera 62, 64
Chet Cholka's Band. 8
Cheyenne Mountain Dancers . . . 14, 183
Chinchilla Bar. 114
Chit-Chat 182
Christianson
    Eleanor 160
    Roy 149
Circle
    'n Star 98, 113, 236
    8 Club 24, 45, 113, 217, 236
    B 95, 103
    D 87, 181
Circus City Squares 218, 223, 236
Clar-Adel Dancers 43, 44, 91, 236
Clark, Martha 9, 17, 18, 48
Clark, Martha—Golden Agers 48
Clark's Woods 38
Classic
    Lanes 113
    Square and Country Dancing 86,
        208
CLOG National Clogging Organization .
        79
Clogging 76, 77
    Association of Wisconsin 79
    Leaders' Association of Wisconsin . 79
Club
    Garibaldi 38
    Leadership Journal 182, 206
    of the Month 197
The Coat Tree 188, 213
Cocke, Enid 132
Cockrum, Larry 27, 219
Col-Sac Ferry 107
College of the Pacific Folk Dance Camp .
        84
Collins, Jim and Pat 59, 116, 201
Comeau
    Sue 97, 114, 236, 237
    Skip 97, 114
Community Dance Program . . . 85, 206,
        208, 216
Conger, Sally 17
Conner, Jim and Jeanette 118
Conrad
    Dot 104, 161
    Otto 104
Continental Can Company 86
Contra 35
CONTRALAB 89
Converse School 31
Cook, Caroline 167
Cook's Nook 117
Corder, Joyce 237
Cote
    Bud 170, 221
    Joanne and Rosy 236
Coulee Region Promenaders 84, 224
Coulthurst, Bernie and Carolyn 181, 182

Country
    Corners 219, 236
    Promenaders 163, 192, 217, 236
    Squares 218, 236
    Swingers 108
    Villa Squares 236
    Western Dancing 226
County Cousins 217
Craig
    Barb Busche 173
    Schlosser Legion Post 41, 42
Cream City
    Buckaroos 24, 26
    Cloggers 79
    Squares 229, 230
Cripple Creek Cloggers 78
Crosstrails 218, 229, 236
    Exhibition Square 72
    youth "Square Dance Club" 130,
        223, 228
Curator of Costumes and Textiles for the
    State Historical Society. 234
Custer High School 47

D

D & L Dancers 76
Dahnert, Bob 236
Daily
    Dorothy 236
    Jack 236
Dairyland's Singing Cowboy 43
Dance-N-Squares 226
Dancing Bears 129
Dawson
    Bob 7, 9, 49, 83, 146, 147,173,
        178, 179, 180
DeBoer
    Norma 135, 136
    Stan 135, 136, 210
Decco Deck 130
DeForest
    Community Center 235
    High School 106
Deinhammer, Steve 170
Dell City Wheelers 74
Department of Natural Resources . . 136
Desch, Gloria 143
Dhuse, Dwayne 221
Diamond
    Rounds 235
    Squares 106, 107, 130, 218, 236
Dilges, Don 229
Dip\N\Dives 236
Disney World 167
Dittner, John 221
Dixie Style Square Dance Shop 188
Dixon School 42
Do-Si-Do On Time 186
Docey Doe Club 24, 26
Doers
    Sue 104, 160
    Vic 68, 103, 104, 197
Dolmer, Glen and Elaine 98
Donnell, Joyce 101, 102
Dorschner
    Clarence 55, 56, 126, 210
    Enid 56, 126, 210
Dot & John's Bar 205
Doucette, Phil 148, 219
Dousman Derby Dancers . . 88, 147, 181
Dow, Ann. 111
Downtown Arts & Activities Center . 228

Drafz, Betty 105
Draize
    Ivan 27, 150, 151
    Margaret 151
Dreyfuss, Gene 179
Drought School 109
Duckham, Dick 148
Dudes and Dolls. 75, 113
    Square Dance Club 109, 163, 217,
        222, 228, 236
Dundon
    Claire 69, 237
    Jim 68
Dunham, Jean 237
Dunn, Ed 179

E

E & D's Grand Square 186
Eagan
    John 48, 55, 56
    Marie 56
Eagle Chain Squares 94, 144, 146
Early American Dancers 70
Eastern Illinois University 90
ECCO 65, 85, 125, 206, 213
Edgar Squares 211
Edge
    Mary 75, 98, 109, 113, 223
    Roger 109, 113
Edwards, Gene and Berla 182
The Electric Company 28
Elias
    Elmer 6, 9, 18, 28, 30, 46, 53, 72,
        69, 83, 179, 180, 219, 225
    Rosemary 69, 179
Elliot
    Arlene 56
    William 55, 56
Elm City Dancers 24
EMBA Square Dance Club 24, 28,
        29, 30, 65, 116, 213,
        217, 225, 233,236
Endres, Larry 100
English Country Dance 35
Engum, Bob and JoAnne 211
Erdman, Roger 69
Eric Tangman's Swingin' Singles . . . 232
Erlandson, Win and Jo Ann 117
Erler, Louise 101, 102
European Association of American
    Square Dance Clubs (EAASDC) . . 128
Evans
    Arnold 55
    Dorothy 55

F

Faelten, Carl 9
Falls Promenaders Square Dance Club .
        . . . . 142, 163, 164, 166, 217,
        222, 236
Family Squares 72
Fancy Pants Round Dance Club 131
Fas-N-Eighters 236
Fashun, Orion 237
Fease
    Bob 92, 173
    Marj 173
    Shady Rest Lodge 92, 143, 173,
        174, 188
Ferderer
    Carol 59
    Will 59, 100, 219
Fiddle and Squares. . 3, 7, 38, 48, 50, 178

Fiftieth Anniversary of the SDAW . . 234
Fink, Herman 140
First International
    Square Dance Festival 18
    Presbyterian Church 101
Flag Foundation 212
Flippo, Marshall 121
Flying Squares 94
Flynn, Dan 237
Fochs
    Howie 55, 148, 219
    Rosie 236
Foggy City Squares 229
Folk Fair Dancers 54, 69, 70
Fond du Lac Square Dance Club . 23, 26
Ford
    Henry 3, 86, 183
    Mrs. Henry 3
Forrest
    Clinton 55, 56
    Vi 56
49ers Square Dance Club . . . 41, 45, 217,
                                          233, 236
The Four Hits and their Mrs 59
Fox
    River Melody Squares 109
    Valley Squares 217, 236
Franseth, Mrs. Paul 130
Frazier, Joe 229, 230
Frederic March Theater 68
Freis, Clarence 43, 44, 91
Friendly Twirlers 218, 236
Friendship Ring 197
Frontier Square Dance Club 45
Fruit, John 219
Fuerst, Dolores 13, 16
Fugina, Joe 9
Fun
    Dance Squares 83
    on the Farm 106
The Future of Square Dancing 74

G

G & L Dancers 76
Gade, Marion 237
Galaxy Rounds 212
Galoff, Marlys 236
Garden State Square Dance Campers . .
    127
Gardner
    John 9, 18, 26, 59
    Mildred 26, 59
    Square Dance Club 26
    Square Dancers 23
Garfoot, Cathy 237
Gates, Jim 115
Gateway
    Square Dance Club 38
    Squares 219
Gatzke
    Joyce 112, 216, 233, 237, 238
    Lloyd 112, 216, 233
Gauthier, Wayne and Judy 233
Gaver
    Jack 87, 111, 112, 232
    Lolly 87, 88, 111
Gay
    Callers' Association (GCA) 230
    Squares Square Dance Club 131
George
    Ralph 59
    Vi 59

Germundson, Nyle 221
Gessner, Wayne 219
Gibour, Joyce . . . 220, 230, 231, 232, 238
Gibson, Royal and Joan 115
Giese, Olive "Skippy" . 161, 163, 170, 176
Gilmore
    Ed 86, 121, 144, 195
    Howard 89
    May Donna 2, 89, 182
Gladding, Ralph 94
Glasgow, John 219, 235
Goebel, Bob 161, 220
Golden
    Cal 90
    Pheasant Game Farm 78
Gonske
    Mary 164, 238
    Steve 164
Goocher, Fay 69
Good Time Squares 218, 236
Gordon
    Maryann 69
    Thomas "Flash" 68, 234
Gorski
    Art 93, 94, 144, 145, 174
    Fran 93, 94
Gorton Machine Tool Company 47
Gotoski, Eleanor 18
Graef, Vic 9, 13, 14, 16, 17, 18, 19
Grand 150, 185
    Avenue School in Thiensville 95
    Squares 115, 236
Grandine, Les 18
Grange Hall 153, 155
Granville School 86
Great Lakes Coal and Dock Company . .
    147
Green
    Bay Recreation Department 27
    Bay Square Dancers (Squares) . . . 23,
                          26, 27, 28, 217, 236
    Mel 217
    Merrylou 217, 236
Greendale
    Village Days Parade 72
    Village Squares . . . 101, 213, 217, 236
Greenfield Avenue Single Adults Club . .
    101
Griggs, Ione Quinby 101
Grobschmidt Senior Center . . . 113, 223
Gruetzmacher
    Amanda 221
    Warren 211, 219
Gulbrand
    Ellery 69, 217
    Karen 69, 217, 238
Guse, Larry 101, 102
Gustafson, Arlene 236

H

H & C Petticoat Junction 188
Haag, Jerry 102
Hagens, Mary 237
Hall
    Lovett 183
    Marilyn 236
Hamann, Elmer 39
Hamm's Tavern 87
Hampden Hoedowners 89
Hansen, Dick and Arlene 109
Hanson, Terry 165
Hap 'P' Hazards 211

Happy
    Rounders Round Dance Club 131
    Steppers 212
    Twirlers 97, 114, 218, 222, 236
Hare, Joyce 237
Harrington, Lou 31
Harry Moertle's Band 8
Hartland Hoedowners Square Dance
    Club 88, 111, 112, 217, 232, 236
Hartlerode
    Gale 221
    Richard 221
Hartmann, Ceanna 237
Harvest Festival 72
Harvey's Square Dance Club 24, 26
Hastings, Irene 42
"Have-a-Heart Dance" 222
Havey
    Sauer Tours 192
    Wayne and Evelyn 192
Hawthorne Square Dancers 24
Hechel
    Judy 237
    Marvin 219
Heebsh
    Brooke 79
    Kelly 79
Heidenreich, Judy 237
Heidi Festival 72
Held, Byron 138
Helsel, Lee 121, 122
Helt, Mr. Jerry 195
Hempe, Lorelei 76
Hendrickson, Connie and Lorraine . 106
Herb Greggerson Milwaukee (Ranch
    Dance) Institutes . . . 37, 38, 39, 47, 48
Here 'Tis 7, 50, 65, 83, 84, 85, 90,
                    92, 116, 117, 178 180, 181,
                          182, 206, 213, 235
Herschman, John 221
Heuer, Roland and Marge 108
Hill
    and Gully Twirlers 224
    Bert and Fern 127
Hilltop Whirlers 84
Hiltgen Hall 138
Hinkley, Janet 236
Hints, Russell 101
Hinze, Fred and Jackie 104
Hitzke, Leroy 92, 143, 174
Hobb, Donna 237
Hodag
    Clam Diggers 92
    Square Dance Club 92, 237
    Twirlers 92, 93, 94, 144, 146, 173,
                          194, 219, 236
Hoedown News 56, 85, 212, 214
Hogan
    Judy Berg 92, 94, 142, 152, 173,
                                          221, 237
    Tom 94, 143, 174, 221
Holiday
    Folk Fair 71
    Inn Southeast 107
Holup
    Bob 88, 143, 188, 211
    Pauline 188
Hooyman
    Bertha 56
    Kenneth 55, 56
Howard Grove High School 140

Hubbard, Deloris 236
Hugdahl
   Hug 59, 179
   Norma 59, 179
Hussey, Dave 90
Hutchens, Laurel 237

I

Igorski, Irv 179
Immaculate Conception School 41
Industrial Fuel Company 147
Indvick, Norm and Jennie 97, 224
Inter-Level Squares 90, 149
International
   Association of Gay Square Dance
      Clubs (IAGSDC) 229
   Association of Round Dance Teachers,
      Inc. (ROUNDALAB) 124
   Folk and Dance Club 84
   Folk Fair 116
   Institute of Wisconsin 79
   Showcase 72
   Square Dance Camporee 223
   Square Dance Festivals 42
Invick, Norm 114
Iowa Square Dance Convention 223
Irwin
   Elaine 236
   Wayne 220, 232
Isenberg, Elizabeth (Betsy) 104, 140

J

J. F. Square Dance Club 24
J. I. Case High School 233
Jacks 'N Jills 91, 217, 236
Jacobsen, Carole 174
Jahn, Erv and Isabelle 179
Jamboree Juniors 72
Janesville
   Fire Department 117
   Senior Center 223
   Swingin' Squares 117, 118
Jashinsky, Harry and Barbara 84
Jeans & Queens 226, 236
Jessup, Mike 231
Jochims, Kevin 91, 220
Johnson
   Bruce 121
   Clifford 78
   Herbert "Herb" . . . 6, 9, 36, 55, 56, 59,
                72, 126, 136, 149,
                210, 212
   Janice 236
   Ken 6, 73
   Laurie 76
   Matilda "Tilda" . . 56, 59, 126, 149, 212
   Ona 237
   Ruth and Harry 179
Justman, Freddie 110
Justman, Patty 111

K

K C Squares 210
Kachelmeier, Jerry and Jan 70
Kaczmarek, Buzz 6, 86, 220
Kallio-Schenzel, Lucille 194
Kelm
   Pat 43, 91, 219, 221, 236, 237
   Bob 91
Kennedy, Bill 86
Kenosha
   County Fair 106
   Eagles 45
   Senior Citizens 232
   Square Dance Club 22, 26

Kenyon, Otto 87
Kerkhoff, Elsie 9, 12
Kernan, Ken 206
Kersey, Bill . 82, 83, 86, 87, 103, 142, 179
Kersey, Betty 83, 103, 179
Kettle Moraine
   Square Dance 23
   Squares . . . 91, 112, 192, 217, 222, 237
   Morraine Bowl 112
Kickbusch, Irv 9, 13, 16, 28, 53
Kielbasa night 112
Kies, Mary Ann 237
Kindschuh, Doug 175
kitchen junkets 35
Kleitz, Ike 69
Klemp, Leona 138
Knoblach, Art 7, 185
The Knotty Pine 225
Knutson, Gene 107
KOA campground 128
Koch, Phil 146
Koehler, JoAnn 237
Koerner
   Robert W. 212
   Verla 236
Konrad, Erwin 55
Koser, Bob 220
Kovach, Jacquie 236
Krakower, Glen. 235
Krautkramer
   Mike 113, 162, 200, 220, 228, 234
   Julie 228
Kretschmer, Joe and Phyllis 219
Kronenberger, Arnie 121, 122
Krueger, Ann 28, 148, 150
Kumm
   David A. 212
   Violet 221
Kuntry Kuzins Square Dance Club . 131

L

La Crosse
   Oktoberfest 97, 126
   University 90
Laczkowski, Ted and Dennette 64
Ladish Company 46
Lake
   Country Swingers Square Dance Club
      . . . . 227, 237
   Shangrila 105
Lakeland Promenaders 94, 144, 237
Lakeside Twirlers . . . 193, 217, 235, 237
LaLone, Les 97
Lamplighters 217, 237
Lamster, Scott 143
Landry
   Brad 90, 117, 127, 144
   Bernie 127
Lane, Frank 121
Langlois, Del 83, 87
Lariat and Lace 140
Larson
   Arlene 237
   Carl 178, 179
Lasata Home 95
Laufenberg
   Delores "Boots" 108, 162, 164
   Maynard 108
Layman, Jim 101
Lazy L & N Riding Club 23
Leatherman
   Dennis 85, 181, 205, 216, 219, 234
   Karlene 181

Leatherman, cont'd.
   Lyle 9, 55, 56, 59, 85, 90, 127,
                     179, 207
   Margaret 56, 59, 85, 92, 127, 179,
                205, 207, 214
Lecheler, R. 99
LeClair, Johnny 110
LEGACY 54, 65, 85, 89, 123, 124,
           182, 201, 206, 213, 238
Legion Hall 138
Lehner, Harold 86
Lemerond, John and Catherine 108
Lenz, Dick and Marilyn 125
Levis and Lace 219
Lewis
   Bob 74
   Joe 83, 121
LGBT 229
Library of Congress 66
The Lightning Trio 200, 223, 227
Limber Timbers Square Dance Club. . . .
      . . . . 131, 172, 218, 237
Lincoln
   Junior High School. 31
   School, Hartland, Wisconsin 111
Lincoln Squares 211, 219, 237
Lind, Harry 75, 113
Lindemann, Bob 221
Lisko's Hall 108
Lloyd Shaw Foundation . . . 5, 54, 89, 132
Loberger, Joe 91
Lodi Valley
   School System 237
   Squares 100, 237
Log Cabin 41, 49, 137
Long
   Elaine 237
   Lyle and Faye 187
Lorenz, Jean 75
Lovett, Benjamin 3
Loyal Circle 8's 219
Luber, Donna 186
Lucey, Patrick J. 62
Lucky, Ginny 102
Lukens, Harry 173

M

M-T Saddles Square Dance Club 95
MACC (Milwaukee Area Callers' Council)
      . . . . 46, 52, 53, 83, 106, 179,
      180, 200, 212, 217, 220, 228, 233
Mader, Norma 149
Madison
   Area Square Dance Leaders' Council .
      54
   Community Center 228
   Recreation Department 36
   Senior Center 223
   Monona Terrace 107
"Magnificent Mile" 37
Maier, Henry W. 62
Mainz Masters Square Dance Club . 131
Majchrzak, Lynn 68
Mammoth Cave 107
Manning
   Jocko 129
   Tim 115, 218, 221, 224
   Charlotte 218, 224
Marascalco 237
Marathon Squares 211
March of Dimes 150
   polio benefit jamboree 39
Marge Merhoff's Band 5, 8

Marinette KC Square Dance Club 24, 26
Markesan Wheels 89, 218, 223, 237
Marquette University 83
Marshall Stars 237
Marshfield Hoedowners 219
Martha Clark Golden Agers 48
Martinson, Eileen 237
Mattson
    Lucy 68, 233, 235, 237
    Wayne 233, 235
Mayfair shopping center 143
McCarthy, Robert 31
McGinnis, Betty 43
McKinnon, John 101
MECCA 62, 63, 67, 116
Meilahn, Arnie 88
Merbs, C. Florian 55, 56
Merhoff, Marge—Band 5, 8
Merkt
    John 128, 130
    Nancy 128
Merry
    8's (Wausau) 89, 219, 237
    Go Rounders 188
    Mixers 218, 237
Metric Squares 236
Metro-News 83
Mid-America Square Dance Jubilee .. 64
Midnight Squares 74
Midwest
    Engraving 186
    Radio 7, 185
    Record and Engraving 185
Mill Inn 96
Miller, Doug and Virginia 98
Millstream Wranglers 217, 237
Milquet, Fae..................... 236
Milton Village Squares 161, 218,
                             223, 237
Milwaukee
    Area Callers Council (MACC) 47,
        48, 50, 52, 54, 86, 180,
                    219, 226, 237
    Clogging Company 79, 222
    Exposition Convention Center and
        Arena 62
    Girl Scouts 152
    Holiday Folk Fair 69
    Journal Green Sheet 101
    Journal Sentinel Rose Festival 71
    Moose Club 49
    Recreation Department ... 15, 16, 23,
                    37, 45, 47, 48
Mini Legacies 124
Minnesota
    Callers' School 144
    Federation Festival 84
Mitchell Park 142
Moertle, Harry—Band 8
Montgomery, Al 221
Mooney, Marion (Schneider) 55
Moose
    49ers 75
    Club 147
    Lodge in La Crosse 114
Morrison, Joanne and Jerry 67
Morse, Marion 237
Mother of Good Counsel School 36
Muecke, Chuck 220
Muscular Dystrophy Telethon 78
Myklebust
    Elvin 106

Myklebust, cont'd.
    June 106, 216, 235, 236, 237
N
N&B Hall 101
National
    Archives 66
    Association of Square and Round
        Dance Suppliers (NASRDS).... 124
    Clogging and Hoe-Down Council .. 79
    Convention 118, 150, 166
    Singles Convention 148
    Square Dance Campers' Association,
        Inc. (NSDCA) .. 46, 87, 89, 125, 127,
                128, 136, 210, 212,
                        214, 223
    Square Dance Convention .. 42, 62,87,
                101, 102,
                    122, 148
    Square Dance Convention Board .. 75
    Square Dance Convention Committee
        124
    Teacher Education Center 90
Neenah Advanced Dancers 235
Neher, Howie 49
Neighborhood House 229
Nelson, Elroy 213
"New Callers' Dance" 231
New Callers' Jamboree 231
The New England Square Dance Caller .
    .... 123, 134
New Glarus Hotel 130
Newland, Coleman "Doc" .. 5, 6, 8, 9,10,
            35, 39, 40, 146, 147
Newstip 102
Nickel
    Kathy 221
    Tom 221, 229
Nicklaus, Glen and Pat 127
Nicolet
    College 94
    High School 86
1998 Wisconsin Square and Round Dance
    Convention.................. 47
1979 National Square and Round Dance
    Convention 66, 116, 118
Niva, Don 100, 106, 195, 202, 204,
                        221, 223
Noeldner, Nathan and June 110
Noonan
    Jim 86, 96, 101, 147, 201, 220,
                    225, 236, 237
    Bette 96
Norbie Baker's Hall 87
NorJen Round Dance Club ... 114, 218,
                    224, 237
North American Coal Corporation .. 147
Northeast Building Inspectors
    Association 88
Northern Star 237
Northernaire 143
Northtown Club 49
Northwest Senior Center 103, 232
Nu Dawn Club 222
O
O'Neill Ruth 105
Oaklawn School 85
Ocean Waves 130
The Octagon Barn 140
Odd Fellows Hall 41
OK
    Squares 83, 87
    Swingers 91. 237

Oklahoma Avenue Unity Lutheran
    Church Dancers 47
Olsan, Jack and Lu 179
Olson
    Alioto, Teresa 79
    Dwayne 70, 72, 76, 101, 140, 200,
                220, 222, 233
    Julie 79
Omro Square Dancers 24
Orahula Ballroom 55
Orchard Inn 96
Osborn, Mildred 237
OSDA 128, 129, 130, 131
Osgood, Bob 8, 86, 121, 122, 123
Oshkosh
    Hilton 130
    Senior Center 208
    Square Dancers 24
Overbye, Vern and Dorothy 163
Overseas Dancer Association 85,
                    128, 237
P
Packman, Jerry 105
Paddock
    Hooker Lake Clubhouse 113
    Lake Squares 106, 113, 131, 237
Pade, Art and Ethel 193
Page
    Bob 121
    Ralph 86
Pairs-and Squares 218, 237
Palladium 43
Palmen
    Doris 105, 106, 220
    Ted 105, 106, 113, 220
Palmer, Jean 238
Palomino Square Dance Service 187
Pampanga Promenaders 130
Pamperin Park 27
Pappy Shaw Institutes 36
Paragon Club 84
Parbs, Ken 186
Parduha, Dorothy 237
Parins
    Fritz 114
    Lou 114
Paris Swingin' Livewires 4-H Club . 106
Park Lawn social centers 39
Pasch, Irv 84
Paull
    Bob 115, 146, 221
    Lu 115
Pauly's Sales 188
Peaceful Valley, Colorado 86, 143
Pearson, John 94
Peckham
    Ellz 59
    Thelma 59
Pelky, Janet 237
Peninsula Promenaders 212
Perfect Squares 74
Petass, Evelyn 237
Petri, Art 17
Petti-Pants Unlimited 188
Pettis, Inez 237
Petunia City Squares .. 32, 165, 218, 237
Pfister, Dewey 88
Phannenstill, Harold 98
Phillipson, Agnes 13, 16
Pierce Park 85
Pietersom, Jim van 9
Pigeon, Clayton A. 27, 212

Pine Tree Square Dance Campers'
    Chapter 002 233
Pioneer
    Chapter 010 .... 127, 210
    Round Dance Club 50, 84
Pionkoski, Phyllis 69, 236
Pischke
    Elissa 29, 186, 187, 220
    Bob 29
Pistol's & Petticoats 236
Pistols 'N Petticoats 237
Placzkowski, Ed 213
Plover Circle Eights Square Dance Club
    .... 182, 211
Plymouth
    Kettle Squares 222
    Square Dance Club 24
Polka Dot Teen Club 94
Polly, Greg and Joan ... 69, 96, 200, 201
Portis, Jerry 221
Prairie Partners 218, 224, 237
Pratt and Whitney 157
Primuth, Dorothy 236, 237
Prison City Squares 218, 237
Promenade Hall 106
Promenaders 72, 87, 237
Promotion Committee 200, 216
Prosser, David 130
Pyramid Squares 237

Q

Q-T Square Dance Club 116
Quade, Ray 6, 118
Qually, Irene 9, 13, 16, 56
Quimby, Velda 163

R

R Squares 75, 96, 201, 225, 226, 231
Rabe, Dolores 188
Radke, Edward.................. 56
Radoll
    Art 6, 75, 86, 109, 228
    Marge 109
The Rainbow Squares 145
Rand, Florence 237
Randall, Ernie 96, 225
Rapid 8s 211
Ratajczyk
    Mary 136
    Paul 9, 40, 42, 136
Ray Smith's School 38
Raymond
    School 109
    Town Hall 109
RC Twirlers 224
Reabe, Barbara 237
Red Carpet
    Bowlero 102, 231
    Hotel 102
Reiser, Doc and Gerene 96
Reiss Coal 147
Reitz, Bert 142
Rennebohm, Governor Oscar 17
Reoch, Howie 83, 86, 142, 220
Rheingans, Joanna 237
Rhinelander Square Dance Clubs .. 237
Rhythm and Rounds 218
Rice
    Dwight 13
    Lake Twirlers 218, 237
Ridge Runners 45, 75, 113, 217, 237
Ridley, Jerry 220, 222, 232
Riebau, Les 138
Rietz, Bert 6, 9, 38, 45, 86, 181

Rindfleisch, John and Gloria . 31, 32, 216
Ripon Twirlers 89, 217, 237
Riverfest 97
Riverside
    Ballroom 27
    Park 85, 207
Rocky Mountain Folk Dance Camp .. 48
Roehr, Jack 213
Rogge, Lois 18
Rolling Thunder 232
Roltgen, Martin 17
Romeos and Calicos 217, 237
    Square Dance Club 212
Roosevelt Junior High School...... 31
Roselle Exhibition Dance group .. 29, 54,
                              59, 72, 116
Rosenbergs 185
Ross
    Ann 93, 144, 173
    Don 93, 144
Rothman, Helen 163
Roundabouts 87
ROUNDALAB .. 122, 123, 181, 188, 212
Roundups 212
Ruf
    Sue 149, 237
    Therese 149
Russell
    Charles..................... 92
    Edith 131
Ruzicki, Diane 236
Ryan, Dale 221, 225
Ryback
    Jodie 101
    Shirley 101

S

S.S. Badger 148
Saints and Swingers 219, 237
Sampson, Sid 68
Sanchez-Reid, Linda 68
Sanderson, Rob 220
Sauer, Don and Alice 192
Sauthoff, Hermine 18
Schara, Bill 163, 221
Scharlau, Rick 232
Schenck, Wendell 175
Schenzel, Vern 194
Schiesl, Yvonne 237
Schmidt, Christine 134
Schneider
    Carlton 9, 56, 59, 127
    Gert 163, 236
    Marion 59, 127
Schoeckert
    Loretta 59, 179
    Mel 5, 8, 9, 10, 13, 15, 16, 17,
           18, 59, 146, 147, 179, 213
Schopp, Harry 95, 220
Schreiner
    Al 64, 65, 216
    Harriet 65
    Vera 62, 64, 216
Schultz, Floyd and Jean .. 188, 216, 218,
                              236, 237
Schumacher, Betty 219
Schwandt
    Lenny 59
    Mabel 59
Scottish Rite Society 148
Scotty's at Five Corners 95
SDAW 35, 46, 52, 62, 66, 69, 85,
           89, 97, 112, 115, 117, 122, 181,

SDAW, cont'd.... 188, 197, 201, 216, 218,
           223, 231, 234, 235, 238
South East Area Callers' Council
    (MACC).... 21, 52, 54, 96, 102, 106,
           112, 160, 196, 197, 200,
           201, 212, 213, 217, 223,
           225, 233, 235, 237
South West Area ... 21, 115, 216, 218,
                              225, 236
South West Area Callers' Council
    (SWA) 54, 118, 218, 221, 223,
                         225, 229, 237
Wolf River Area Callers' Association
    (WRACA) 55, 56, 85, 125, 126,
           210, 212, 214, 219
Wolf River Area Dancers' Association
    (WRADA) 21, 85, 90, 117, 152,
                         217, 237
Seminary Springs School 228
sesquicentennial of Wisconsin 131,
                              233, 234
Sets in Order 8, 85, 121
Seventh Day Adventist Church 158
Shadow Viner's Round Dance Club . 113
Shady Squares 92, 173, 237
Sharpe, Barb.................... 237
Shaw
    Dr. Lloyd "Pappy" 4, 5, 8, 14, 16,
           17, 22, 37, 40, 41,
           42, 47, 48, 86, 137, 183
    Lloyd—Foundation 54, 89, 132
    Loren 102
Shawano Lake 126
Sheboygan
    Falls Square Dancers 24
    Square Dancing Club 24
"Shindig in the Barn" 103
Shipps, Barbara 27
Shirts & Skirts 91, 106, 237
Shirts and Flirts 142
Shootn' Stars 59
Shoreview Lanes 135
Shorewood
    Recreation Department 38
    Square Dancers 39
Short, Christine 236
Siegmann
    Dan and Paula 112
    Family Singers 69
    Len 29, 30, 108
    Ruth 29, 220
Siewers, Lloyd and Carol 127
Silver
    Buckles 228
    Dome Ballroom 110
    Spur Award 8
Silvers, Harold 82
Silverspring House 87
Singer, Loni 237
Single Square Dancers USA 101
    Dance-a-Rama 102
Skolaski, Margaret 236
Skudlarcyzk, Marge 108
Smith
    Charles 66
    Ray—School 38
Snowmobile Dance 94
Snyder, Lewis "Lew" 6, 140, 212
Somers Town Hall 105
South
    Milwaukee High School 40
    Milwaukee Middle School 46

South, cont'd.
Milwaukee Recreation Department 26
Southeastern Minnesota Caller's Clinic .
.... 84
Southgate Shopping Center 39
Sovereign-Aders 90, 210
Spoolhoff, Pat 227
Spoor
Alice 213
Milt 213
"The Spotlight Shines on" 116
Spring
City Squares 217, 237
Swingers 224
Sprosty, Doug and Don 222
Square Benders Square Dance Club....
.... 103, 104, 140, 160, 161,
163, 166, 213, 217, 220,
222, 235, 237
Square Dance
Association of Wisconsin .. 13, 17, 26,
27, 47, 48, 58, 65, 108,
178, 212, 213, 214, 238
"Capitol of the World" 97
Hall of Fame 121
Month 124
The Square Dance Shop 186
Square Dancing (Sets in Order) 123
The Square Dancing Encyclopedia by Bill
Burleson 176
Square Generations 91, 237
Square Swingers 36, 212
Square Wheelers 75, 218, 228, 237
Squarely Yours 83
Squarenaders 83, 87, 218, 237
St. Boniface Parish 222
St. John's Lutheran Church 105
St. Joseph Catholic Church 150
St. Mary's
in Hales Corners 42
of the Lake Church 99
St. Paul Square Dancers 39
St. Veronica's in Milwaukee 42
St. Vincent Hospital 118
Stardusters 72
Starlight Theater 96
State
Fair Park 63
Historical Society 66, 235
Square Dance Convention 106
Statehood Days 193, 216
Steblik, Nancy 162
Steckmesser, Art 142
Steil, Gladys 130
Stein, Nancy................... 237
Stein's Garden Center 68
Steinich
Marilyn..................... 235
Ray 164, 221, 235
Stillson
Cal 163
John 163, 219
Stipe, Harvey 26
Stoner Prairie School 229
Stuart, Robert.................. 45
Stubbe, Harry 221
Suburban 8's Square Dance Club... 201,
217, 222, 223, 228, 237
Summer Sounds 226
Sweetheart Swingers 218, 224
Swing Easy 45
Swing-in-Families 217

Swingin'
Beavers 218, 229, 237
Families 74
Seniors 223
Singles Square Dance Club ... 67, 75,
101, 102, 104, 140, 147,
150, 160, 213, 217, 220,
222, 226, 231, 232, 235, 237
Swedes 106
Swinging Stars Square Dance Club . 74,
147, 186, 217, 227
Swingsters 24
Swiss Miss factory 130

T
T-P Taws & Paws 113, 237
T-P Camp 'n Dance 106
T-P Teens 72, 106
T-P Trailers 106
Tanglefoot, Clyde 110
Tangman, Eric 75, 102, 104, 140,
220, 230
Tannis, Herb and June 227
Tans
Pat 220
Randy 101, 200, 220, 227
Taws & Paws 217
Taylor
Dave 121
Ralph 213
Teen Twirlers 72
Teen Twisters 237
Temple of Music 37
Tess, Eric 96
Tetzlaff
farm 103
George and Evie 140
Thaney, Tom 68
Thanks for New Dancers night 112
Thiensville
Firemen's Picnic 95
Gardens 95
Thingvold, Buford and Chris 165
Thirty-ninth Wisconsin Square and
Round Dance Convention 112
Thompson, Earl 6
Thorp
Carol 161, 162
Milt 59, 71, 72, 129, 225
Verna 59, 72
Thrap, Howard 144
Thurner
Agnes "Aggi" 162, 216, 233
Max 104, 162, 233
Thursday Night Hoedowns 205, 208
Tiefert, Chris 68
Tim's A-Team 218, 224
Timber Toppers Square Dance Club ...
..... 36, 135, 136, 143, 149, 210,
212, 213, 217, 237
Tjepkema, Ida 141
TNN 75
Tock, Dolores 172
Todd American Legion Post .. 29, 73, 223
Tom, Rose 236
Tony's Club 45
Toth
Johnny 45, 47, 75, 86, 142, 233
Louise 45
Triple Scooters 170, 218, 237
Truax Field Service Club 129
Turner
Cecil 68

Turner, cont'd.
Hall in Fillmore 138
Square Dancing Club 23, 24
Twenty-eighth National Square Dance
Convention 89, 117
Twenty-seventh Street Social Center ...
.... 40
Twilight Twirlers 168, 170
Twin City Squares 90, 212, 217
U
Udovich, Charlotte 236, 237
Uecker, Ray.................... 165
Ulbing, Tiffany 79
Ulichny
Art......................... 10
Ruth 10
Underwood, Jim 115
University Lake School 88, 112
University of Wisconsin 36
Milwaukee 79
Oshkosh 68
Urban
Eddie...................... 211
Mary 211
USAF Contrails Squares 129, 130
UW-La Crosse 90
V
Valley Carousel Round Dance Club . 149,
212
van Pietersom, Jim. *See Pietersom,*
Jim van
VanAntwerp, Bob 121, 122
VanderLangt, Red 163
Vanderpool, Dick and Betty 127
Vanderzee, Joel 221
Venture Inn 96
Verona Square Dance Club .. 64, 71, 72,
130, 228, 237
Vertz, Lloyd 27, 219
Veteran's Park 113
Veterans Home in Waupaca 42
Vetter, Alex and Mona 125
VIP's 45
Vircks, Bob 143
Voltz
Gladys 131
Steve 131
W
W & F Square Dance Shop 188
Wagner
Dale .. 3, 6, 8, 9, 10, 13, 16, 46, 73, 86,
142, 143, 146, 147, 158,159,
179, 227
Florence 10, 159
Wagon Wheels 228
Walker
Chet 86
Diane 213
Wangerin, Chet 9, 38, 39
Washington Park 37, 49, 232
Temple of Music 45
Watermelon Squares 218, 229, 237
Waubeka Fire Hall 138
Waukesha
County Square Dancers 24
High School 83
Waunakee American Legion Hall... 100
Waupaca Squares 205, 217, 237
Waupun Old Time Square Dancers .. 24
Wausau Daily News 88
Wausau Merry 8's 222
Waushara Starlight Promenaders ... 48

Wauwatosa
  East High School 147
  Fundamentals 24
  Recreation Department 15, 48
Webster, Bill 74, 75, 228, 231
Wegart, Charlotte 188
Wegner, Art and Dorothy 116
Weisensel
  Art 6, 9, 59, 99, 100, 142, 163,
                 178, 179
  Billie 74, 163, 223, 228, 236, 237
  Deanna 74
  Mary 59, 74, 100, 178, 216, 229
  Vern 74, 221, 223, 228
Wellhoefer, Romaine 43
Welsh Singing Festivals 89
Wenglewski
  Ceil 109
  Jerry 109, 163
Wertels Hall 27
West Allis
  Grand Squares (WAGS) 65
  Recreation Department Dancers 24, 26
West Bend
  High School 138
  Square Steppers 238
West Central Area Callers' Association. .
              . 21, 218, 221, 224
West Turners Square Dance Club . . 212,
                217, 238
Westfield Jolly Squares ... 89, 181, 218,
               223, 238
Westosha Central High School 113
Westport
  Square Dance Club 99, 100,
               218, 238
  Town Hall 99, 100
Wettstein
  Marilyn 72
  Steve 72, 73, 87
Wheaton, Ralph and Faye 185
Wheel and Deal 143, 219, 238
"Where to Dance in Wisconsin" . . 66, 181
Whipple, Jeff 220, 233
Whirl-A-Way Club 117
Whirl-A-Ways 144, 217, 238
"Whirlaround" 108
Whirling Wheels 72
White
  George....................... 97
  Wes and Eileen 173
Whitefish Bay Square Dancers . . . 24, 39
"Whitewater Express" 67
Wild
  Bob 146
  Gwen 66
  Wilbert "Bill" 66, 212
Wilklow, Vi 237
Williams
  Bill 47
  Elmer 113
Willow-O-Way in Grant Park 113
Wilson
  Bob 98, 131
  Judy "Hot Pepper" 74, 112
  Laurie 236
  Liz.......................... 131
Wilton
  Bill 180, 181, 234
  Colleen 180, 181
Wine, Clarence 92
Winkelmann, Shirley 101

Winnebago
  County Fair Grounds 127
  Dip & Dive Square Dancing Club ...
              . 22, 23, 26
  Mental Health Institute 213
  State Hospital 36
Winnemueller, Bert and Alice 104
Wisconsin
  Avenue Social Center 26, 36, 37,
                39, 84
  Building Inspectors 88
  Callers' and Leaders' Council 223
  mini-LEGACY 125
  Physician's Service 118
  Regional Writer's Association..... 28
  Round Dance Leaders' Council ... 54,
            188, 212, 224
  Senior Olympics 148
  Social Center 48
  Square and Round Dance Convention.
         . 37, 52, 58, 59, 63, 67,
        83, 117, 205, 214, 216,
          223, 230, 233
  Square and Round Dance Convention
    Corporation 58, 214
  Square Dance Flag............ 212
  Square Dance Flag Foundation ... 66
  Square Dance Leaders' and Callers'
    Council (WSDLCC) .. 15, 18, 47, 48,
          53, 54, 58, 210,
        212, 213, 214
  Square Dance Leaders' and Callers'
    Council (WSDLCC) Work Spree . 38
  Square Wheelers 74
  State Fair 200
  State Square and Round Dance
    Convention 71, 87, 102, 143,
             148, 206
  Teachers Conventions 90
Wisconsin Squares and Rounds..... 180
Wishau, Jean 236
Witt, Ruth 237
WLS—Prairie Farmer Station 18
Wolf, Pat 69
Wolf River Rollers 72
Wolf's Hall in Allenton 112
Wood County Normal School 141
Woodlawn Cemetery 214
WPA 154
WRDLC 181
WSDLCC 85, 89, 206, 228, 233
WSRDCC 85
WTMJ Television 17, 28, 200

X

Xavier High School, Appleton 90

Y

Yellow Rockers 231, 232, 238
Yellow Rockers Plus 232
YMCA 97, 148
Yorkville United Methodist Church . 109
Younger, Glenn A. 162, 163, 221
Youngs, Darryl and Emily 186
Youth and Adult American Cloggers . 79
Ystad, Milton 111, 164

Z

Zaragoza
  Air Base, Spain 85
  Bimillennium 85
  Promenaders 85
Zemski
  Fritz 104, 162
  Marie 104

Ziemann
  Carol........................ 59
  George 18, 47, 59
  Gordy 76, 112, 220
  Mary Ann 112, 220
Zimmerman
  Bernice 236
  Dawn 237